ALLEGIANCE TO WINDS AND WATERS

Allegiance to Winds and Waters

Bicycling the Political Divides of the United States

Anne Winkler-Morey

ISBN 13: 978-1-63489-516-3

Library of Congress Catalog Number has been applied for.

Printed in the United States of America

First Printing: 2022

26 25 24 23 22 5 4 3 2 1

Cover and interior design by Patrick Maloney
Cover illustration by Emily Donovan
Interior illustrations by Tori Hong
Maps by Heather Spates
Author photo by Eric Mueller

Wise Ink Creative Publishing
807 Broadway St NE
Suite 46
Minneapolis, MN, 55413

In memory of Stefan Siegfried Winkler, from whom I learned to be wary of flags, and Marjorie Green Winkler, who loved wetlands and salty winds.

To Emily Winkler-Morey, my heart, and David Winkler-Morey, my home.

What happens to nationalism, to political boundaries,
when allegiance lies with winds and waters
that know no boundaries, that cannot be bought or sold?[1]
—*Robin Wall Kimmerer*

1 Kimmerer, Robin Wall, *Braiding Sweetgrass*. Minneapolis, MN: Milkweed Editions. 2013, p 112.

CONTENTS

AUTHOR'S NOTE

ON MEMORY, TRUTH, AND CONSEQUENCES

People break rules about talking to strangers when they meet someone with luggage on their bike. Perhaps they assume you are fulfilling a life dream, and they want to share theirs. Or they see you are bending life's responsibilities, and it inspires them to take a risk. Or maybe it's the stranger-on-a-plane syndrome: they know you won't be in town long.

Loaded bicycles elicit intimate conversations but make official interviews difficult. I brought a tape recorder and notebook, but on the second day, after fumbling with my bags while nurse Wendy Dart made profound connections between "clean air, water, literacy, and public health," I decided to listen carefully instead. When we weren't biking, I would write what I remembered. Sometimes that was days after an encounter. For this reason, few quotes are exact.

After completing the trip, I circled the US perimeter in the library. I wanted to understand the forces moving the country toward greater inequity, less sustainability, and more amnesia. I looked for resistance. That research is reflected in stories about localities and hidden histories.

In the process of writing, I explored my relationship with my partner and traveling companion, David Winkler-Morey. The chronology of those insights isn't linear on the page. David went through similar processes, and I interweave some of his post-trip insights.

In 2017 my child, Emily, announced they were nonbinary. Nothing about their gender identity changed, only the terminology to describe it. I use the pronouns *they* and *them*, even when talking about Emily as a baby.

My mother died on July 23, 2019. During the last five years of her life, our best times together were when I read her drafts of this book. Her death changed my understanding of our relationship.

As I wrote, exploring fear, nationalism, and the possibility of social change, I was influenced by events unfolding around me. The Great Recession that sent me on the road looked tame compared to the economic tsunami that attended the COVID-19 pandemic. The wealth divide that the Occupy Movement exposed had only deepened, as had resistance.

In May of 2020, Minneapolis police officers murdered George Floyd ten blocks from my home. His death unleashed a social movement that spread worldwide. A year later, our social inequities were laid bare. We were discovering what was essential and what was expendable. Evidence of our mutual self-interest was everywhere, yet those in power were scrambling to erect new barriers to our solidarity. Understanding how to thrive with insecurity as we dismantled oppressive systems had never been more critical.

Anne Winkler-Morey
May 28, 2021

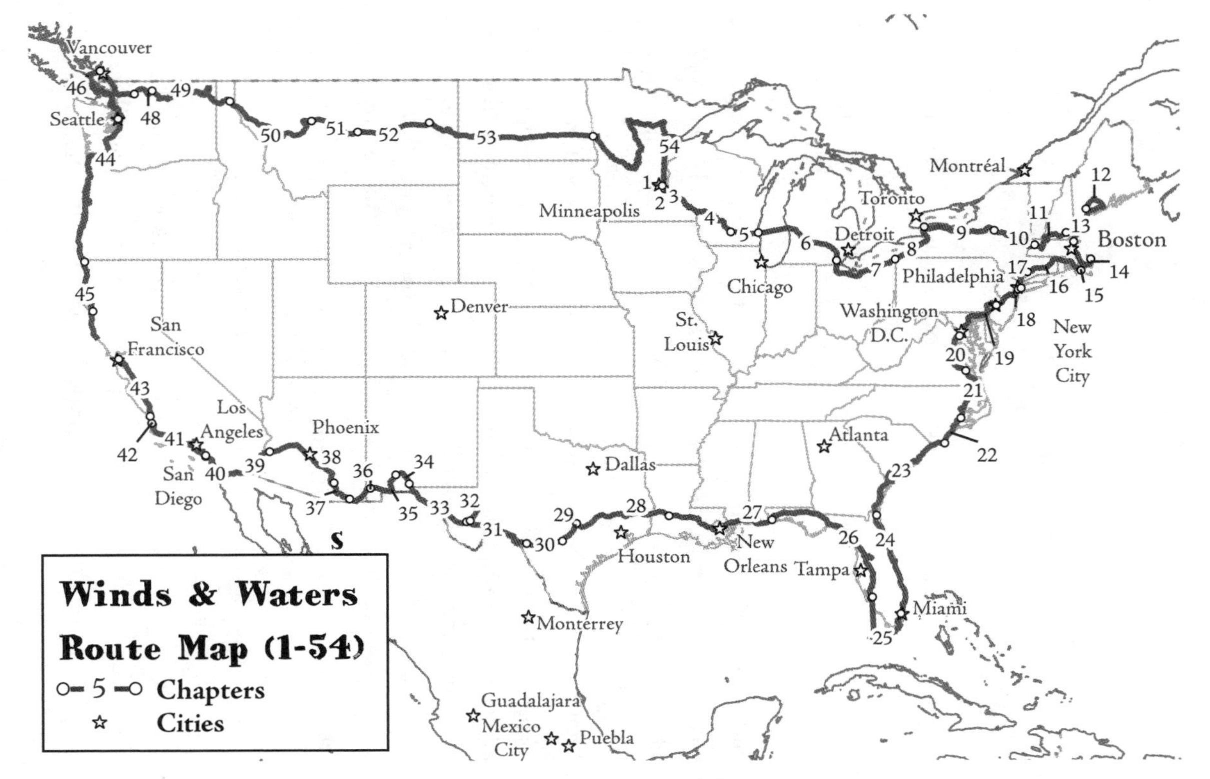
Winds & Waters
Route Map (1-54)
5 Chapters
Cities
Vancouver
Seattle
San Francisco
Los Angeles
San Diego
Phoenix
Denver
Dallas
Houston
Minneapolis
St. Louis
Chicago
Detroit
Toronto
Montréal
Boston
Philadelphia
Washington D.C.
New York City
Atlanta
New Orleans
Tampa
Miami
Monterrey
Guadalajara
Mexico City
Puebla
1
2
3
4
5
6
7
8
9
10
11
12
13
14
15
16
17
18
19
20
21
22
23
24
25
26
27
28
29
30
31
32
33
34
35
36
37
38
39
40
41
42
43
44
45
46
48
49
50
51
52
53
54

I

SPRING ICE

. . . [O]ur personal suffering [is] a political condition.[2]

I don't believe in ghosts. I believe in history. But I am haunted, and I lean on imaginary thinking to keep specters at bay. Sometimes I escape. I picked up my fleeing habit from my dad. When he was a child his family snuck across political borders, living in refugee camps and homes in half a dozen nations and states before settling in an apartment in Queens, New York.

When I was little, and Dad a young adult, we moved often. By age twelve I had lived in thirteen places in four states. For me, it was an adventure. We were escaping together. We settled in Madison, Wisconsin, where Dad began to escape without me, into his thoughts. He spent much of my high school years in his easy chair, eyes fixed on some place I could not see, fingers circling paper scraps into soft balls. He would emerge after a few years, but by then I had left home.

After graduating from high school in 1975, on my seventeenth birthday, I moved to Oberlin, Ohio, for college. During January term, I signed up for a modern dance intensive in Minneapolis, Minnesota. For a month, I slept on an unheated porch, danced seven hours a day, and ate only cottage cheese. When it is a choice, extreme living for short periods can lead to euphoria, especially if

2 Manifesto, Redstockings Women's Liberation Movement, 1969. https://www.redstockings.org/index.php/rs-manifesto.

you are seventeen. When I returned to Oberlin, the exhilaration disappeared. I wanted it back. I dropped out and caught a bus back to Minneapolis.

My parents did not like my chosen city. They worried about me, and, I suppose, they had reason. I had more conversations with strangers on the street than in safe social venues. I looked even younger than I was, and religious cultists and pick-up artists saw a target. Mom came up once to beg me to come home. We made a scene, my Brooklyn Jewish mother and I, taking our high-voltage fighting methods to the streets of Scandinavian Minneapolis. Her disapproval made me more determined to stay.

Besides, I was falling in love.

To get to dance class from where I lived, I would cross the 10th Avenue Bridge over the Mississippi. In the winter, I'd check the progression of ice building on the water's edge; and in the warmer months, I'd watch barges headed for New Orleans and dream I was on them. Minneapolis still felt like a borrowed city, but the river was becoming mine.

THREE YEARS AND EIGHT moves later, I found an apartment a block away from Ralph and Jerry's grocery store on 4th Street, where I worked as a cashier. It was a ground-floor efficiency with a bathroom down the hall that I shared with five men. A family of mice lived in the stove. The place was a dump, but I loved it. I had a record player and candles, a bed and a table, windows that looked out onto the street, and postcards taped to the wall. There were no rules about what I could put up. This space was mine. I imagined myself staying awhile.

In early March, the sheet of ice on the sidewalk was giving way to puddles. It was still light when I finished my grocery shift, and I decided to go for a run. I jogged toward the river, pausing on the 10th Avenue Bridge to watch a log break through the ice, then on to the West Bank, past the cascade of frozen icicles hanging from the cliff, crossing again on Franklin Avenue, touching Saint Paul—a seven-mile circle.

Back in my apartment, I put Jimmy Cliff's album *Follow My Mind,* on the record player. While he sang "Look at the Mountains," I changed into my nightgown, lit a candle. A man's frame filled my bedroom doorway. He wore a ski mask, tied my hands with a rope, put a knife to my neck. We negotiated: I wouldn't scream again. He would put the knife away and untie my hands. He would rape me. He wouldn't kill me. Afterward, he paced, eyeing the window and me on the floor. When the record ended, he lifted the needle and replayed it.

He finally fled. I banged on the door of my bathroom mates, and they called the police. "Did he penetrate?" the male cop asked. The two male ambulance attendants talked over me as I sat between them, my ripped nightgown stained with blood. At the Hennepin County Medical Center, a male doctor examined my pelvis.

A volunteer from the Rape Crisis Center appeared at the hospital and helped me figure out who to call, told me it wasn't my fault. She continued to meet with me for the next two years. I became part of her research on the long-term effects of sexual assault. In 1979, twenty-four months was considered a reasonable time for this kind of study. PTSD was not yet understood.

I slept on a coworker's couch that night, went to work in the morning wearing a borrowed pair of too-tight jeans and someone else's boots. Marv and Charles, who lived in my building, came into the store for cigarettes. "We heard the scream, saw the ambulance," Marv said. "Are you OK?" A cop called, asking for me. I answered the phone in my cashier's cage, while Marv was still standing there waiting for his change. The officer said since the man had a mask, there would be no further investigation.

I had not asked for an investigation, and now I had no choice in its ending. In the following days, my hair fell out. I wouldn't have been surprised if a limb had fallen off. I felt as if I controlled nothing about my life. Everything happened *to* me.

Friends and family offered safety advice: lock your door, don't share a bathroom with men, don't live on the first floor, don't run at night, live in a secure building. I did move—next door—into a newer development with a security entrance, a roommate, and a third-floor apartment. My parents were appalled. They wanted me out of Minneapolis. Why would I refuse to move off the block? "There is no safe place," I argued. "No rapist is going to force me to move from my neighborhood."

I was asserting control in a life that seemed to be dictated by others. I was also staking a claim, saying, *This neighborhood is mine.*

I quit dancing, unable to contain the vulnerabilities and mood swings it released. And I stopped running. But I still walked, sometimes at night. I was most afraid inside enclosed spaces. I had a new job at a co-op grocery store on the West Bank. The half-mile sidewalk on the 10th Avenue Bridge, with its concrete barrier to the road and suicide drop to the river, had no exit. Crossing the river to work, I still imagined escapes—but not to exotic places. Gripping my keys, I planned how I would break free from the clutch of any man behind or in front of me.

THIRTY-SIX YEARS LATER, A laid-off history professor stood on a bridge over the Mississippi with a loaded bike, and whispered to the river, "See you in New Orleans."

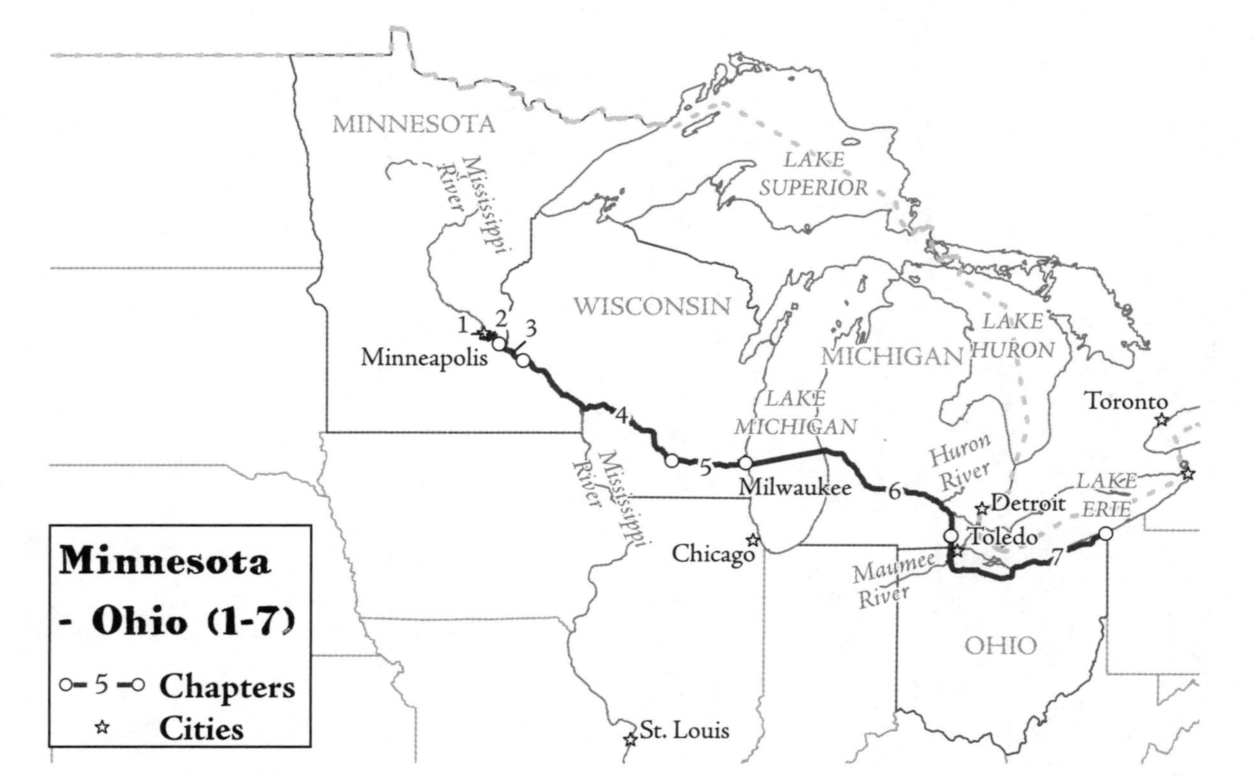

MINNESOTA
Mississippi River
LAKE SUPERIOR
WISCONSIN
1
2
3
Minneapolis
MICHIGAN
LAKE HURON
LAKE MICHIGAN
4
5
Milwaukee
6
Toronto
Huron River
Mississippi River
Detroit
LAKE ERIE
Chicago
Toledo
7
Maumee River
OHIO
St. Louis
Minnesota - Ohio (1-7)
5 Chapters
Cities

2

LEARNING CURVES

Minnesota

"In a twelve-person lineup, you'd be the last one I'd pick to ride a bicycle around the country," a friend said. I knew what she meant. At fifty-three, I wasn't athletic. In my friend's lineup, I'd be the disheveled one with wispy hair and dirty glasses, hands over ample chest, eyes darting, trying to disappear. To find me, you'd have to be looking for the one who wants to escape.

The desire for an epic voyage had been with me since the days when I dreamt of adventures on the 10th Avenue Bridge, but fears and responsibilities got in the way. Now, those responsibilities were disappearing. My child Emily left home for college in New York City. My college instructorship at Saint Cloud State University was not renewed. It was the nadir of the Great Recession, and no one else was hiring.

It was easy to convince my husband David to come with me on a fourteen-month bicycle escapade. In my friend's lineup, he would be the slim, positive, eager, sociable guy standing in the center, looking ready for adventure. Besides, he was worried about me. My post-employment depression was worse than past lows. The day I mouthed the idea of riding the perimeter of the United States, he gave me no chance to think twice. He signed up for a leave of absence from his job as a Minneapolis Public Schools social worker and posted our house on a for-rent site.

Even after the plan was set and renters found, I spent afternoons in bed, my body becoming less capable of the feat of bicycle-touring. But the more the trip defied physical logic, the more acute my need to flee became. I felt I had little to lose—a condition that can engender a foolish kind of determination.

As the end of David's school year approached, we studied maps, joined host networks, asked friends to ask friends if we could stay with them. We reserved the last week for final packing decisions and a practice ride. But days before departure, both of our mothers fell ill. Instead of testing our load, we shuffled to hospitals in Minnesota and Massachusetts.

When the young renters arrived, they found us standing in the living room surrounded by a pile of possible take-alongs. Into our bags we threw assorted spandex, camping gear, snacks, laptop, William Least Heat-Moon's *River-Horse,* vitamins, chain bike lock, camera, tape player. We agonized over a sweatshirt, grabbed more socks, argued about an extra pair of blue Lycra pants. The drama distracted me. Rolling the bikes down the front steps, I didn't notice unwelcome hitchhikers climbing into my panniers—emotional baggage I intended to leave behind.

FIFTY POUNDS, HASTILY STUFFED, rides differently than an unloaded bike. I struggled to balance on two wheels. Thinking neighbors might be watching, I whispered to David, "Let's walk to the end of the block." Three houses up, it sprinkled. At the corner, it was pouring. We stopped to dig for raincoats. The wind rose. Branches cracked.

Soaked, cold, not hungry, we made our first purchase: cups of warm decaf coffee at Turtle Bread. I tried not to look at David, hoping he didn't remember painful days of caffeine headaches to prepare for my trip budget plan: "We will drink only tap water!"

The June 2011 edition of *Southside Pride* was on café tables. In its centerfold, a middle-aged woman outlined plans for a 12,000-mile bike escapade with her husband. She sounded confident, looked tough in her side-angle photo. The reader couldn't discern the bum knees, the extra girth, the withdrawn demeanor, the tendency to imagine every disaster that made her an unlikely candidate for fourteen months on a bicycle. I slumped in my chair, hoping no one saw the resemblance between the woman in the article and the drowned rat making a puddle on the floor six blocks from her home.

A man approached our table.

"How far ya come?"

WHEN THE THUNDER SUBSIDED, we left the warmth of the café, following the paved bike path snaking along Minnehaha Creek to the Mississippi River. Despite the rain, I stopped on the Ford Parkway Bridge and stretched my arms and legs at the bridge's apex, straddling two halves of a nation. I whispered to the river.

We descended five hundred feet into downtown Saint Paul, past barges, freight trains, parks, and condominiums, until we became ants beneath a tangle of towering bridges. From there, our bikes entered new territory. Fifteen wet miles of wrong turns and a mile from our destination—unable to follow the blue ball on the new iPhone we had bought the day before—we stood in the rain, shoes saturated, and called my friend Ruth.

"Oh, honey," she said with a laugh. "I'd better come get you."

Ruth's car inched along the highway toward her Cottage Grove home, two cyclists following in her exhaust stream. She insisted we bring our wet bikes into her living room. When we opened the panniers, every item was soaked.

Ruth taught liberal arts at the Minneapolis College of Art and Design. When we met, in the 1980s, I was director of the Central America Resource Center in Minneapolis. Ruth got involved when Efraín Ríos Montt was reigning terror over Guatemalan Indigenous communities.[3] I joined the Central America movement after four US religious women were raped and murdered by US-backed death squads. I saw the movie *El Salvador: Another Vietnam?* and learned that thousands of Salvadorans had suffered the same fate. When I discovered my tax dollars contributed to the mass violation and slaughter of women, the Central America movement became my passion. For a time, putting my experience as a rape survivor into a political context felt like the way to exorcise my own ghosts.

Ruth and I would commiserate about men in the movement who deemed it their job to educate us. Their mansplaining was especially outrageous in the case of Ruth, a brilliant Native American anthropologist, and a founding scholar of the University of Minnesota's American Indian Studies program. When I returned to college and then graduate school, studying Latin American history and US social movements, Ruth was the kind of activist-scholar I wanted to be.

Every surface of my mentor's home not decorated with student art or photos of children and cats was covered with our wet belongings. In one hand, Ruth held a hair dryer to my soggy documents; in the other, her phone, soliciting advice from her bike-touring sister on packing panniers so that stuff stays dry.

"Twenty-eight miles?" Ruth snorted. "Honey, you're gonna have to do more than that to make it around the country!"

"Of course!" I mumbled, hobbling to her guest bed. "But we wanted to stay with you."

3 In 2013, Montt was indicted by one Guatemalan court for genocide and crimes against humanity. The case was still being litigated when he died in 2018. The Reagan administration was never indicted for aiding and abetting his reign of terror.

3

MR. SUNSHINE AND DISASTER BRAIN

Wisconsin

Eager to be in another state, we ignored recommendations to hug the riverbank on the Minnesota side, where hills were less steep and shoulders wider. Instead, we crossed into Wisconsin at the confluence of the St. Croix and Mississippi rivers. Picturesque bluffs—so lovely from a car—were excruciating to ride. I'd set my sights on the top of a hill, calibrating my expectations, only to discover a small plateau and another crest. We gathered no speed on the descents. I rode in front, braking hard, inching around sharp corners as though slowing down would erase the chance of a truck toppling, creating a bicyclist pancake.

Ten hours, thirty-nine miles. The Bay City Campground on the edge of Lake Pepin was a sight for sore legs.

LAKE PEPIN IS NOT really a lake, but a widening in the Mississippi River. Robert S. Duncanson, an African American landscape artist from Ohio, stopped to paint its tranquility while fleeing to sanctuary in Canada during the Civil War, capturing its surrounding cliffs, marshes, forests, and lush fields.[4] Sitting on its banks, the view did not make me gasp like a western

4 We discovered Duncanson's painting in the Cleveland Museum of Art.

mountain or eastern sea might. Instead, it settled my breath, dissolving knots I didn't know were there.

The other campers, forced there by economic circumstance, were not feeling the peace. A man with two fishing poles and a boy, walked by as we erected our tent. I heard him say to the child, "We'll eat when we catch something." A middle-aged couple overfilled the site next to us, car and pickup loaded with worldly possessions. The woman wore a blue dress suit over wide hips. She pulled off her pumps and rubbed her feet.

I asked her, "Can you tell me where the shower building is?"

She shook her head and pointed at the lake.

Rain impeded our plans to cook an oatmeal breakfast. Raw oats and a swig of water did not satisfy. After a three-mile hill, we asked a couple taking bikes off their car rack about food options. Wendy Dart, a nurse from Marshfield, Wisconsin, looked a few years older and more bicycle-fit than me. She was excited about our adventure.

"You don't look old enough for retirement," she said. "How are you able to do it?"

"I got laid off," I said.

Wendy nodded empathetically. "So many people lost their jobs or suffered pay cuts here in Wisconsin."

I took the opening, told her about Saint Cloud State University taking advantage of the Great Recession to remove instructors and quadruple class sizes.

"We traveled to Madison to protest Governor Walker last winter," Wendy responded. "A hundred thousand of us! He's destroying health care in this state. Clean air, water, schools—everything he cut connects to our health."

The intimate and overtly political nature of this conversation surprised me. We had similar rule-breaking interactions with strangers as the day progressed. At a scenic wayside, a man from Superior dispensed with pleasantries about the weather, the view, our adventure. Hearing we were educators, he railed against the state's governor. "Did you ever imagine teachers would become the bad guys?"

We found breakfast at a bakery tucked into cliffs a block from the main road in Maiden Rock. Two customers were parsing collective bargaining rights. "Those teachers want benefits I've never had," said one of them.

"Union contracts lift all boats," the other responded.

David grew up in rural Wisconsin. I went to high school in Madison. The election of Governor Scott Walker, his attacks on public sector workers, the unprecedented revolt his policies sparked, and the recall vote he now faced had transformed a state whose rural/urban dichotomy we thought we knew. I had friends who participated in the Madison capital occupation—a protest that smashed records and made global headlines—but I had not realized the extent to which Walker and his detractors had transformed the rural lexicon. Union phrases had become as common as "wind chill factor" or "cheese curd."[5]

BACK ON THE BIKE, I girded myself for another steep decline, holding on to my fears like a shield, as though they could protect us. David pumped along behind me singing.

My partner operated under an aura of invincibility. His positive outlook attracted, puzzled, and infuriated me. Our child, Emily, once diagnosed our divergent worldviews: "Dad's a preacher's kid. If he's good, he goes to heaven. You're the daughter of a Holocaust refugee."

Family history was undoubtedly part of it, but my disaster brain could reach absurd proportions. I didn't just worry about being assaulted or the rise of fascism. Sometimes I'd stand on the top of a flight of stairs and imagine

5 Walker won the recall election in June 2012 and the election in 2014. He ran again and lost in 2018.

myself falling. I leaned on David to balance my negative outlook, but his worldview was no more realistic. If we were hungry, he'd remember a café that wasn't there. If we were broke, he expected a paycheck, already spent. Sometimes I bathed in that pretend world, though I knew its logic was leaky.

But who could fault a man for singing? David had a habit of turning conversations into lyrics, something he shared with his dad and siblings. "Being with your family is like being in a musical," I'd say. But his incessant ditties irritated me. I suspected something sad behind all that sunshine, though I figured that was my disaster brain talking. It was I who went into therapy, took antidepressants, racked up diagnoses: PTSD, autism spectrum, ADHD. David occasionally accompanied me to a session "to work on our relationship," but I was the sick one. He was the healer.

When we first met, in the winter of 1982, our disparate outlooks and origins did not concern us. We'd arrived at the same crossroad. David had just returned from six months in Central America, where he tried to join a revolution. The Salvadoran revolutionaries told him, "If you want to do some good, go home and organize. Stop your government from arming ours."

I was a year deep into the activist life by then. We met in the Northrop Auditorium dressing room, folding leaflets on El Salvador to hand out at a Joan Baez concert. He was the young man with green eyes and a mass of brown curls rubbing knees with me during the performance. Skinny from parasites and unemployment, he devoured the folk singer's backstage spread while lecturing her on the Farabundo Martí National Liberation Front. We spent our first night together. David said I was beautiful and wrote a poem about my bookshelf. I gave him *The Dispossessed* by Ursula K. Le Guin. We debated revolution, interrogated dystopian realities, and imagined utopian possibilities. Three months later, we went on our first camping trip, had our first fight, and decided to get married. Intimacy led to rape flashbacks. Guilt and resentment topped with fear made for an explosive mix. Thirty years later, dodging those minefields was part of our normal.

Suddenly exhausted, I braked on a hill outside of Pepin, Wisconsin. Behind me, David took off his helmet, slathered sunscreen on his bald head, and handed me the lotion. The break felt good, until a swarm of mental mosquitos descended. We wanted to average forty-five miles a day. We had to be capable of seventy. Our plan for this day was forty. Halfway there, at the crest of the next hill, we stopped at a fruit stand. The muscles in my extremities melted. I lay atop a picnic table, legs shaking. The peaches we bought felt heavy. I lifted one, held it, chewed it, dropped the pit in a bag like a bodybuilder dropping weights at the gym. The weakness did not wear off with rest.

I shuffled spaghetti legs three blocks to the Pepin RV campground, distraught that twenty miles had slayed me. The campground manager squinted at my unlikely profile. "You rode from Bay City? How'd ya climb Three Mile Hill? There's a racer who comes every year to train on Three Mile. He doesn't carry a load like you."

4

THE BRAIN IS A FUNNY MUSCLE

Wisconsin

Outside Anderson's Village Market in Cochrane, Wisconsin, an old man leaving the store slipped and fell. Milk and corn puffs spilled onto the road. I, David, and a motorcyclist scrambled to help him to his feet and retrieve his purchases.

The motorcyclist was from Traverse City, Michigan, on his way to a woodturning conference in Saint Paul. He insisted on paying for our groceries. "At eighteen, I took a bike tour of the Great Lakes," he explained. "People were kind to me. I'm paying it forward." We accepted his gift gratefully, awed by the instant intimacy that came from uniting to help another, and the human desire to be part of someone else's adventure.

An hour later, we were stepping out of a park bathroom when a woman yelled from the seat of her 1970s station wagon full of children, "You know there's a tornado coming? Follow me if you need a place to stay." Before David could open his mouth, I said, "Thanks, we have a place," though our planned shelter was a tent.

A siren sounded as we arrived at our campsite. A gust ripped the rainfly from David's hands. We retreated to the brick restroom, talking across the bathroom wall until the storm drowned out our voices. Squatting on the cement floor listening to the wind whistle and the crack of falling trees, I realized my fear of strangers and unfamiliar indoor spaces was more of an impediment to this trip's success than my physical limitations. I wasn't conscious of what I was doing when the woman in the station wagon approached; I just instinctively resisted being stuck in a strange place. Now, I questioned the sanity of my hierarchy of fears. Staying with others was part of our financial plan, and, in cases like this, central to our safety.

Merrick State Park was a refuge for endangered wood turtles. Like us, they believed this was a protected place. In the morning calm, they congregated under our picnic table, laying eggs. Crows circled.

RAIN WAS INCESSANT. WE sought refuge at a café in Fountain City with six counter seats, two tables, and a stained-glass eagle over the door. A man with a camouflage cap took in our wet biking clothes. "Bike trails are political," he said, eyeing us as if we embodied them. "Some believe they revitalize dying towns. Others see them as invasions of property and interruptions of our way of life."

With our loaded bikes, few ignored us. The Nelson's Creamery cashier eyed us suspiciously and put our twenty up to the light to see if it was counterfeit. A man buying gas in Onalaska handed David five bucks and wished him well. I began to feel like a character in one of those Yiddish folktales my dad used to read to me. We were seekers on the road, attracting strangers with profound messages.

At a private RV campground in West Salem, a man with a large motor home asked if we needed anything. David picked up our pot. "We could use some hot water."

The man returned with boiling water. A young father camping with his family was watching. He brought a burning log to our pit.

Water and fire. Elemental gifts.

RAIN FELL INTO OUR bowls. The next morning, the nylon tent floor sat on an inch of water and threatened to spring a leak. We showered, hoping time might bring the sun, only to emerge from warm restrooms into a cold deluge. We were low on food. Hungry, tired, we took our discomfort out on each other. I filled a pannier. David redid it. We fought.

I looked for somewhere to get away from David, but the only dry place in this West Salem campground was the laundry room, large enough for two people if they stood side by side. David left to knock on motor-home doors for coins for the washing machine. Unshaved, wearing his hood against the rain, no one would let him in. While he was gone, a woman with brown curls and red lipstick found me in the laundry room, drove me to her RV, and served me tea. She was planning a trip to Tennessee for a Kenny Chesney concert. She showed me her new cowboy boots. Though I knew nothing about country music, to sit with a hot mug and a best friend and talk Nashville seemed the normal thing for a fifty-three-year-old woman to do. Too soon, however, she gave me a handful of quarters, a cup of detergent, and a ride back to the laundry room.

We didn't leave the campground until 2:00 p.m. At the Jolivette Family Farms store where we stopped for provisions, the cashier snapped, "Some people have to work and can't go on a ride for a year."

"We are lucky," I agreed, though I wasn't feeling it.

The first tunnel on the Elroy-Sparta State Trail was a fifteen-minute walk: dark, slippery, forty degrees, damp. I didn't think to don a layer. The path from the tunnel to the Norwalk campground descended gently, so we never warmed up. The evening temperature was fifty-eight degrees. In the icy park shower, a sharp stab shot through my right knee. In cold air, my right leg would not hold weight. Holding on to David, I hopped into the tent. I thought the trip was over, and that flipped a switch in my brain: now I was desperate to continue. David elevated my leg with a pannier and wrapped it with the extra pair of blue Lycra pants. Scared and cold, we made peace.

The next day, my leg took the weight. Still, we took it easy, lingering in downtown Norwalk. David asked a man on the street about breakfast options, slipping into a small-town way of talking. As a preacher's son, David had moved with his family from one small rural white Christian Wisconsin town to another every four to six years. When we met, college in Saint Paul and travel in Central America had fractured his small-town perspective. It fascinated me to hear him return to his roots when we left the city.

The homogeneity of David's childhood—when diversity meant Methodists, Lutherans, and Catholics—was disappearing. Here in Norwalk, Immanuel United Methodist Church, a stately brownstone with stained glass, filled a block. Its windowless competitor, Iglesia Evangelica, sat low on a corner.

"I moved to Norwalk from Los Angeles," the owner of Los Tres Garcias Bakery told us. When she had bought the store, there was a sign in the window: *Closing for Good 1/20/11*. She had turned it over, written, *Big Bakery. Mexico. Fresh Donuts*, and stuck it back in the window. Her business catered to the two hundred men and women who worked at the Valley Pride meat processing plant outside of town. We ate her corn muffins and watched as men ordered "para llevar."

In the 1980s, large-scale agribusiness decimated Wisconsin family farms. A decade later, the United States took advantage of NAFTA to dump cheap corn south of the border, destroying Mexican livelihoods. This one-two punch to family agriculture in the Americas transformed Norwalk. Foreclosed Wisconsin farmers left. Valley Pride recruited displaced Mexican campesinos to process meat in rural Wisconsin.

Valley Pride had been cited with dozens of safety violations. One of the workers who paid the ultimate price for the company's neglect was Edgar Rodriguez Bacerra, who came to Norwalk for work, settled for love, and had three children. In 2011, faulty plant wiring electrocuted him. He was the second Valley Pride worker to die on the job that way.[6]

IN WONEWOC, WISCONSIN, WE found a coffee shop on the path. In the window was a stack of booklets, an illustrated history of the town. We looked through it, searching for mention of the local Methodist church.

A man approached us. "That's my book," he said. "I'm the town historian."

"My father was the Methodist minister here," David explained.

"Reverend Morey? I remember him! He was the one who burnt down the parsonage." His eyes got wide, as if talking about an infamous character, not a pillar of the community.

From Wonewoc to Reedsburg, we rode side by side on the 400 State Trail. David's pace slowed. I could tell he was upset. As we passed lovely rock formations on the outskirts of town, I tried a memory I thought would soothe him. "When I first met your dad," I said, "he pointed out the beauty of those rocks, the way their jagged edges looked like faces and animals."

David didn't want soothing. "That fire wasn't Dad's fault. The house had a leaky gas pipe. He was defrosting the freezer with a hair dryer, got a phone call, ran across the street to get a file, and forgot to turn it off. I don't think that was a manic episode."

We rode silently for a bit.

"When did you first realize your dad was bipolar?" I finally asked.

"He was diagnosed in 1978 after he punched out the Volkswagen dealer.

6 In June 2012, the Occupational Safety and Health Administration ruled on Edgar's case, recommending a fine of $186,000. https://www.riverfallsjournal.com/lifestyle/health/1057018-osha-fines-beef-plant-safety-violations.

He was hospitalized then and got treatment. But I knew there was something wrong when I was fourteen, at the cabin, when John caught the bullfrog."

I'd heard fragments of that story before. Now, there were new details.

"Dad was halfway across the lake in a rowboat," David continued. "He heard John yell and thought we were in trouble. He rowed furiously, and one of the oars broke. By the time he got to shore, he was in a full rage. Instead of being relieved, he cursed John and me for crying wolf.

"I took John up the bank, away from Dad, and turned on our portable radio, hoping for a Twins game. I thought baseball would mellow Dad out. But the news was on. Eagleton was resigning from the Democratic ticket because he had seen a therapist. The next story was about Vietnam.

"Dad must have conflated the two stories, and it set him off. Though he had yet to be diagnosed, he knew he was ill, and he feared he, like Eagleton, would be targeted because of it. He told us to hide because Nixon's men were coming to send us to Vietnam. I reminded him I was fourteen and John only nine, but it didn't register. He told me to get our guns."

"You never told me that," I said.

"I know how you feel about guns. We were hunters. You don't get that."

Your grandma killed herself. I kept that thought to myself. "Did you get them?"

"I don't remember. The next morning, everything was back to normal, as though nothing had happened."

"Did you ever talk about it with him or with your mom?"

"No. But for the rest of my years at home, I saw it as my job to protect John. If Dad went manic, I'd try to distract him, get him singing or walking in the woods. That's how I learned to de-escalate situations."

"Like you do with me."

WE AWOKE BEFORE DAWN to the smell of excrement. Camping in the Reedsburg Park was free, accommodating, and next to a sewage plant. We'd planned to leave early, get as close to Madison and my mom's house as we could. But eggs, potatoes, and eavesdropping at Greenwood's Café were too delicious.

"Did ya hear 'bout that judge Walker appointed, who punched a guy?"

"Yep. Punched another judge!"

We weren't on the road until nine.

I DRAPED MYSELF ON the small table at Mason's Grill in Prairie du Sac. The bartender was impressed. "They use Route 12 to train for the Tour de France," he said. I eyed the sticky barroom floor. The desire to lie down was overwhelming. But Mason's Grill wasn't an inn, and there was no place to tent among these suburban tracts.

"You can do a couple more miles," David coaxed.

"A couple more miles" became nine, ten, eleven. As we approached mile twelve, David busted a tire—or so he thought. Mr. Never Gets Tired was experiencing his first "internal flat." Already an expert, I explained the phenomenon: "You work hard, but you're slowing. Soon, you can barely move. You think the tire got soft, the road steep, the terrain rough, but nothing's changed—except you."

At the top of Collins Ridge Road, David eyed the wooded corner of a long front yard.

"Do you think our tent would be seen there?"

From the ridge, we could see Madison in the valley, where Mom's abandoned house was, where we could rest for as long as we needed.

Day eight: sixty-five miles. The brain is a funny muscle.

5

CHOOSING TO REMEMBER

Wisconsin

How does a city choose to remember its past?
—America's Black Holocaust Museum[7]

I awoke to a house inhabited by ghosts and a refrigerator full of rancid condiments. Two summers earlier, Mom had left her Wisconsin home to visit my brothers in Massachusetts. She never returned. The house had become untenable due to her diabetes. Unwilling to give up hope she would be healthy enough to come back, she had refused help to prepare the home for sale. Weeks became months. Fall became winter, seasons, years.

Dusty rooms were stuffed with decades of accumulation, mostly books. Henry David Thoreau leaned on *Little Bear*. Agatha Christie and *The New England Journal of Medicine* shared space with a bowl of pinecones, rocks, and shells. A massive eclectic collection of records—Pete Seeger, Jimi Hendrix, and a full set of Wagnerian operas—sat in a closet, cardboard jackets mildewing. Toys, saved until too musty to pass on, spilled out of closets. Photos of four children and five grandkids were stuck without frames wherever they might stand. There were memories in every corner.

It is the 2000 Oscars. Mom faces the TV. I face Dad, watching his lithe frame melt into the velour couch. I don't expect him to live through the night. Angelina

7 This quote can be found here: https://www.abhmuseum.org/rememberance/.

Jolie thanks her parents, her producer, her boyfriend. Dad raises his arms like a ballerina, face breaking into that childlike grin I have loved all my life. He is so thin it appears he might levitate. He lifts and lowers his head, takes his final bow. His body laughs, tickled by his cosmic joke. I hold my breath to elongate the moment, but he is down again, an expressionless pile of bones.

Dad escaped Nazi Germany at age six, with his mother and sisters. He succumbed to colon cancer in his sixties. While I was small, he finished medical school in Boston and a residency in North Carolina before taking a position as a radiologist at Madison's VA hospital. This house—the first one my parents owned—represented a settling down and economic leap for my family.

Shorewood Hills sits on a corner of Madison's largest lake. Residents enjoy the city's vast public waterfront but keep their own lakeside private. A postage-stamp beach with a boathouse is one of two public access points. The path to the beach is dark. Trees block the sun. Halfway down, you pass under a bridge undergirded with thick wooden posts. When I was thirteen, a man hiding behind one of those posts placed his giant hands around my mouth and throat. Later, the Shorewood police force—all two of them—questioned me in our kitchen. Guns hung from their belts. In the coming years, those cops would leer at me, comment on my looks and how I had grown.

"He was not from Shorewood," Mom said while I was in the process of writing this book and called to ask what she remembered. It was a strange comment, but I knew what she meant. My attacker was an aberration, she thought. What happened to me was not likely to happen again.

We all create imaginary safety walls to protect ourselves and those we love. My wall was even flimsier. I thought that if I kept moving while heavily burdened, I would be invisible. Four months after the assault, I started high school. I walked three miles each way, weighed down by an oversized backpack. The load humped my back, curved my shoulders, hid my growing breasts from view. After I was raped, the backpack got heavier. Even now, as I sit in a coffee shop and write, a heavy load sits beside me, ready for our walk home.

Dysfunction or not, walking became a refuge in high school. Movement directed my restless mind. I wanted to be a modern dancer and took a dozen classes a week, but I also sowed the seeds of the activist-historian I would become. I was fascinated by examples of integrity under fire: German Christians who harbored Jews, Black liberation activists who risked incarceration and death, artists unbowed by the House Un-American Activities Committee.

In eighth grade, I read *The Autobiography of Malcolm X*. The story of transformation in prison spoke to my obsession with fortitude. I got my friend to remove books and toys from a small room in her house and lock me in. Solitary confinement on a plush carpet lasted forty-five minutes, and my plan to read the dictionary like Malcolm, didn't get past *aardvark*. But his story opened a door. Angela Davis, jailed for her politics, writing her truth, walked in. So did Studs Terkel, a chronicler of people's stories, and I. F. Stone, a journalist sleuth for justice.

IN MADISON, I HAD lunch with three of my high school friends. They were all teachers, in Governor Scott Walker's bull's-eye, who took circuitous routes to the classroom. Donna had been a translator for Sandinista dignitaries in Nicaragua in the 1980s. She returned to Madison for graduate school when her children were small and became an education professor. Beth traded a lucrative career in historic preservation to become a Spanish bilingual elementary teacher. Larry quit corporate engineering to become a high school math instructor.

"Walker is increasing class sizes, making teachers' jobs untenable," Donna told me. "You add five students; kids fall through the cracks."

Larry and Beth had participated in a four-day work stoppage organized by the Madison teachers' union and lost a week's pay. "This movement lacked the violence of Vietnam anti-war protests I remember as a kid," Larry asserted. "Everyone was polite and cared for each other."

Beth also compared the uprising to protests of our childhood. "The anti-Walker movement tapped deeper and wider roots," she said. "My undocumented students and their families participated."

WE PLANNED TO SPEND two weeks getting Mom's house ready for sale. We scrubbed and painted and even met with a realtor, but Mom rebuffed our work. So, after three days, we left Madison, riding east on the Capital City and Glacial Drumlin trails, to the home of Nancy and Mitch, hosts in an international friendship network we had joined for the trip.[8] I was nervous, but Nancy was so kind on the phone. They were going to a concert. They would leave the door open and fish pie on the counter.

We miscalculated the distance to their Pewaukee home. Sixty miles on, we were still fifteen miles away and it was dark. At a closed Mobile gas station, we called, and these strangers picked us up in their truck and set us up in their second-floor guest room. Embarrassed at our obvious incompetence, I tried not to let them see me wince as I climbed their stairs, burning sensation shooting through my knee.

In the morning, after hugs and promises to keep in touch, we discovered our first flat. Eager to show our gracious hosts we had things under control, I made a show of stuffing a 700c tube into my twenty-six-inch tire, and—when that didn't work—David tried to force his Schrader valve into my Presta rim,

8 SERVAS, a global host network, encourages two-day stays so people can get to know each other.

until Mitch had enough of our tubes and valves routine. He loaded our bikes into his truck, and drove us to the nearest bike shop.

ON THE NEW BERLIN trail at the edge of Milwaukee, a cyclist with a threadbare tee and white beard offered to shepherd us to the Hank Aaron State Trail. Our new friend braked to glean raspberries and paused to point out fall delicacies: wild grapes, black walnuts, and apples. His cycling adventures were just as frugal. "You heard of RAGBRAI?"

Yes, we knew about the Iowa state bike extravaganza.

"I rode the opposite direction for free. Empty roads across the state, against the ten-thousand-cyclist tide."

As we parted ways, he recommended a shortcut. His directions took us past empty factories covered in graffiti, barely visible through new green growth along an abandoned railroad bed. But after a mile of gravel and sand, we met the Menomonee River and the promised bike path.

Information placards lined the Hank Aaron Trail, tracing the area's transformation from industrial powerhouse to wasteland to urban green space. As I read them, I thought of my mother's stepfather, my Grandpa George, who worked in a Milwaukee bread factory when he was young. I imagined him beside me, holding his hat against the Lake Michigan wind.

At age eleven, Grandpa George was exiled from his Russian village. "Why?" I would ask. "I burned the rabbi's beard," he would say. He arrived in New York City alone and found a job in a shipyard. In 1915, he boarded a boat headed west on the Saint Lawrence Seaway and landed in Milwaukee. "The 'sewer socialists' ruled Milwaukee then," he would tell me, referring to reformers with a local focus, who fought for public housing, utilities, food markets, and parks.

AT THE ENTRANCE TO Milwaukee's historic district, a Lake Michigan gale forced us off our bikes. Ahead of us, a cyclist riding a wind tunnel created by buildings lost control. His lithe body was unharmed, but his carbon fiber bike snapped in two. After that, we walked, holding tight to our loaded clunkers, taking shelter from the wind in the lobby of the Milwaukee Art Museum. The eclectic building's rooftop wings were retracted; a giant bird hunkered in a gale storm.

The wind died down and was moving with us when we left one museum in search of another. I wanted to visit the historical gallery created by Dr. James Cameron, the lone survivor of an infamous lynching in Marion, Indiana.[9] We found the building. The windows were covered with plywood. The marquee letters were no longer there, but the wood was lighter where the letters had been, so that we could still read the words: *America's Black Holocaust Museum.*

Walking toward the dock to catch our ferry across Lake Michigan, we passed a plaque marking the spot where, in 1886, 1,500 ironworkers filled Milwaukee streets demanding an eight-hour day. Then-Governor Jeremiah Rusk called in the militia to quell their uprising, and seven people died. The iron workers' strike ushered in the period of labor activism and radical politics that had so impressed my Grandpa George. Now my high school friends, educators Donna, Beth, and Larry, faced a governor as determined to snuff out workers' collective bargaining rights as Jeremiah Rusk had been over a century ago.

Rolling my bike onto the ferry, I thought about who and what we choose to remember.

---

9 A photograph of the Marion Indiana lynching, with white crowds gathered to watch, is well known. Cameron survived because someone untied his noose (http://www.blackpast.org/aah/marion-indiana-lynching-1930). He got the idea for the museum after a visit to the Holocaust Museum in Washington, DC.

At the end of his life, Grandpa George remembered two things about Milwaukee: the sewer socialists, and the smell of yeast.

By defunding America's Black Holocaust Museum, Milwaukee had chosen to erase not only the memory of white supremacist atrocities, but also the anti-Black legacy of many of Milwaukee's early labor leaders.[10]

Someday history's gatekeepers will choose how we remember the Wisconsin Uprising of 2011.

10 When James Cameron died in 2006, the Milwaukee City Council canceled support for his museum. In 2008 it was foreclosed. In 2017, people began raising private funds to build a new building and reopen. Check out their website: https://www.abhmuseum.org/about/. The early sewer socialists of Milwaukee were members of the wing of the early twentieth century Socialist Party who advocated for the white working class at the exclusion of Black and Asian workers.

6

PAVED PARADISE ON THE ROAD TO HELL

Michigan

The pretty beach cottages surrounding the Muskegon, Michigan, harbor were like a row of trees hiding a clear-cut. A block away, boarded buildings and relentless potholes announced, "Welcome to Michigan: Your Recession Is Our Depression." An abandoned store marquee still advertising spring deals spoke of recent hard times. Rutted roads wreaking havoc on my bicyclist butt, told of years of infrastructure neglect.

The newly paved twenty-five-mile Musketawa Trail took us away from this visible hardship and into an area of lush vegetation, until we stopped at Conklin, midway on the trail. The town's mini-mart had a welcoming porch. Noting the ten-pound bags of masa harina (corn flour for making tortillas), David asked in Spanish about cafés in town.

"Cerrado," the cashier said. "Everything closed. We bought and reopened this market two months ago."

Eating mangos and bananas on the store's porch, I flipped through a calendar, free at the cash register, put out by Farmworker Legal Services. It had a multiplication table to calculate paychecks, a guard against growers who stole farmworker wages.

Leaving the path, we got lost and arrived an hour late at the home of Leigh and Kris, Warmshowers hosts who lived in Grand Rapids.[11] Kris put a perfectly grilled burger in front of me, my first after thirty-five years of vegetarianism. That and the pie that followed were manna from heaven. At breakfast, Leigh printed out a Google map with explicit directions out of town. A car accident forced us to detour from Leigh's map, but we found a parallel road. Making good time, we dallied at an East Indian café, cooing, as a customer whose business card read *Grandpa. Services: Hugs and Kisses* showed us photos of his job security.

Back on the road, a man in a suit ran out of his office and pointed at a harrowing intersection. "I apologize for Grand Rapids," he said. "A horrible place for a bicycle. We're trying, but we're broke."

Absorbed in surviving those dangerous roads, it was late afternoon before we realized we'd taken a wrong turn on 60th Street, making a thirty-mile circle around the city. The road out of town might have been fun if I had been fresh. But I was tired, and the narrow curves frightened me. Climbing a hill to the Indian Valley Campground at sunset, we took in the faux-Native décor and missed the *Sorry—Full* sign. David's cajoling did not persuade the owners to give us a corner for our tiny tent. As we left in the dark, he spun a sunny view to console me:

"We're lucky not to get stuck in that racist place."

Entering Middleville, Michigan, we passed a cemetery. David chirped, "We have a last resort."[12]

"Everyone's last resort," I replied, grimacing.

We passed a steepled church and spilled onto Main Street. On the other side of downtown was a bench by a trail next to a creek, with a pole embossed with *May Peace Prevail on Earth* in four languages. We agreed to wait until

11 Warmshowers is a bicycle host network: warmshowers.org.

12 Bike tourers like cemeteries for stealth camping because they can usually get away with it, and there is a water source.

dark to set up camp by the peace pole. After manicotti at Faro's Italian Pizza, we washed and changed in the restaurant bathroom. Fireworks colored the sky on the other side of the marsh as we erected the tent.

Planning to leave unnoticed, we arose early, but people were already streaming past our tent, walking, running, biking. A man crouched with his camera to capture swans and their reflection. A father and son fished from a canoe. A professional photographer emerged from the trail and took our portrait. An elderly woman out for her morning walk exclaimed, "Using this spot as a campsite! What a great idea!"

A man in his sixties stopped jogging to question us. "I'm an educator too," he said. "Would you like to take a shower? My townhouse is the first one on the right. I'll get you fresh towels."

Clean and renewed, we had breakfast at the Big Easy, a deli with a New Orleans theme. Conversation crossed tables. Was the food fabulous, or just very good, with creme-de-la-community sweetening each bite? We had camped at the entrance of a three-mile paved segment of the Paul Henry—Thornapple Trail along the Thornapple River. Leaving on the path whose entrance was our home for a night, we passed human fishers sharing the creek's bounty with a blue heron. I thought, *Apologies, Joni Mitchell: sometimes, paradise is paved.*[13]

A TINY WOMAN WITH long gray hair sat next to us at Booksellers Books & Coffee in Mason, Michigan. Her husband joined us. He was slight like his wife, with a gray ponytail. The two had married in 1983, when they were in their late fifties, and they acted like newlyweds. She leaned over and lowered

13 Reference: the lyrics in "Big Yellow Taxi", Joni Mitchell, 1970.

her voice. "I lost a grandchild," she said. "It is worse than losing a child, watching your baby experience this ultimate tragedy. Nothing you can do to take away the pain."

Before I could find the appropriate response, she wanted to exchange feminist awakenings. For me, it was realizing all the identifiable characters in John Dos Passos's *USA Trilogy* were male. For her, it was reading the Shakespearean play *Henry VIII*. Her voice shook with fresh anger as she told me of her girlhood revenge fantasies against the misogynist king. I wondered if the ancient story of matricide pierced something personal and traumatic.

We returned to our food and our husbands.

A few minutes later she tapped my shoulder and whispered conspiratorially, "I'm responsible for the Mackinac Bridge!"

I looked confused. She clarified. "Between Michigan and Wisconsin, in the Upper Peninsula. I visited our senator, who planned to vote against it. Acting like a stupid woman—it *was* the fifties—I asked, 'Is the rumor true? Does Wisconsin get the UP if the bridge isn't built?' The next day, Mr. Senator voted for the bridge."

"You need to do your stupid woman routine again," I said. "Trick today's politicians into filling Michigan's potholes and fixing its bridges."

She smiled.

WE ARRIVED IN DANSVILLE, Michigan—population 500—before dusk, ready to stop, but our options didn't look good. The general store owner—happy to sell us his frozen treats—changed his tone when we inquired about camping. He pointed out the door. "There's a campground ten miles down the road."

Outside the store, a young man with a gentle face, shoulder-length brown hair, and a gray ARMY shirt, out for ice cream with his dogs, his wife, and his eight-year-old daughter, gestured toward us. We stood together, five humans licking cones, two dogs catching drips.

"You need some water for those bottles?" ARMY shirt asked. David nodded.

As we walked the suburban tract road to the family's home, the young man pointed at each house, telling us about each resident who was currently serving in or recently returned from Iraq or Afghanistan.

WE SLEPT IN A strip of Department of Natural Resources land outside Dansville, covered in waist-high grass. Third day in a row going to bed without bathing. At 5:20 a.m., mosquitoes chased us out of our temporary home and onto the road, fueled by a scoop of oats and nuts. We sleep-rode, enjoying the early morning despite our need for food and showers. Aware we'd begun to smell, I worried about obtaining the former without the latter. The sign *Come As You Are* on the bright blue diner in Gregory, Michigan, seemed written for us. Inside, three male customers were telling "Nam tales" as though the war had ended yesterday. David asked, "Can you give us directions to Doyle Road?"

"Go to Hell," they answered as one.

Signs to Hell, Michigan, led us in a circle on unpaved roads to a roadside park not far from Dansville, whose outhouse we'd visited in the morning.

"It's the ride, not the destination that counts," David philosophized.

His Zen attitude irritated me more than our purgatory circuit. I held on to my foul mood until we crossed the threshold of Dexter's Foggy Bottom Coffee House outside Ann Arbor. It was a world away from Gregory, or Hell. Helmet off, I ran my fingers through my sweaty locks and read about "hair healers" in *Southeastern Michigan's Conscious Living Magazine*.

Huron River Drive into Ann Arbor reminded me of the River Roads along the Mississippi in the Twin Cities, but here, bikers and cars competed for the same slice of pavement. Hiding above the river was a phenomenon we had yet to see in Michigan: luxury homes of the fabulously wealthy. We shared that observation with our host Janet, a journalist for the *Ann Arbor News*. She nodded, saying, "The growing wealth divide is most visible in the housing market. We've seen an explosion in foreclosures and multi-million-dollar mansions."

After a restful night, we thought we'd spend the early hours hanging out in a funky Ann Arbor café. Maybe I'd get a massage or have my hair healed. City traffic, narrow roads, and no bike lanes put an end to those plans. On a sidewalk out of town, a man handed us a leaflet protesting the collusion of the United Auto Workers and bosses. I expressed solidarity and a desire to learn more. He shrugged. He was a man without work, paid by activists to hand out literature he had not read.[14]

In front of a Toyota plant on the outskirts of Ann Arbor, the asphalt got smoother before returning to Michigan-norm. As we got close to the Michigan-Ohio border, the rutted gravel on Petersburg Road rattled my spine, and my speed fell to five miles per hour. But traffic was light, and we weren't lost. David made a game of missing the holes I hit. I joked, "I'm getting that massage I dreamt of in Ann Arbor."

---

14 In the 1930s, autoworkers in Flint, Michigan, sat down and built a mighty union, forcing General Motors and Ford to invest in Michigan communities. After the 2008 stock market crash, Presidents Bush and Obama salvaged GM while forcing a downsize of wages and workers. Autoworkers still on the line in 2011 no longer made a send-your-kid-to-college living, and the roads their product relied on were barely passable.

7

PAY-PER-VIEW

Ohio

Money . . . can [not] induce us to sell the lands on which we get sustenance. . . . We know that these settlers are poor. . . . [D]ivide therefore this large sum of money, which you have offered to us, among these people. . . . If you add also the great sums you must expend in raising and paying Armies, with a view to force us to yield you our Country, you will certainly have more than sufficient for the purposes of repaying these settlers.
—Western Indian Confederacy, 1793[15]

Every new town, field, and wood we biked through belonged to us, our memories, our deed of ownership. Now, we owned the dewy morning on the Michigan-Ohio border. Despite my internationalist heart, I hummed. *Spacious skies, amber waves of grain,* feeling a catch in my throat as we passed endless fields of wheat and hay. *Amber, yes. And gold, orange, rust—even purple.*

The rural peace ended at the state border as we entered the Toledo metropolitan area. At a busy intersection, a hardy woman named Cheryl, wearing a bike jersey, pulled up beside us. Before the light turned green, she offered to escort us around the outskirts of the city. We followed her. No arguments, no

15 Western Indian Confederacy to the Commissioners of the United States, August 13, 1793, as excerpted by the author. http://nationalhumanitiescenter.org/pds/livingrev/expansion/text6/negotiations.pdf.

getting lost, no decisions. Cheryl was fast, efficient, and eager to show off her bicycle skills, which she had won the hard way.

"At forty-one, I had back surgery," she explained. "Biking was therapy. First, I could only make it around the block. Fourteen years later, I do sixty-mile rides. I sewed a quilt with fifty panels. Bike a state, fill a panel. Twenty-seven so far."

Cheryl wanted us to appreciate her homeland. "See the black dirt? Back in the 1880s, European settlers drained these wetlands and created the richest soil in the world." When she left us at the Shops at Fallen Timbers in Maumee, she directed, "This mall sits on historical ground. Look it up."

Tired from keeping up with Cheryl, I found a plush seat at the Barnes & Noble and entered the 1790's. To stop white settlers from moving west across the Ohio River, the Western Indian Confederacy proposed a generous compromise signed by twelve Indigenous nations. The United States chose invasion. Native warriors, led by Miami Chief Little Turtle, Shawnee Chief Blue Jacket, and Lenape Chief Buckongahelas joined forces to fend them off. On August 20, 1794, US General "Mad Anthony" Wayne led his troops in the Battle of Fallen Timbers.[16]

Toledo celebrates Anthony Wayne with a bridge, memorial statue, school, freeway, and annual family-friendly bike ride. In addition to this shopping center, a movie theater, golf course, and environmental center have adopted the Fallen Timbers appellation. On our way out of the mall, we passed a rack of Cleveland Indians T-shirts with cartoon heads.

We left the parking lot and crossed the Maumee River, where Wayne's troops burned Shawnee and Miami villages.

We didn't get far. Desperate to get out of the sun, we accepted the *Public Welcome* sign at the Riverby Hills Golf Club. Retreating into the icy dark

---

16 Ibid. One of the Indigenous leaders involved in the Fallen Timbers battle, Shawnee Chief Tecumseh, continued building a pan-Indian force to fight US encroachment until he died fighting the US in the War of 1812.

of the clubhouse to drink overpriced tomato juice, we watched men in white shorts flirt with the woman bartender.[17] I picked up the newspaper. "The Tribe Is Not Doing Well," the headline read, referring to baseball, not the aftermath of Fallen Timbers. Inside was a small article titled, "New Program for Sandusky Homeowners: Mow Foreclosed Lots, and the Land Is Yours." I showed it to David. "The Homestead Act gave Shawnee and Miami land to white settlers. Sow to own. Now, it's mow to own."

TEN MILES FARTHER, THE landscape pancaked. I had discovered this flat Ohio plain in the fall of 1975, when I rented a bicycle to escape the loneliness of Oberlin College. A few pedals and the bike rode itself, away from the college I would soon leave for good.

At the Sunoco gas station in Haskins, guys in pickups gathered to eat pizza and buy twelve-packs. I saw one young man place a can between his legs under the steering wheel, eleven more within arm's distance on the passenger seat. We joined the guys on the pizza. I immediately regretted it. In Bowling Green, I insisted that we splurge at an upscale vegetarian place where waiters described each ingredient. It was dark by the time we left the restaurant. With an image of man, car, and beer still lodged in my head, I ruled out biking five miles to the campground. Bowling Green State University was hosting a marching band contest at their football stadium. Hotels had jacked up their prices. David was ready to pay $130 for an overpriced room at a Best Western. I was not.

17 In Wisconsin, I lived down the hill from the Blackhawk Golf Course. Like the Western Indian Confederacy at Fallen Timbers, Sauk Chief Black Hawk's struggle for sovereignty in 1832 ended in a massacre of Indigenous people. Both crimes of racial violence and land theft opened the way for statehood and white settlement.

We rode through town to the soundtrack of drums, horns, and cheering crowds, searching for a place to camp. David wanted to hide. I argued we should stake a claim, act as though we belonged. I spied a thirty-two-foot RV parked in a campus lot.

"Let's do an Arlo Guthrie," I said.

"What?"

"In *Alice's Restaurant*, he saw a pile of trash and added his to the heap. We'll join the RV and call it a campground."

Arlo had gotten arrested for littering. Like him, I wasn't thinking this through; and David didn't remember the movie. We set up in full view, next to the RV and under a streetlight. At 2:00 a.m., I had to pee. Imagining myself getting arrested for indecent exposure, I grabbed a plastic bag and squatted by the door. The squatting encouraged the vegetarian spinach and eggplant dish to dislodge the pizza. I crawled into the spotlight to look for a place to dispose of the bag.

Back in the tent, awake and unclean, I resented the man sleeping sweetly beside me: for being anatomically equipped, for being right about finding a dark place, for being right about taking the hotel, for being able to sleep without a shower, for focusing on the best outcome while I imagined every possible wrong turn.

At 4:53 a.m., we broke camp. David went to find a bush to pee into while I strapped the tent to my bicycle.

"You in that tent?"

I looked up at the campus cop. Underneath me was a square imprint of smashed grass. I nodded.

He looked me over. I was disheveled, pungent, old enough to be his mother.

"How far you come on those bicycles?"

I looked at my odometer. "Seven hundred sixty-two miles."

"That's something. You need anything?"

"Huh. A bathroom?"

He raised an eyebrow and an arm, as if to say, "*That's obvious!*"

"Follow me."

We followed the police car as it snaked through campus, stopping at the stadium where thousands had cheered their young musicians the night before. The cop got out and beckoned, then hesitated.

"Are you two married?"

We nodded. He unlocked the women's locker room door. "Roll your bikes in here so no one will mess with them. When you leave, close the door. It'll lock automatically."

As a middle-aged white woman of short stature, I was used to being considered unthreatening. With David, the aura of heterosexual respectability surrounded me. Now, wandering across lines of legality, we leaned on various forms of privilege, never knowing the extent to which our demographics protected us—aware that, without showers and laundromats, we could lose assumptions of innocence. The officer trusted us. His gift of showers erased our growing scent of indigence.

Bowling Green athletes had posted inspiring quotes and pictures of people they admired on the hallway wall. The bicycle woman in her fifties—cleaned, dressed, and feeling new—posed in front of the wall of fame.

AT AN ITALIAN EATERY in Clyde, Ohio, owner and waitress served us minestrone and a local tale of malfeasance. "The school superintendent had this knack for fundraising," the owner explained. "The newspapers loved him— 'til he was caught siphoning funds. In jail now. Got seven years."

"His salary was two hundred thousand dollars," the waitress interjected. "What'd he need the money for?"

"Funny thing," the owner continued. "He's still in the headlines, now as the villain." He shook his head. "You don't expect that kind of greed in a small town."

"I do," the young waitress said.

Not wanting a repeat of Bowling Green, we decided to get a room in Clyde. The Winesburg Motel—named after the book by native son Sherwood Anderson, in which a young man grows up in a town rife with secrets and corruption—was owned by an extended family from India. They lived there and grew peas and potatoes in a tiny patch in front of the office. We opened the door wide and took our seats on the edge of the sidewalk, watching brothers, sisters, aunts, and grandmothers move from one room to another, carrying food, laundry, and children.

Leaving Clyde, we transitioned from farmland to waterfront. We were never more than a quarter mile from Lake Erie, but we rarely glimpsed it. Most of the shoreline was private. At Firefly Campground, twenty-five dollars bought us a piece of grass and a sunset over the lake—pay-per-view.

A TALL, YOUTHFUL RETIREE in Vermillion, Ohio, made reckless circles around us, showing off his athletic prowess. He stopped to chat with a blond woman on a one-speed. The two caught up with us in a park as we changed a tire. The woman—younger than me by a decade, but more used up—wore white pants, a tie-dyed tee, and fancy blue flip-flops. She gave me a woman-to-woman squeeze, took a horn etched with a smiley face off her bike, placed it on my handlebars, and offered me a sip from her coffee cup. "It's not spiked," she said. "It's a good morning. I'm still sober."

Later, as we watched a Canadian cargo ship go under the Black River drawbridge, the woman rode by us, tanked up and barefoot. At the Root Café, west of Cleveland, I labored to write about her. Did she trade her flip-flops for a drink? As we left the café, her gift smiled at me from my handlebars.

IN CLEVELAND, A COUPLE with a home full of kids invited us to stay two nights. In their backyard, David rounded out a dodgeball team while I changed the height of the plastic basketball hoop per the wishes of pint- and quart-size players. The father slow-cooked a meal so exquisite that even eight small children focused on eating. Though the adults were younger than us, I felt like one of their offspring. We played, ate, and went to bed early. As I drifted off to sleep, I thought, *halfway between Minnesota and New York—we biked to Cleveland*!

The family's home was six miles from downtown Cleveland. We had a day to see the city. David wanted to take the bus, but I insisted we go on foot. I was eager to take in urban infrastructure, public spaces, and diverse multitudes. Walking, we could admire Cleveland's waterfront parks and public art.

Cleveland confounded and entranced me. On a block of brownstones that looked like a scene from a 1940s movie, *There's No Place Like Om* advertised naked yoga for men. We ate at a tiny soul food lunch counter that could have been in Harlem, yet people on the street walked slowly like they do in the heartland. As we entered downtown, a brick wall mural mirrored the magnificent urban visage of bridge, lake, and skyline. In front of the Cleveland Art Museum, I admired swans, and lovers, while David retreated into the cool of the building. I sat on the grass alone, relishing the moment. Catching up with him, I gushed, "New and old, Northeast and Midwest—we've cycled to an in-between place!"

David scowled. "No more days off, walking in the sun!"

"But think of what we would have missed," said I, a walker who bikes.

Leaving the next morning on the Cleveland Lakefront Bikeway, we bewildered other cyclists when we paused to photograph a Cleveland Public Power billboard. John D. Rockefeller made his first million from this region of Ohio, in North America's first oil boom. Cleveland "sewer socialists" extracted some of that petroleum wealth and poured it into museums, parks, and, eventually, a publicly owned utility.

On the east edge of town, mansions big as city blocks blocked our view of the water.

IN A SMALL TOWN outside of Cleveland, a couple of bicycle activists waved us over.

"There's a bridge out ahead. We'll get you permission to walk across and avoid the twenty-mile detour."

The foreman at the site wasn't happy to see our loaded bikes, but he relented. When I saw the steep and slippery ravine, I wished he hadn't. Seeing the terror on my face, a construction worker with pectorals the size of a cyclist's thighs lifted my loaded bike over his head and carried it across. I followed, squatting and sliding down on my butt. As I began the upward climb, I felt his mighty arm lift me gently to the ridge. He shrugged off my thanks. "This is what I do all day: carry stuff from one side to the other."

THE YOUNG COOK AT the Lighthouse Café in Conneaut, Ohio, was excited to hear where we were from. "I was in Rochester, Minnesota, once. Had a job sandblasting and painting water towers. I brought my gun—thought I could do some hunting. But it was a city with a big hospital! It was kinda sad, people visiting relatives dying of cancer."

"Sandblasting is like coal mining suspended in midair," he explained. "We used six tons of sand and black lightning to clean inside water towers. I liked the travel and the money, but it wasn't good for my health. When you're spraying, it's so dark you can't see. You're breathing in the chemical, like having black lung disease."

He placed an artfully made-to-order veggie sandwich on the table. "Not making much here, but I enjoy it. I've got a high school certificate in Culinary Arts."

Before the sandwich disappeared, a young man from Texas, biking from Seattle to Maine, joined us and ordered an orange juice. "How did you like Minnesota's bike paths and campgrounds?" I asked, expecting an enthusiastic response—unaware that the Minnesota legislature, in a showdown with the state's governor, had shut down public amenities.

He grimaced. "State parks were closed, private campgrounds full. Minnesota was the worst part of my trip."

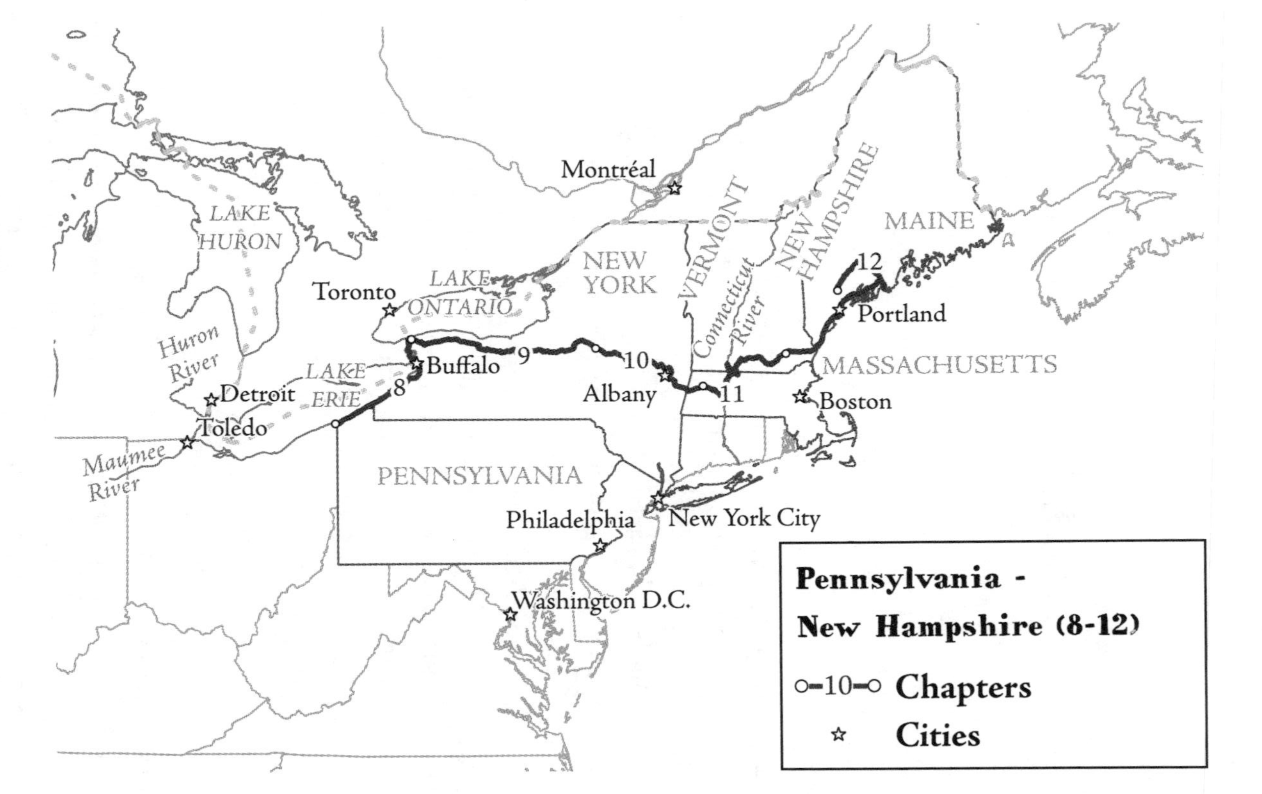
LAKE HURON
Huron River
Detroit
Toledo
Maumee River
Toronto
LAKE ONTARIO
LAKE ERIE
Buffalo
8
9
10
11
12
Montréal
NEW YORK
Albany
VERMONT
Connecticut River
NEW HAMPSHIRE
MAINE
Portland
MASSACHUSETTS
Boston
PENNSYLVANIA
Philadelphia
New York City
Washington D.C.
Pennsylvania -
New Hampshire (8-12)
10 Chapters
Cities

8

SISTERS IN A BROTHER'S PLACE

Pennsylvania, New York, and Ontario

Over the Ohio/Pennsylvania border, we hit the 1,000-mile mark and I got a flat. Sitting at the bottom of an acre of lawn, we fought.

"You are not patient enough to let me change it," I whined.

The truth? I wasn't either. I had learned this basic repair at the Hub Bike Co-op in Minneapolis, using a bike with looser tires. My hands weren't strong enough to pull out my tightly-fitted one. But the tire was no longer a tire; it represented patriarchy itself.

Professor and school social worker sat on the corner of someone's yard using their outside voices, volume expanding into space. After a while, David changed the tire. While he worked, my mind drifted, frustration dissipating. I stared meditatively at a brick silo that appeared too old to be in the Midwest. Had we just entered the Northeast?

ERIE, PENNSYLVANIA, WAS AN industrial city without exurban sprawl. Leaving the smokestacks behind, we crossed the border between urban and rural quicker than expected. By the time we desired indoor relief from the heat, all options had passed. Shades Beach Park on East Lake Road, a few miles from the New York border, had woods deep enough to dump clothes and a creek hidden enough to skinny dip. Afterward, I slipped on a sundress. Clean and rested, we laid our mats under a willow. Our caressing was interrupted by two nearly identical men in their fifties, skinny, shirtless, graying blond hair, towels in one hand, smokes in the other. They approached, standing close. One of them said, "Have you ever seen a more beautiful place in the world?"

I sat up, resting my back on the tree. Lake Erie flowed on one side. Grape arbors snaked along the other. I nodded to let him know I could see the landscape from his perspective.

The other man, standing a foot from my underwear lying carelessly beside me, finished the reverie. "More concord grapes grow here than anywhere else on earth. Next time you put Welch's on your sandwich, you think of us." He leaned over, extended his hand eastward. "You won't have problems with people here, but you watch out in New York. They ain't all wrapped too tight."

"Wackos, if ya know what I mean," the first fellow chimed in.

By now we had gotten used to people warning us about the next neighborhood, town, or state. But I wondered if there was a specific history behind these men's distrust of the other. Decades earlier, Welch's recruited Puerto Rican, Black, Mexican, Seneca Indian, and European migrant workers to process their grapes and bunked them in segregated dorms, playing on racial animosities to keep workers from organizing. Did that divide and conquer strategy still pay dividends for the company? In a month Welch's would lay off two-thirds of their Michigan employees and transfer work—but not workers—to this Pennsylvania plant. Did these men know they had bigger things to worry about than "wackos" across the border?

As we entered the Cattaraugus Reservation, at the New York border, cars with fifty-foot boats took advantage of tax-free tobacco and gas. We stopped at a fruit stand and took advantage of freshly picked blueberries and a slice of shade. "Do you have an outhouse?" I asked the woman staffing the stand.

"Sort of," she said, inviting me to share her bucket and shower curtain.

Resting at the Breezy Point Café, I watched local TV. The Buffalo newscaster was shocked! The reservation sold tax-exempt cigarettes! This ancient news was the total of airtime devoted to the Seneca Nation. There was no mention of an upcoming reservation festival with dance contests, historical enactments, and Seneca language classes. The rest of the news was a police blotter: fires, pedestrian deaths, robberies. If it divides, it provides. No wonder our Welch's friends feared those "on the other side."

SHERRY WAS SIXTY BUT looked forty—the first woman we met touring solo—cycling New York's Great Lakes Seaway Trail from one campground to the other.

"No stealth camping without a partner. That's where I draw the line," she said as she joined us around our firepit at Lake Erie State Park.

I had taken one bike trip alone: a five-day Wisconsin circle. Instead of relishing the solitude, my mind had fixated on defending myself against attackers. But I had one thrilling encounter on that trip. A woman riding with her male partner had asked me for advice about bike repair and long-distance riding. To be seen as that kind of woman! The self-esteem buzz had lasted for weeks. Now, I looked at Sherry with those same eyes. I was jealous. I didn't want to ditch David. I wanted to ditch the feeling I couldn't do what Sherry was doing. I wanted a soul mate, a traveling companion, not a protector. I had both. It wasn't David's fault that his presence provided more safety for me than mine did for him, but I still resented that fact. There was no path out of this dilemma, only dependent compromises.

ALL MILES ARE NOT equal. The first five can fly by. Sometimes a quarter mile can be nearly impossible. Bikers call it *bonking*. No food or drink—DayGlo blue or otherwise—will help. You need to stop. Exhausted by traffic, hills, and curves with no sightlines, I bonked as we entered Hamburg, New York. The owner of the Hamburg Pleasant Market didn't know of any nearby campgrounds. We stalled, buying blueberries, then peapods, then banana bread. As we sat down on the edge of the parking lot to eat, de-bonk, and figure out where to sleep, the owner approached. I prayed he wouldn't make us move.

"I talked to my caretaker," he said. "They agreed. You can camp in the back of my store."

The grassy knoll behind the market and the caretaker's house overlooked a slope of orchards and vegetable fields, with Lake Erie on the horizon. In the morning, the caretaker put on hot water for tea and ushered us in for showers. Colleen was a strong woman with voluptuous hair. She was recovering from a motorcycle accident. The driver who had run into her had been on a cell phone. Her injuries had forced her to quit her job.

I hugged Colleen hard before we left. We both cried as I tried to explain what her hospitality meant to us. It wasn't the first extraordinary kindness extended to us by strangers, and it certainly wouldn't be the last. But at this point in the trip, I was still overwhelmed by such treatment. I thought back to the woman who had offered us a place to stay during the tornado in Wisconsin. I was accepting assistance now—some of it surely lifesaving—but it still amazed me.

Colleen shook her head. "I'm a nurse without a job," she said. "We need to help people. You are doing me a favor."

DESERTED DOWNTOWN BUFFALO WAS easy to bike, but the shuttered inner city with abandoned buildings turning green was eerie. As we entered a neighborhood, a few people sat on porches and in front of bars. We passed a colorful sign that read *Seneca Street Community: A Proud Past and Promising Future*. No mention of the present, which appeared shockingly depressed. In Buffalo's twin city, Niagara Falls, we passed the infamous locus of environmental injustice, where William T. Love had promised to build a canal linking Lake Ontario and the Niagara River. A one-mile trench was all Niagara got. The Love Canal became a dumping ground for toxic waste.

In a Black and Latino neighborhood in the shadow of the Rainbow Bridge, we stopped at a McDonald's to cool off. Here, life seemed more hopeful; people were engaged in living. A few blocks later, we saw signs of organizing. A billboard of human silhouettes surrounded by a rainbow flag announced *Pride Spoken Here*. Lawn placards in apartment windows read *Ya Es Suficiente, Yo Soy Pacifista* and *Enough Is Enough, I Am Committed to Peace*. We'd need to stay longer to witness residents growing community gardens, organizing car and bike sharing, creating something new and people-centered out of the toxic rust, but we were headed across the border.[18]

We thought. For an hour we circled barren alleys and parking lots, before we found the pedestrian entrance to the international bridge. We joined the line, jittery with frustration and excitement.

"Where have you been?" the customs official asked.

"Buffalo," David said, in that obedient tone you use at border crossings.

The US officer raised her eyebrows, looked sideways, and waited. We

18 Evidence of these people-centered efforts can be found in the alternative newspaper *The Public*, at the African Heritage Food Co-op, in the organizing of Buffalo Food Not Bombs.

followed her gaze toward the sign, *Sidewalk to Canada,* and the giant arrow pointing the other direction.

On the bike path along the Canadian side of the Niagara River, people sat in folding chairs next to their vehicles. No cell phones, Frisbees, or other distractions. Impressed by this popular embrace of public space, we decided to spend the night at a public park with a large picnic area.

I asked a family enjoying a meal, "Is a restroom—I mean, washroom—nearby?"

The woman pointed to the woods.

Behind a tree, I slipped on a long sleeveless dress. David locked the bikes, and we went in search of a shower and a drink. Under a hose attached to a maintenance building in a nearly empty public golf course, we drank our fill and soaked our heads. I slipped off my underwear and sprayed under my dress.

At dusk, the Ontario Provincial Police cleared cars out of the lot. Only then did we realize our "park" was the private lawn of Marineland. We hid behind a tree until they left and put up the tent in darkness. Lying awake, I listened to the dolphins sing.

At 7:00 a.m., we had Niagara Falls to ourselves.

For breakfast, five Canadian dollars got us "two plates with brown toast" at Simon's Restaurant, a 110-year-old diner filled with old newspapers and men over eighty. The waitress gave me a sisters-in-a-brothers'-place smile.

ON THE LEWISTON-QUEENSTON BRIDGE, in the customs line with all the other non-cars, we followed trucks, RVs, and buses onto the New York freeway. Off at the first exit, we headed down a mountain the wrong way. Forgetting our morning pledge not to veer from our path, we continued north on the Robert Moses State Parkway, with the flow and against the plan.[19] A minister on a bicycle from the Assemblies of God church stopped in the middle of the parkway and asked if he could pray for us. I thought he meant he would add us to his daily prayers, but he bowed his head right there on the street and motioned for us to do likewise.

He prayed for our safe journey.

I surprised myself, praying, *Let it continue to be this good.*

19 The name of Robert Moses State Parkway was changed to Niagara Scenic Parkway in 2016.

9

PROGRESS AND STRUGGLE

New York

If you seem to not have a bed to go to, you are more likely to be harassed for sleeping in public. Striving to appear not to need the afternoon nap we needed, we slouched in matching armchairs at the library in Porter, New York, bicycle repair books covering snoozing faces. We did not fool the sharp-eyed librarian. When I rose to use the restroom, she showed me a county map and encouraged us to move on. We did, but I forgot my bike gloves. When I snuck back to retrieve them, she accosted me.

"Where ya headed tonight?"

"Lockport."

She shook her head disapprovingly. "Lockport is landlocked!" She handed me a scribbled note: a map to Four Mile Creek State Park on Lake Ontario. "This is where ya want to stay."

Joining the crowd amassing on the hill overlooking Lake Ontario to watch the sunset, I thanked the librarian. The silhouette of Toronto's CN Tower on the northern bank was yellow, and then crimson purple. City lights rose and bled rainbows across the water.

THE ERIE CANAL TOWPATH—A dusty tree-lined lane along a creek bed, dotted with towns at perfect intervals—promised a serene ride to Albany. Mules and men once sweated here, towing barges from the Atlantic coast to the Great Lakes to profit global traders. Today, capital still extracted wealth from this upstate corridor in the form of produce and cheese.

We ate a pound of local tart cherries next to a twelve-foot concrete red apple, a monument to the fruit growers for their contribution to the local economy. A sign at the Cambria city limits read *Right-to-Farm Town*, warning urban interlopers enjoying Upstate New York beauty that they had no right to complain about agricultural noise, smells, and sights.

As we entered Cambria, we saw a cabbage grower on his tractor, overseeing three farmworkers. We found no monument or posted ordinance to honor or protect the rights of these men weeding cabbages, or their 80,000 fellow workers, who had been marching on Albany for years, demanding "overtime pay, a day of rest per week, and workers' compensation when injured on the job."[20]

LEAVING THE TOWPATH'S COOL, we joined trucks and commuters on steamy, shoulderless thoroughfares into Rochester, New York, through impoverished neighborhoods that made our destination—a stately mansion—even grander. Tom McCart, a laid-off Episcopal priest, offered ice water, showers, pasta with tomatoes and pine nuts, a glass of wine, and a tour.

The city was depressed. The Service Employees International Union called for wage increases to fight Rochester's poverty, but town bigwigs had other

20 "Legislative Memo: Regarding the Farmworkers Fair Labor Practices Act," NYCLU: The ACLU of New York, last modified May 18, 2015. https://www.nyclu.org/en/legislation/regarding-farmworkers-fair-labor-practices-act.

plans. "The Erie Canal used to run through downtown," Tom told us. "They moved it to the edge of the city a century ago. Now they want to move it back to attract conventions."

"More residents here than in town," he observed wryly, as he drove us through the historic Rochester cemetery. We visited the gravesites of Susan B. Anthony and Frederick Douglass. Anthony's white tombstone was knee-high, with no special inscription. Douglass's sons had made sure he had a stone worthy of his stature. On it, visitors left versions of a favorite quote: "Without struggle, there is no progress."

"UNPRECEDENTED HEAT WAVE: DON'T go outside," the weather reporter said.

The heat index was 105 when we arrived at the Muddy Waters Café overlooking the canal in Palmyra, New York. We stayed longer than socially acceptable, then crawled up the hill into downtown seeking another cool place. A local newspaper publisher had printed the first *Book of Mormon* in Palmyra. The Church of Latter-Day Saints offered a free, air-conditioned tour. Our guide—a serious young woman from Seattle completing her two-year mission—saw me staring at a painting of Christ and followers on stone steps with Aztec-looking carvings and a pyramid in the distance.

"Jesus visited South America after the resurrection," she explained.

She showed us how they had printed the Book of Mormon in 1829. "When they skipped proofing a page and sent it straight to the chase to make copies, they called it cutting to the chase."

I told her, "On this trip, we are learning *not* to cut to the chase: not skipping steps like reading street signs, checking the map, putting on sunscreen, stretching, looking at the view, telling people our story, waiting to hear theirs."

"You and I are on the same journey," she said.

OUR NEXT STOP WAS the Palmyra library, a Victorian house filled with children recording their summer reading and moms drinking fifty-cent coffee. When it closed, it was still over one hundred degrees. Two blocks away, we found conditioned air, a sink bath, an ice machine, and chocolate shakes. We snuck in blueberries. The golden arches reopened at 5:30 a.m. We planned to camp on the trail and be their first customers.

The McDonald's scene got less celestial as the hours passed. A young father parked his van with windows open at the drive-through and desperately tossed Happy Meals® to crying kids in the back seat. A toothless man and his daughter with sad eyes breathed cool air and ate fries. They had just taken his wife to the emergency room. "Dehydrated," he explained. "She works at Kraft Foods. She didn't get a water break during her shift."

At dusk we returned to the towpath to find a place to camp. The entrance sign read, *Trail Closes 9:30 p.m.* We considered breaking the law, but some teenagers beat us to it, so we broke our own law against riding at night, cycling nine miles to Newark, New York, where the Canal Park sign spoke to me:

Closed 10 p.m. Except for Boaters.

"We'll dock our bikes with the other boats," I ordered my shipmate, "and get up before dawn to avoid trouble and take advantage of the morning cool."

The night air was thick with heat. Leaving the rainfly off and doors open, I lay without cover, head hanging out the door. Air conditioners cooling the town funneled hot fumes onto me. I baked. David slept.

At 4:30 a.m., David reached into yesterday's bike shirt for his wallet. "I had it last night. Someone stuck their hand in the tent and took it!"

His irrational and uncharacteristic panic had a calming effect on me.

Seizing the chance to be the logical one, I adopted a measured tone. "I was awake all night. I would have noticed."

It was six thirty before he found the wallet in his shorts. Still, we made our thirty-mile, get-out-of-the-heat destination by 9:40 a.m. Self-satisfied, we stopped for breakfast and planned to settle until evening. But Port Byron, New York, was a no-nonsense town. We needed nonsense—a library, an open museum, a laundromat, a coffee shop. We pushed through mid-morning heat to the next town.

Weedsport, New York, intersected with the State Thruway, so it had a truck stop. I slumped into a corner table with a sixty-four-ounce cup of ice and tea. What happened next, I do not understand. It looked like smoke. It smelled like sulfur. It singed my nose hairs. I tried to explain my dragon trick to my scientist mom on the phone:

"Am I internally combusting?"

"Get a hotel!"

We listened to Mom, paying highway ransom for air conditioning, a shower, a toilet, two queen beds, and curtains to block out the sun. Seventeen hours and four cold showers later, we found the towpath trail behind the Weedsport Arby's. It was barely a path here. At 6:00 a.m., riding overgrown grass beside a marshy canal, it was already ninety degrees. We dripped—perfect food for swampland mosquitoes. I made myself more delicious, pouring a bottle of water on my head.

Fifteen miles later, at the Sims' Museum store inside Camillus Erie Canal Park, we asked to use the bathroom. I guess we didn't look good, because the employees led us into a cool room and told us to sit. One woman brought snacks and little bags of ice for us to rub on our necks. Another called for places to stay. A third tried—unsuccessfully—to fit our bikes into her van to drop us off in Syracuse. The attention was a salve. Despite rising temperatures, we left of our own volition.

At the corner of Erie Boulevard and Genesee Street in Syracuse, we found shade under a tree and surveyed our options. A young Black man two streets away, slice of pizza in hand, ran toward us. "I'm going to bike to California someday," he said. "Do you ride at night?"

"No, and we also don't bike during the midday heat," I said.

"Do you know of a place where we can sit out of the sun?" David asked, finishing my thought.

Our desperation must have been visible. "Wait here," he said, and then sprinted into a nearby Denny's. He emerged with a white woman. "She's the manager!"

The manager managed. "Park your bikes on the side rail. I'll put you in the back by the air conditioner. Stay as long as you like."

SYRACUSE'S CLINTON SQUARE HAD a sculpture of men busting open a jail, freeing William Henry the barrel maker, who had escaped slavery. "Syracuse was a sanctuary city," I explained to David. "They refused to cooperate with the Fugitive Slave Act that required northern states to return people to enslavers."

A young woman reading *Nickeled and Dimed* on a park bench interjected, "Harriet Tubman hung out here back in the day."

NAVIGATING CITIES SAFELY TOOK a mental toll on us. I tried to establish walking as our modus operandi when bike paths and lanes were scarce. David found this frustrating. I won in Syracuse. A few blocks from the towpath, we retreated into the cool of an Indian restaurant. A woman from

Bangalore, holding a newborn, was curious. "My brother biked India without a map. Do you use maps?" I showed her how the phone tracked our moves, choosing not to mention we still got lost. An hour later, the iPhone took us on an extra ten-mile circle on hilly county roads. In the morning, we discovered the entrance to the campground our phones missed.

"Ah, well," we philosophized. "Practice for the Berkshires." A twenty-degree temperature drop precipitated this new positive attitude and allowed us to enjoy a wild and peaceful stretch of towpath into Utica.

OUR UTICA HOST, SYLVIA de Swaan, wasn't feeling well. Her refrigerator was empty, and she refused to partake in the grocery meal we bought. But she brightened as we talked. Sylvia was a renowned photographer. Her current project was a 365-day collaborative, reflecting on the news. On this day she had photographed graffiti on a bathroom stall that read, *The rape arena is global.* Hearing about Sylvia's process and examining the fruits of her labor was like visiting a great museum. She inspired me to listen and look more carefully. I realized it wasn't my job to record all events, but to capture my slice of the truth.

Windowless factory carcasses pockmarked Utica. The town's economic anchor, General Electric, had closed in the 1990s. We ate breakfast at a slip of a diner facing a stone church with half its stained glass out, wild prairie flowers where its lawn used to be. Five dollars bought us two plates of eggs, toast, and cups of tea. On Schuyler Street, an African American neighborhood, road signs were rusted artifacts. On Bleecker Street, an immigrant enclave, we rode slowly to miss the potholes. A man ran out of a small storefront and invited us inside. "Clothes, toys in good condition," he said. When we hesitated, he added, "It's all free."

At Continental Cleaners, the manager monitored the parking lot to help elders with their laundry. He told us about his youthful bicycle trips to

Montreal and Texas, then gave us his phone number. "In case you run into problems," he said. "I have friends all over the country."

Now, I thought, *we do too*.

ON THE OUTSKIRTS OF town was Remington Arms, still in business. Small row houses lined the street in front of the two-hundred-year-old rifle factory.[21]

21 On February 12, 2018, two days before the mass school shooting in Parkland, Florida, Remington filed for bankruptcy. Gun enthusiasts, believing restrictions wouldn't pass under Trump, had stopped stocking up. In 2021 it opened again, under new ownership.

10

TEMPTING FATE

New York and Massachusetts

When I was pregnant, I played Sweet Honey in the Rock's rendition of Kahlil Gibran's poem "On Children" to my fetus, preparing to embrace a child different from myself. It did not occur to me that I would give birth to an offspring like me in ways I had not figured out. As Emily grew, we spent afternoons color-coding and filing each other's school materials to tame our wandering brains. Emily danced. We walked distances together.

The day after I dropped Emily off at college in New York City, my Saint Cloud State position started. Absorbed in teaching other eighteen-year-olds, I thought—smugly—I had skipped the pain of the empty nest. But when the job ended, a hole in my heart opened.

As we crossed New York, "riding to Emily" kept me on the bike. We planned to meet in Northampton, Massachusetts, and again in New York City. I was looking forward to crossing the Hudson River, the same waterway they walked in Manhattan. But when we reached the Green Island Bridge over the Hudson in Troy, New York, I was too tired to glimpse the river that connected us. I used my last ounce of concentration to find a place to collapse.

Miraculously, after an hour in a Greek café, we left Troy, rested, fed, and de-bonked.

Entering Albany, exhausted again, we had to get out of the capitol city and find a place to camp, but the Dunn Memorial Bridge over the Hudson was under construction. We crisscrossed underneath its twisted concrete branches, following bicycle detour signs leading nowhere, until darkness forced us to seek shelter at the Red Carpet Inn up the riverbank, in north Albany.

In the morning, we rode back down the hill to catch a bus across the bridge. The driver grumbled as we held him up, unpacking our bikes and climbing on and off to retrieve ten bundles. "You moving to the other side of town?" he sneered. "You're taking all my seats. Get a taxi!"

David stood close to the front to show he wasn't using a seat while I sat with the bags. By the time we were across the bridge, the driver told David of his travel dreams and his daughter's biking exploits. He let us off at an irregular stop to save us a foothill and insisted on shaking our hands. Despite this unexpected, sweet send-off, our last twenty miles in New York were hell. State Bike Route 20 had holes on the shoulder big enough to camp in, forcing us to swerve into traffic on the narrow, winding road.

IN LITTLE FALLS, NEW York, we mailed my mom fifteen pounds of luggage—mostly the chain lock—to "lessen our load for the Berkshires." Still, as we approached our first mountain, my anxiety rose, manifesting itself as a pit in my stomach. At a sweet shop, I filled the hole with frozen bananas covered in chocolate and nuts, then added an ice cream chaser. Thirty minutes later, we stopped at a store where men on folding chairs blocked the doorway. One told us of his adventure in 1975 and the "trail angels" who had helped him. He insisted on buying us cones.

I approached Mount Lebanon with a belly full of sweet milk fat and an outsized notion of how these ten miles differed from the 1,700 preceding them. As we climbed, our mileage fell to walking speed. We rested every two miles. It took three hours. Cresting in Pittsfield, Massachusetts, I looked around for a cheering crowd.

Mundane survival swiftly overtook pride. What would we eat? Where would we stay? David rode off to investigate, leaving me in front of a brick building. My eyes drifted upward to a message in a top-floor window, written like a supermarket ad for pork loins.

Ready to Eat Pride.

"Rub it in," I mumbled.

Another message, in the next window, mocked me.

Cheap Thrills: 3 for 25 Cents.

"Not so cheap," I retorted.

Every window had a message that taunted.

Tempting Fate: All Sales Final.

Aerosol Trauma.

Fast-Acting Regret.

When David returned, we checked out a possible sleeping spot behind a park statue. Cheap but not thrilling. At the Marketplace Café, a folk music trio fed a hungry heart. Tears fell into my black bean burger. Through Google, David found camping at the Massachusetts Audubon Society's Canoe Meadows, which was a couple of miles away, but better than tempting fate at the city park. When we reached Canoe Meadows, it was too dark to appreciate its beauty but light enough to see the *No Camping* sign. Cursing the website, we set up in the parking lot. David used wet wipes to clean himself and was satisfied. They just made me stickier. He slept; I itched. Fast-acting regret.

The next morning, David returned from the Pittsfield Visitor Center, hand full of maps. "Here is the important part," he said triumphantly. "A handy-dandy chart of campgrounds. No more parking lots! No more nights without showers!"

We used the chart to find camping twenty-five miles and another mountain pass away. The climb topped on a small plateau with a convenience store, owned by an East Indian family, that had liquor, cigarettes, soda pop, and samosas, hot out of the oven, served with fresh mint sauce. In 1981, Dad and I had climbed a mountain on the Poland-Czechoslovakia border. At the top, a hut had served homemade soup. Now, hot samosas tasted like Polish cabbage.

Across the street from the convenience store was the Windsor, Massachusetts, library/town hall/police station. As we walked in, a twelve-year-old boy was checking in library books. I talked to his supervisor, Margaret, the volunteer librarian. "We have a small collection," she noted. "But it's still essential, especially in winter, when the mountain is too slippery to travel. It takes no time to close a library. It'd take ten years to reopen it."

When I asked her how to get to the campground, half a dozen library patrons gathered to correct her directions and assure us of the park's beauty and amenability. Buoyed by their enthusiasm and hospitality, we flew down the mountain and turned off at the park exit. Lovely, it was. A bubbling brook, giant pines, wildflowers, and a welcoming sign: *Windsor State Forest.*

In smaller letters was another sign: *Facility Closed for the Season.*

It had been a long season. Whole trees had grown up in fire pits. Sure of our isolation, we bathed naked in a mountain stream, got the tent up, and climbed inside before it began to thunder. Rain played music on the tent's nylon. Dry and warm, we laughed, thinking of the people at the library who boasted the delights of the campground. We took a picture of ourselves. Safe in our aloneness, we cuddled. I fell asleep.

At 2:40 a.m., a rush of cars careened the campground. Bar closing? Factory shift end?

An hour later, coyotes howled.

11

THIS IS LIFE

Massachusetts, Vermont, and New Hampshire

Phone Surveyor: "Do you plan on moving in the next six months?"
David: "Constantly."

At seventeen, before I dropped out of Oberlin College, I stole an orange beanbag chair out of the library to impress a boy. I carried it across campus to the door of my dorm before a police car rolled up. For my punishment, I spent a week accompanying a policewoman on her rounds. The officer schooled me on Oberlin outside the ivory tower, a working-class world the college took pains to shield from its students.

Entering Northampton, Massachusetts, we stopped at the Kentucky Fried Chicken to use the bathroom and ask for directions to Smith College. We were six blocks away, but none of the customers who gathered around us, eager to help, knew how to get there. From the KFC, we turned a corner and entered the university district of coffee shops, reflexology studios, and day spas. At a vegetarian café, I bought an organic mesclun salad for the cost of three finger-licking buckets of chicken.

NORTHAMPTON WAS A DESTINATION for us. Our niece and her infant lived here. David's sister Nancy was in town visiting her new grandchild. Best of all, Emily was here, up from New York City to attend a week-long dance workshop at Smith College. All that pleasure made what I did even more inexplicable.

On our first day in Northampton, I wanted David to know I had to be off the bike. He didn't get my silent message. He knew I needed a break, so he arose early and removed our panniers, preparing for an easy ride. When I came outside, he offered me the denuded bicycle with a giant grin—a gift.

The ride into town was seventeen lightly-descending miles on the edge of the maple-studded Berkshires, the kind of cycling people boarded planes to experience. And it was a gorgeous day: blue sky, puffy clouds, tailwind. But I needed a day off. I wanted to arrive clean and fresh in comfy civilian clothing, have a meal with Emily, window-shop, sit, and write. There was a public bus that went into town. Let someone else navigate!

Resentment inflamed my tired muscles. Anger played staccato on my temples. Moving onto a paved bike path, I stopped, forcing David to brake hard. I climbed off, picked up my bike, and hurled it into a stand of pines.

David retrieved the bike. He spoke gently. "It doesn't look damaged. We are almost there. Shall we walk the rest of the way?"

The rest of our Northampton stay was blissful. Our bikes went to an overnight spa for new tires, chains, and sprockets. We visited a hot tub, relaxed with family, watched Emily dance.

Back on the road, however, I felt unmoored. I didn't realize how much getting to Northampton for this family rendezvous had been motivating me. A blubbery sound escaped my throat. David rode silently behind me, monitoring my sobs, wary of the possibility of more erratic behavior.

Entering Vermont with the setting sun, I tried focusing on the task ahead. We couldn't afford any wrong turns if we were going to get to Fort Dummer State Park before dark. At a roadside store with empty shelves, we asked for directions. "It's seven miles," the store clerk said. "Watch out for the mammoth hill at the end." Two miles later, we posed the same question to a man raking his yard.

"Six miles. Good luck with that hill."

If we ask directions every two miles and each time they add a mile, how far would it be? I wondered. The calculation distracted me from the steep climb into the park.

THE NEXT MORNING, WE floated down the mammoth hill. At the bottom we stopped at a memorial stone that read *Kyle, 20, Who Made the Supreme Sacrifice in Iraq.*

On Brattleboro's Main Street, quaint shops filled the bottom of historical buildings, but their abandoned upper floors had glassless windows. A banner across the road proclaimed it *Breast-Feeding Awareness Week.* Yards and store windows sported yard signs that read *VY for VT!* and *Nuclear-Free Vermont!*

We asked a guy at a bike shop about the yard signs. "Vermont Yankee is a nuclear power plant," he explained. "The Regulatory Commission just renewed its contract, but the state legislature voted to make Vermont nuclear-free." He shrugged. "The conflict keeps newspapers in business."

The bike shop guy provided directions to a path east, through New Hampshire. He sized us up. "Some flatlanders find our trail rough. They're used to pavement."

It *was* rough. And no one else was roughing it, just two Minnesota flatlanders, pushing eighty pounds through mud and brush thick with mosquitos. After ninety minutes, we met the road and a *Welcome to Massachusetts* sign.

Pretending to be tough Yankees, we'd missed the trail going east and instead slogged five miles backward.[22] Never one to turn around, I insisted we

22 I'm still not sure what trail the bike store guy was sending us on. Perhaps the Wantastiquet Monadnock Trail? If so, we were probably better off slogging the river path. At least it was flat.

continue backward so as not to waste the effort. We went south another ten miles, before heading east and north again, up a mountain, through Warwick, Massachusetts. Forty-five miles to progress fourteen.

A mile from a public campground in Keene, New Hampshire, a man got out of his red sports car and waved wildly. "Camp in my yard!" he shouted. Our unexpected hosts, Erik and Debra, had taken their eleven-year-old son Tyler on a four-month bike trip from Boston to Seattle. Tyler told us, "I remember this moment when I realized, this isn't a trip—this is life!"

Tyler articulated a phenomenon we were just beginning to understand. On a trip, one can eat pizza every day, suspend sleep, lose touch with relatives, forget to floss. When a trip becomes life, the extraordinary becomes ordinary and one can no longer suspend the things one needs for mental, physical, and emotional maintenance. When we left Northampton, the trip was over. But we had yet to figure out life on the road.

WE RODE SOUTHERN NEW Hampshire foothills from one hamlet to another, enchanted by green peaks and church steeples. In Harrisville the red roof of a windowless woolen mill where immigrant girls once toiled created a brilliant accent to our blue sky. From there we drifted down, down, only to climb again to Hancock, where another café porch awaited.

Five miles from Greenfield State Park, we admired the late summer peaches and ruby plums of a roadside fruit vendor. An ice cream truck driver drove up. "Need a good blueberry source?" she asked the fruit man. "You sell. They get half the proceeds, no upfront money."

The fruit man seemed dubious. "My second sale of the day," he said when we decided on a pound of cherries. "You are my third," the woman said when he handed her a dollar and picked a creamy treat.

The fruit man addressed us then, pointing to the ice cream driver. "We've been doing business a long time. You heard of *USA Today*? She was my supervisor, accounting department. Before we got laid off, I had company stock worth ninety thousand dollars. Today it's worth twelve dollars and fifty cents."

As we rode off into the Monadnock pine forest, the two resumed negotiations, bartering and borrowing another day.

DAVID'S LACK OF DIRECTIONAL sense was legendary. As a teenager, he had missed a weekly dinner with his parents because the Steak House had—in his mind—moved. In his twenties, he had circled a workshop site and lost a job with the City of Minneapolis. In his forties, he had set out to plug the parking meter in Montreal and left me and Emily to order his dinner. When he found us again, his crepes had long been consumed.

I took pride in knowing where I was going, but my absentmindedness was as serious as David's directional challenge. Combining our deficits, we rode a north-south zigzag up New Hampshire hills and off our eastward route, landing at the Main Street Café in Wilton, New Hampshire. The proprietor shook her head. "Minnesotans are crazy," she said. "It's the long winters. They get a little sun, and they don't know what to do with it."

She stood over us while we ate her spinach omelets and baked beans, bragging, "Our Granny D was more amazing than you. Lived to a hundred. Walked across America at ninety for campaign finance reform!"

I agreed. Granny Doris Haddock was more amazing than us. We left Wilton satiated and inspired, but our collective disorientation quickly resumed. At Baboosic Lake, we ran into a dead end and turned back the wrong way. Scaling the lake's length three times, we stopped to blame each other, using precious energy. At home, one of us would leave. Now, that wasn't an option. We were stuck with each other, not as lovers or adventurers but as one dysfunctional entity.

"We always yell at each other when it rains, or when we are tired or hungry. What couple wouldn't?" wrote bicycle tourer Barbara Savage.[23] So true! In New Hampshire, however, the weather was perfect, and we were eating like royalty.

I think we'd reached a more existential level of tiredness—the kind when rest is not in your future, and the reason for your effort has come into question. Mom was in the hospital again, and though my brother Daniel said it wasn't serious, part of me wanted to head directly to her. I couldn't focus. At a wayside restaurant off the freeway, we called our Auburn, New Hampshire, host to explain our delay. "Detour's my middle name," he commiserated. "Luckily, my wife knows how to read a map."

23 Barbara Savage, *Miles From Nowhere: A Round-the-World Bicycle Adventure* (Seattle, Washington: Mountaineers Books, 1983), 49.

12

MAINE MAGIC

New Hampshire and Maine

We didn't talk about it. We both hoped the trip would provide a salve for a sex life so rife with land mines it didn't feel worth trying. I thought the ghosts would disappear on the road, that I would out-cycle past trauma and leave disorder in the dust. I hoped living outdoors would counteract the claustrophobia decades had not healed. But our tiny tent only compounded that problem. And I had not considered chronic vaginal infections. They don't talk about those things in *Adventure Cyclist*. We talked about infections. We did not talk about our relationship. Just surviving took most of our energy and dominated our conversation.

Survival consumed us in touristy Portsmouth, New Hampshire. Food was pricey. We needed rest but used precious energy searching for something cheap that would sustain us. We found it at Dos Amigos Burritos near the Piscataqua River. The bridge over the river was closed to cars while two states fought over who would pay for repairs, so we had it to ourselves as we entered Kittery, Maine.

Five miles out of Kittery, David's derailleur cable snapped. We walked to the Meet Market in Eliot, Maine, to ask about bike shops or hardware stores. A sailor named Ray gave us the number of his friend, Bicycle Bob.

"Bicycle Bob!" Emily exclaimed with a laugh when I made my nightly call. "There's a Bicycle Bob in *Fudge-a-Mania* who lives in southern Maine!" [24]

24 *Fudge-a-Mania* is a 1990 children's novel written by Judy Blume.

Fiction or fact, Bicycle Bob was not answering. Sailor Ray apologized for not having a place for us to stay. He pressed forty dollars into David's hand "for bike repairs" and suggested we ask the Eliot police if we could camp in their backyard.

The police officer was excited. "Never had a request like this before!" he exclaimed.

An hour later, another bicyclist saw our tent and asked if he could join us, and what never happened in Eliot happened twice in one evening. The newcomer called himself "Bike to Australia." He had been riding for two years, going where the wind took him, looking for sponsors to help him live up to his chosen name. He was a sweet guy, but he scared me. I wasn't afraid he'd hurt us. I worried the road would do to us what it had done to him. To David, however, he was a magician. Hearing our dilemma, Bike to Australia pulled a derailleur cable out of his back pocket. David looked as though he had pulled out a rabbit.

While the two men managed a temporary fix, I put bedclothes on my unwashed body. Conscious of my bralessness, I headed to the outhouse on the edge of the field, wondering if any women lived in Eliot.

AT 2:00 A.M., THE police officers lined up their vehicles and washed them.

At 3:00 a.m., it poured.

At 8:00 a.m., we left Eliot in the rain. We rode three hours before seeing another human being—a man selling berries in his front yard. He offered us a plump sample. "They're a hobby," he said. "I work for a pharmaceutical company in Kennebunk."

"How's business?" I said between blue mouthfuls, expecting the usual tale of woe.

"We're one of the few local companies hiring. People with master's degrees are begging us for entry-level positions."

"Why are you doing so well?" I asked.

"Got a government contract for an anthrax antidote."[25]

WE FOUND A LAUNDROMAT in Kennebunk to rest, eat, and clean clothes. I asked a lanky fellow in his thirties loading a dryer about the words on his tee shirt. "What is a *Kneading Conference?*"

After Noah finished describing the joy and science of communal bread baking, he invited us to spend the night on his farm.

The farm was sublime, a rainbow of vegetable rows, flowers, and fruit trees. We slept in a barn repurposed for WWOOFs (organic farm apprentices). To use the compostable toilet, we stepped into the dew. The comfortable, indoor-outdoor feel of the barn relaxed me. I felt expansive, safe, and intimate.

In the morning, around our host's broad kitchen table, we shared tales of living outdoors. Noah recounted an NPR story about a man who spent seventy-one days living on a puddle of water and what lived in it. I helped myself to another slice of fresh-baked bread slathered with butter.

WE HAD BEEN FOLLOWING the Maine coast without ever seeing the ocean. Now, our route wound through a sleepy fishing village. We took a wrong turn, wooed by a path through an arboretum salt marsh. A woman with a glorious head of salt-and-pepper curls biked alongside us. "Got a place to stay?" she asked. "Do you like eggplant parmesan?"

An offer to tent in the yard of her Higgins Beach vacation rental progressed to a bed off the kitchen. After a swim, the sky turned the color of the strawberry daiquiris we were drinking, and we learned the intimacies of our host's life. A teacher, Damari had worn a black armband to school at the start of the Iraq war and was "relieved" of her position. Her husband of thirty-one years

25 After 9/11, letters laced with anthrax were sent in the US mail, sickening seventeen people and killing five. The "Amerithrax" investigation closed in 2010, but, apparently, the government was still worried about another bacterial attack.

had died in May. Today was his birthday. She was mourning and beginning to date—a woman in transition.

Before dinner we held hands. Damari said, "A friend asked why I, an atheist, say grace at the table. I told her, 'I'm grateful!'"

I was grateful too. Grateful we had taken a wrong turn in a salt marsh, so we could hold hands with Damari on Higgins Beach.

PORTLAND, MAINE, WAS UNDER construction. We took detours through new immigrant neighborhoods. A Salvadoran pupuseria tempted us, but it was late, and we left the city more tired than miles warranted. At a fruit stand, a father with a *Share the Road* bumper sticker and two kids in car seats eating berries, eyed our load. "Should take you an hour to get to Brunswick," he said. We figured two. When Mr. Share the Road left, we admitted to each other we'd hoped he'd invite us home. Maine was spoiling us.

A mile further, we saw a van parked on the side of the road. It was Mr. Share the Road. He handed David his address.

His children helped us set up the tent. Little Oliver dragged a sleeping bag to the backyard. Five-year-old Lilly boasted, "He's the strongest three-year-old in the world."

Our host set our bikes on end to give them a tune-up. "I used to run a high school bike repair program in Portland for the Bicycle Coalition of Maine. I worked with kids with names I couldn't pronounce and life stories that blew me away. I loved the work but couldn't afford to live on nothing once we had kids." He nodded at Lilly, drawing me a bird with a party hat. "Now, I teach bike repair at a college."

His wife, Katie, came home to a campground in her yard and a couple of strangers sitting on her couch. After the kids were in bed, I asked her about her work. Without cracking a smile, she explained, "Laughter yoga. I teach people to ha-ha. It kicks in their endorphins."

In the morning, Katie passed us bowls of fortified oatmeal. "The hemp seed will keep you satisfied," she said. And it did. We sought second breakfast later than usual: a pint at one of Maine's roadside fruit stands.

OUTSIDE OF BATH, MAINE, David's back rack fell off after a bolt snapped. We turned into a service station. A man wearing an explorer hat and tool belt was pumping gas. He introduced himself.

"AJ, certified Maine guide. I take people into the wilderness to hunt and fish."

He wanted to know the economics of sourcing food on an adventure that didn't include a fishing pole. He pointed at the price on the tank: $3.85 per gallon. "Sure, you save on gas, but how do you feed yourself? You need an awful lot of carbs."

"Simple carbs are cheap and plentiful," I said. "Getting fresh produce is hard. Easier in Maine." We told him about David's rack. AJ pulled a tool from his belt, and presto! It was fixed. I expected him to click his heels, tip his explorer hat, and disappear into salty air.

Shortly after AJ fixed the back rack, David's front rack broke. Detours to escape the endless parade of tourists on Route 1 slowed us further. To cross the Sheepscot River, we had no choice but to join the traffic-filled highway, which narrowed as it approached Wiscasset. Rain blurred our vision. We skirted stalled cars for a mile. I hoped they could see better than we could. I had one reference for Wiscasset, Maine, stuck in my disaster brain: James Weldon Johnson, an NAACP leader who wrote "Lift Every Voice and Sing"—and whose life I studied for my dissertation—had died in a car accident here. I saw how it might have happened.

Stopping before the bridge, we joined a line for lobster at Red's Eats. We stayed close to our bikes, thinking maybe someone would take us home. A New York Fire Department therapist specializing in care for 9/11 responders invited us to stay with him when we got to Brooklyn. I wanted to talk to him, but we were shivering. We traded lobster bliss and conversation for a dry indoor seat across the street, where clam chowder was all-you-can-eat, if not good.

With no Certified Maine Guide, organic farmer, or angel with salt-and-pepper curls to save us, we climbed onto our wet bikes, rode another mile, and got a tiny room at the Pioneer Motel across the bridge. David dried his bike shorts in a microwave and pranced around naked. Remembering Katie, the laughter yoga healer, we ha ha'd away a hard day.

OUR RIDE THE NEXT day was short, to Waldoboro, Maine, where my brother Michael had a house. Not far from our destination, an old man laboring toward his front door nearly dropped his groceries when he saw us. "Come in, come in!" he said. "Would you like something to eat?"

He fed us fudge bars, orange soda, and then rainbow sherbet. While we ate our three-course meal, his wife sat silently in an easy chair.

"She has Alzheimer's," the man said.

The couple had been teachers. "Married fifty-six years." He sighed. "I don't go places anymore. No desire to go without her. I don't even want to go to the garbage dump." He realized that sounded funny. "Well, who does? But still."

He gestured toward us. "This is what's important: talking to people."

ALONE FOR A DAY at my brother's cavernous house in Waldoboro, I insisted we leave the bikes and walk to Friendship, Maine, a lobster fishers' village five miles away. Remembering a bike tossed like a Frisbee in Northampton, David agreed. Friendship had a café with the town's happy name and a marquee that read: *Liars Go to Hell*. In the library a little girl was checking out *Blueberries for Sal* and *One Morning in Maine*. At the Friendship harbor, cars had right- and left-wing bumper stickers, and one popular with both sides:

Eat More Lobster.

In the tiny Friendship Museum, I found a century-old Maine Grange pamphlet. In the late nineteenth century, Grange farmers united with factory and railroad workers to stand up to bankers and price-gouging railroad tycoons. In 2011, the National Grange advocated for rural health care and education. Like their forebears, contemporary Grangers also decried bank bailouts and corrupt foreclosure practices. I'd noticed Grange halls in Eliot, Bath, and Wiscasset, still hosting dances and community meetings. I asked the docent about the pamphlet. She had never heard of the Grange.

The next day, my brother and his family arrived. We ate my sister-in-law Katherine's homemade pizza and dug clams with Michael. David taught our nephews how to play poker. The comfort of family made me question the sanity of our ride. I could no longer stomach the traffic on Route 1. Michael and Katherine had friends we could stay with fifty miles northwest in Belgrade, and they helped us map out a route into Maine's interior, along hilly, empty roads. We left late and rode fast and strong without a break, through tiny towns where Baptist churches had outhouses in their parking lots. We passed Augusta, the capital city, memorable for its killer hill.

Belgrade became our northernmost point on the East Coast. Our hosts had three homeschooled children, heads in books. Sabrina, age thirteen, gave us a blow-by-blow account of a new novel she was reading about "the future of America," in which "a girl from a coal-mining region fights the rich."

FROM BELGRADE, WE HEADED south and west to Lewiston, Maine. I had shown a documentary film about the town to my classes when I was teaching at Saint Cloud State. Lewiston had been economically depressed since the 1950s, when textile factories closed. East African refugees settled there in the 1990s, and impoverished white residents resented them. In 2002, the mayor wrote an open letter telling the refugees to stop coming. White supremacists across the nation flocked to Lewiston to support the mayor. So did anti-racists.[26] The movie struck a chord in Saint Cloud, where Somali immigrants faced ridicule in schools and discrimination in housing and employment. My students were mostly white, from surrounding small towns, growing up hearing lies about Somali Muslims coming to Minnesota to impose Sharia law. The movie opened conversations and provided essential validation for the one or two Somali students I had in each class.

Lewiston was pretty, with massive stone churches perched aside steep hills along the Androscoggin River. Immigrant shops had revived the otherwise shuttered downtown. In the library—a multiracial space in a white state—I watched tweenagers put their names on a waiting list for *The Hunger Games*.

We lost track of time. A horse veterinarian and a retired teacher whom we met at a Korean restaurant a week earlier had invited us to their home in New Gloucester, twelve miles south of Lewiston. We were late. As we got on our bikes, a celestial giant dumped her bucket, turning the road into a raging river. Swimming down a steep hill and wading up the other side took my last drachma of strength. Three miles from our destination, we found a truck stop hotel and called our hosts to say we wouldn't make it. The veterinarian unloaded the mobile office he used to make house calls to make room for two loaded bicycles. His wife, Bonnie, erased our embarrassment at needing a ride.

"How did you make it?" she asked. "It rained three inches in two hours!"

We left our wet panniers in the laboratory and our bikes in the donkey barn. Bonnie lit the kitchen fireplace, erected a drying rack for our wet clothes, and laid warm quiches and bowls of fruit on the hearth. The comfort was overwhelming.

After dinner, she gave us a tour of the 1799 stone home. "We like to imagine a previous owner standing before the kitchen fire, saying, 'President Lincoln's been shot!'" Bonnie said.

---

26 *The Letter: An American Town and the 'Somali Invasion,'* directed by Ziad Hamzeh, 2003.

"The house is my office," the veterinarian said, then corrected himself. "*Our* office. When Bonnie retired, she became my accountant."

Bonnie handed me a photo labeled *Kindergarten Class of 1946*. She pointed to two children standing side by side.

"That's us."

I looked up from the photo to the two of them, standing side by side.

THE NEXT MORNING, WE rode southeast, through a region of craggy, diverse farmsteads. It was lovely, but the rain was Maine-steady. We found a place to dry out in a conference center meeting room where a group of women, ages thirty to one hundred, spun wool with pedal wheels.

"Fiber is huge in Maine," one woman told me. We listened to pedals clack and stories weave.

Maine - Maryland
(13 - 19)

●16● **Chapters**
☆ **Cities**

13

HUNGER GAMES

Maine, New Hampshire, and Massachusetts

In downtown Portland, Maine, people wearing clothes too warm for the weather waited for shelters to open. We stopped at an art gallery and viewed a global photo exhibit that mirrored the deprivation on Portland's Congress Street, including portraits of coal miners from my dad's hometown in Upper Silesia,[27] and a series on a New York City elder rendered homeless by a cascade of health care costs. The exhibit was called *Portraits of the International Crisis of Capital.*

Route 1A took us out of Maine, along the coast, into the eastern edge of New Hampshire known as the Hamptons, where mansions with gilded *No Trespassing* signs and turrets provided exclusive views of the sea. Acres of manicured lawns belched fertilizer into the ocean. A man in his crimson convertible barked into his cell phone as he reversed into our bike lane. He missed me by inches. I called him "portrait of the internal crisis of a capitalist."

Rain pummeled us as we crossed into Massachusetts. I squatted on a smelly Porta Potty in a park, dizzy with images of deprivation and excess and exhausted from intermittent storms and heat. A chortle gurgled from my belly—half-sob, half-laugh. I was so tired I didn't want to leave the foul confines of this urine-splattered seat and reenter the rain. I called myself "portrait of a woman who needs a break from the road."

---

27 Upper Silesia is a region on the border of Germany and Poland. My dad's hometown, now known as Gliwice, is part of Poland today. When he lived there, it was Gleiwitz, Germany.

14

TREMORS AND CYCLONES

Massachusetts

I got my break in Arlington, Massachusetts. Like students back from college, we filled my brother David's home with dirty laundry, insatiable appetites, and a thousand stories. Brother Daniel sent over spring rolls and woke us early for yoga.

On our way out of Boston, we visited the Brookline neighborhood where I had lived when I was little. "I was six when I got my first two-wheeler," I said, pointing my spouse toward the driveway of a duplex my parents had rented. "I tried it once, wobbled, and refused to get on again until I was nine. Michael wasn't even four yet. He rammed the bike into that tree, tumbled, and got back on, and the bike was his."

Riding through Jamaica Plain, we waved at people sitting on stoops on Walk Hill Street. We passed office parking lots filled with people and waved at them too. At a bike store outside of Boston, we exchanged passions with a letter carrier, admiring pictures of his jazz guitars. Opening my phone to share photos with our new friend, I saw a text from my brother: "Evacuated my building. Sent us home. You OK?"

"?!" I texted back.

"We had an earthquake!" he responded.

A tremor rattling the East Coast did not register on the Richter scale of a couple of cyclists absorbed in their minutia.

THE SAGAMORE BRIDGE SOARED above the Cape Cod Canal. The sidewalk leaned into traffic. A sidewind pushed us toward the road. As we held tight to our heavy bikes, fear morphed into anger. At a volume to best the wind, I yelled at David about conditions neither of us controlled.

At Ginny's Café, the parking lot was empty, save a rusted van, its flat tire sunk into the sand. The café's owner was filling her refrigerator and sink with ice. "Not a good time to be on the Cape," she said. "Hurricane Irene's coming. Nothing like it since No-Name in '91."

A hurricane?

We raced the rest of our sixty-eight miles. I walked through my mother's door in South Wellfleet like a kid. "Hey, Mom," I said. "We biked 2,148 miles to visit you!"

MOM MADE HER MARK on the natural history of Cape Cod, coring the depths of its freshwater ponds, measuring climate change before the term was coined. Now she lived in the house that my brother Michael built on the end of a sand road. But her diabetes was debilitating, and I worried about her ability to care for herself. To prepare for the hurricane, I moved her house plants inside. David brought in her bird feeders so they wouldn't slam into the windows. We filled the bathtub, collected flashlights, found candles.

With time before the storm's arrival, we walked along Cape Cod Bay. An oyster farmer harvesting a double supply greeted us warily, protecting his crop with friendly banter and watchful eyes. He looked less grizzled than most Wellfleet oyster farmers.

"I used to be a photographer," he said, answering my thought. "Digital came in, and I saw the writing on the wall. On assignment with *National Geographic* to shoot oyster farmers, I got hooked. I lease an acre from the city, buy my oysters from Upstate New York, put 'em here, and they're Wellfleet oysters." He held a smallish one. "I'm harvesting when they're not mature. The tourists demand it. They want their 'Oystah Rockafellah' now. They won't be here in September when these babies are ready."

As night fell, the wind rattled the house. Irene moved inland, dumping her payload on Vermont. In the sunny, still morning, we emptied the tubs, put out the bird feeders, removed fallen branches. Most Cape homes lost power. Since electricity operates the Cape's wells, those homes lost water as well. At the Hot Chocolate Sparrow, people on cell phones negotiated with the electric company: "Next Tuesday? I can't make it 'til then. Please make it Friday."

We spent two weeks on Cape Cod. I tried to assuage my guilt for being on the road, talking to social workers and nurses to get Mom more help. We argued. She and I had been doing some version of this dance for decades. I didn't like the way middle-aged adolescence looked on me.

My nephews came to visit. We took seven-year-old Benjamin for a walk. He fell on the cement and scraped his knees. Afterward, he took David's hand "for balance." Back at the house, I noticed Benjamin wasn't the only one leaning on my spouse for support. "David, could you fill the bird feeders?" Mom asked, skirting her recalcitrant daughter to have her needs met.

Later, I fell off my bike. I lay on the ground and contemplated the irony. I had pedaled freeways, slick mud, narrow curves, and rocky paths without one spill. Now, on this flat, paved, smooth Cape Cod Rail Trail, over I went. True to form, David found the safe eye in the raging storm: "You learned you could fall and be all right."

I stayed in the cyclone. I was more off-kilter with Mom than on a mountain precipice.

TROPICAL STORM LEE HIT Cape Cod the day we left. Like Mary Poppins, we blew in with one hurricane and went out with another. Unlike the magical nanny, I did not fix anything. No cure for diabetes, no solution for the elder who needs help and craves independence. No peace for mother and daughter negotiating their adult relationship.

Poppins rode the gales when the sun was setting on the British Empire. *The moral of her story is still apt,* I thought. *Rein in the empire and the banks, and follow your passion—be it kites, jazz guitars, or farming oysters. And listen to Mom: Feed the birds!*

15

ISLAND MENTALITIES

Massachusetts

Arriving early for the island ferry in Hyannis, we visited the Zion Union Heritage Museum that celebrates the history of African Americans, Cape Verdeans, and the Wampanoag people on Cape Cod. Museum founder John Reed welcomed us, though we dripped mud onto his floor. A high school teacher with deep roots on the Cape, he raised private funds, designed exhibits, and secured the historic Black church to house the museum. "I don't want us to be beholden to anyone," he said. I nodded, thinking of the foreclosed Black Holocaust Museum in Milwaukee.

John's museum honored the history of the region's working-class people, who picked cranberries and worked as domestic laborers. One exhibit told the story of Eugenia Fortes, a housekeeper in Hyannisport who refused to leave a segregated beach in 1945. Like Rosa Parks, Fortes was an organizer, and a leader of the local NAACP for decades. "This is not about Oak Bluffs," John noted, referring to the better-known history of middle- and upper-class families who created an African American vacation enclave on Martha's Vineyard.[28]

TROPICAL STORM LEE RAGED as our ferry landed on Martha's Vineyard. Shari and Bob led us by car to their dry home. Shari and I had sludged the murky waters of graduate school together, sharing Latin American history

28 In the nineteenth century, a biracial group of abolitionists organized on Nantucket. By the twentieth century, Black elites had established an enclave on Martha's Vineyard.

classes, advisors, and a love-hate relationship with the academic world. We had kept each other afloat. Now my eyes swam across her bookshelf, catching phrases from a past life: *Slave and Peasant, Nations and Nationalism, Reform and Revolution, Island Mentalities.*

The next day, Shari took us on a tour. We passed a Vineyard Haven church marquee that read: *Food Bank—November to April.*

"Does poverty have a season on this island too?" I asked.

Shari knew what I meant. On the Caribbean islands we studied, the "dead season" was the time between sugar harvests.

She nodded. "Here it's when the tourists leave."

Martha's Vineyard was as gorgeous as its reputation, even in the rain. I had expected the beaches, cliffs, and lighthouses. The woods and small farms surprised me. "Our source of vegetables without the off-island surcharge," Shari noted. "It's ninety bucks to take your car on the ferry in the summer when the politicians, movie stars, and tourists flood the island. The Obamas just left—cut their vacation short due to the hurricanes."

Shari made stuffed quahogs and invited friends. One of her guests, a middle school teacher, explained the island mentality to me. "Year-rounders divide time into on- and off-season, the world into on- and off-island. Often, my students' geography papers begin, 'Germany is off-island.'"

We assured Shari that we could get to the New Bedford ferry ourselves, then rode to the wrong port. On the way to the right port, the ocean rose to meet the rain. Echoes of Tropical Storm Lee soaked our legs and the bottom of our bags. It was exhilarating. Danger has a different flavor when a friend is close.

We missed the boat. In Oak Bluffs, David changed a tire in the doorway of a shopping complex selling cotton candy and emu oil. I found a corner table at Biscuits. Dirty water trickled off me, creating a puddle around my chair. I hoped the waitress believed me when I said, "I'll wait for my husband before ordering."

At the next table, two professionally dressed Black couples visibly transitioned from city-quick to island-slow. They ordered the menu, expressing hope that Biscuits lived up to its reputation for serving authentic southern soul food. Spying on them, I didn't notice them spying on me. When David walked in, they clapped. One of the women shook her head at my wet partner: "We wondered if you existed."

The sun emerged before the ferry arrived, and we got a chance to see what inspired a steady stream of tourists to board the boat for the Vineyard. It wasn't cotton candy, codfish cakes, emu oil, or even Biscuits' famous chicken and waffles. Rays of yellow light played with sand, rock, and water. A gay Dutch couple gasped at the beauty as they disembarked. They were curious about us. "Where are you going next?" asked one. "Why are you leaving now?" asked the other.

We struggled to answer.

16

STAY OUT OF THE STATE OF CONNECTICUT

Massachusetts, Rhode Island, Connecticut, and New York

In the end, it's some lone detail that kills a venture. . . .
Every small occurrence is a potential last straw in wait.
—William Least Heat-Moon[29]

Once, while I was riding my bike with sixteen-year-old Emily along the River Road in Minneapolis, a car full of college boys threw eggs at us. One landed on Emily's hair. I was furious. But the incident did not change my view of the bike path I had ridden so many times, or of Minneapolis. Such disaggregation is not so easy when you are passing through a place.

A NEW BEDFORD FISHERMAN wagged his finger. The freeway abutting the harbor was no place for a bicycle! He gave directions to calmer waters, and we were relieved to be out of town, until David's bike tire refused to stay inflated. We were far from bike shops or hardware stores.

---

29 William Least Heat-Moon, *River-Horse: The Logbook of a Boat Across America* (Boston: Houghton Mifflin Harcourt, 1999), 75.

"My rim keeps cutting the valve stem," he explained. I nodded, pretending to understand.

We stopped every three miles so he could inflate his tire, then every two. David pumped and sweated. I enjoyed the breaks. *This was the pace I wanted.*

It started to rain. When the tire refused to stay full for any distance, it was dark, and we were wet and ten miles out of Providence, Rhode Island, our destination. We decided the lawn of an eighteenth-century wooden church on a hill outside of Dighton, Massachusetts, was a serviceable camping spot, and called our young Providence host.

"I'll be right there," Alexis said.

Alexis commanded the situation, tossing our bikes onto their car rack, stuffing luggage in their hatchback. In Providence, they pushed aside a strand of yellow curls and carried our bikes and gear to their second-floor apartment, laying our wet sneakers by a fan to dry. Before leaving to spend the night at their boyfriend's, they introduced us to three shy kittens who hid their furry faces but left us a gift on each pannier that—despite numerous launderings—stayed with us for the next 8,000 miles.

A QUICK FIX AT a bike shop in Providence made David's bike ride, but not like new. As for me, two weeks in Wellfleet had softened my bike legs. We were climbing Berkshire foothills again, and they felt like mountains. Struggling into the state of Connecticut, we arrived late to the home of our bicycle hosts in Eastford, but not too late for garden tomatoes and strawberry rhubarb pie. Our new friends asked how we planned to cross the Connecticut River, which was breaching its banks due to post-hurricane rains. We gulped like spring visitors to northwest Minnesota who don't know there's a Red River. Incredulous, they brought out maps to educate us.

Our Eastford friends kept cycling magazines in a bathroom basket. David sat on the toilet and read, "How to Fall Off a Bike."

We limped through the next day, stopping to refill David's tire, moving slowly to compensate for my failing brakes. Come evening we sputtered into an RV park in East Hampton, Connecticut. It was the tenth anniversary of 9/11. Above a three-foot faded photo of Richard Nixon in the RV rec room, a banner read *Never Forget*. Below it, a man repeated an anti-gay slur to an appreciative audience. In the campground, twelve-year-olds on a daddy-kid camping trip bullied each other while their fathers drank. A woman shouted, "I'm going to call the local TV, 'cause you're news!"

We didn't feel like news. We felt like aliens in enemy territory.

TERRIFIED OF MY FAULTY brakes, I insisted we walk the eleven miles to the nearest bike shop, riding only up hills. It was tiring, but also a relief. I felt safer and had time to think. Crossing the Arrigoni Bridge over the Connecticut River, I took a deep breath, watched a sailboat arrive and disappear. Behind me, David banged his ankle on his pedal and swore. He brushed away my attempt at sympathy with silence, and then:

"This is the worst day of the trip."

We walked the last blocks to the bike shop in silence. The repair took hours. They replaced David's cracked rim. His brakes were more shot than mine, which confounded me. How could he want to ride without brakes? But I said nothing, determined to help us toward peace.

We left the store in better spirits, but the morning walk and afternoon wait made getting to our destination in Waterbury, Connecticut, before nightfall impossible. A white couple at the bike shop warned against riding there after dark. Entering the city at dusk, we passed a downtown building with a smashed-in roof covered in green growth. In the fading light, it looked like the face of a hairy giant.

At a convenience store in an immigrant and African American

neighborhood, the customer ahead of us couldn't remember what he was there to buy. Shoppers and workers leaned on counters, helping the seven-year-old figure it out. As I watched the child walk the dark hill alone, exhaustion took the space where fear had been. We promised each other: "Tomorrow we will take a day off!"

Our Waterbury host, Blair, fed us fresh vegetables, apples, chicken, and heroic stories of handcuffing bosses who abused their workers. Blair investigated errant employers for the Connecticut Department of Labor, including those who take advantage of undocumented workers or abuse independent contracting. "Can a FedEx driver haul something other than mail?" he asked rhetorically. "There's nothing independent about these workers except their health care."

I expressed surprise at Connecticut's commitment to workers' rights.[30] He corrected my assumptions. "We had a thirty-five-hour workweek until the last decade. Came close to single-payer health care. Today, however, towns like Waterbury are in economic shambles."

"My grandparents emigrated from Forlì, in northern Italy," Blair continued. "When I was born, Forlì was a post-war pile of rubble and Waterbury the brass capital of the world, with strong unions, progressive taxes—a cultural and architectural mecca. On my last visit to Italy, Forlì was thriving, with equitable wealth and fabulous public amenities. Waterbury's economy today? A jail, a hospital, a halfway house. They recently refurbished the theater to its old glory—the one reminder of our prosperous past."

30 In 2021, Connecticut activists continued to lead the nation. The Connecticut Connecting Families Coalition were the first to push their governor and legislature to make prison calls free, eliminating a source of impoverishment and recidivism. https://worthrises.org/pressreleases/connecticut-makes-history-as-first-state-to-make-prison-calls-free.

BY THIS TIME IN the trip, I had succumbed to David caring for me. I was more tired at the end of the day, and I needed to write. He put up the tent; washed, folded, and picked out our clothes; repaired the bikes; carried things; assuaged my fears.

When I awoke in Waterbury, David was already dressed and had laid out my bike jersey and shorts.

"We're taking the day off," I reminded him.

"Automatic pilot," he said. "Can we do a short one?"

We agreed to a fifteen-mile ride, to Kettletown State Park, but argued about walking to the edge of town. I was sick of rushing, danger, exhaustion—sick of feeling pushed. In the middle of heated negotiations, a man on a motorcycle stopped traffic to shout at us, "Far out! You two are so cool!"

Out of the city, on a wooded dirt bike path, we felt happier, until a fallen tree forced us to backtrack. Hills grew as we got closer to our destination. The last three vertiginous miles required all the effort and concentration I had. It wasn't until we reached the top of Maple Tree Hill Road that I relaxed. From there, the State Park was a mile away. Judging from the landscape in front of us—early-changing red and yellow maples embellishing a green valley—it would be gorgeous. I let my new brakes go, gained speed swiftly, took chances. Time slowed. Exhilarated, I swerved left at the intersection and glided to the stop sign at the corner of Georges Hill Road.

A guy in a pickup leaned his head out to ask my breasts if they wanted a ride, alerting me that I was alone. David must have stopped to take pictures. He did not come. My cell phone was dead. I returned to the Maple Tree Hill intersection. I heard the air horn that Erik in Keene, New Hampshire, had given David to scare away dogs—but I was unsure which direction it came from. Had David turned right at the bottom of the hill? I heard the blast again. This time I felt sure it was coming from back up Maple Tree Hill. I climbed quickly, as if on flat ground.

Halfway up, I saw a woman leaning over, holding David's hand.

"He hit the lip on the side of the road," she said. "Flipped over his handlebars! I heard him yell. Found him flat on his back in the raspberry bushes."

David stood, holding on to the woman. His face was scratched and bleeding. I pulled his bike out of the brambles, my thoughts a contradictory thicket. *I violated our rule about sticking together; I shouldn't have let go on the hill. Too much joy is never safe. David is injured; I ruined his life with this selfish, meaningless trip. David isn't dead! This is a sign we should quit while our child's parents are still alive.*

In most of my scenarios of disaster, it was me bleeding on the roadside. It was the same for David. "I read that article about how to fall off a bike for you," he told me later. "I never thought I would need it." He had remembered the article's advice and had continued to roll, absorbing the shock of the fall.

We walked slowly toward the park. David moaned with each step.

"Where does it hurt?" I asked.

"Back. Ribs. Gut."

A forest ranger nearly ran into us. He parked his truck, called 911, and joined us on foot, walking David's bike for him. The ambulance was waiting for us at the park entrance. David did a cost calculation: A ride from a camper tomorrow would be free. An ambulance would break the bank. "I feel better," he lied, walking his bike into the campground. I followed.

Most campers at Kettletown State Park were hurricane refugees who couldn't go home due to downed power lines. One tired-looking man, seeing me struggle to put up the tent myself, brought us wood. Once I managed to get the tent together, we looked for the restroom. It was up a small hill. I took David's hand. His bravado from a half-hour earlier, when an ambulance awaited, was gone. He struggled to walk.

It took David forever to come out of the bathroom. When he did, his face was ashen.

"There's blood in my urine."

There was more blood in the morning. A group of college students stared blankly when I asked for a ride to the clinic three miles away. The campground staff wouldn't entertain the idea. Suddenly in charge, I collapsed the tent, locked the bikes, and called an ambulance. Instead of heading to the nearby clinic, the volunteer attendants strapped David into a gurney and drove slowly, without sirens, twenty-five miles to Danbury. Turning onto Hospital Avenue, the ambulance driver told me, "Good thing you weren't here last week. The road flooded, and we couldn't get through."[31]

At the hospital, the physician's assistant was brisk. "I'm willing to bet you broke a couple of ribs and punctured your kidney. We'll take an MRI."

What trauma does to a face! David had become lean and tan. Now, his thin visage looked gray and vulnerable. He smiled at me, but his eyes—deep in their sockets—shouted fear.

"Read to me," he said.

Steadying my voice, I picked up where we had left off in *River-Horse*. Behind in their schedule, Least Heat-Moon and his companion had sailed their boat into a "wall of water—still pursuing, still waiting for us to falter and then have us."[32] David's lips quivered.

David cries easily for others. He will comfort an abused child, then come home and weep. A sappy movie will bring him to tears. But he rarely cries for himself.

"Should I read ahead?" I asked. "To where they arrive safely and eat in some warm, inviting place?"

"No!" he answered.

MY GRANDPA WINKLER'S LAST words: *stay out of the state of Connecticut*, uttered in a hospital in New York City, were a mystery passed down to me without explanation. At the campground, after calling Connecticut bicycle

31 Survivors of the Sandy Hook Elementary School massacre on December 14, 2012, were transported to this hospital.

32 Least Heat-Moon, *River-Horse*, 73.

hosts, Connecticut family-of-family, and Connecticut friends-of-friends, each "regretting they were unable to help," I thought about Grandpa's dire warning and decided to call for help across the state border.

The soft-voiced bicycle host in Carmel, New York, did not hesitate. I called him again from the ambulance. No problem, he told me. He would come to Danbury when he got off work. The third time I called, it was 3:00 p.m. and I was crying. The doctor was still examining David. I knew nothing, suspected the worst. My new friend reassured me.

"Call when you're ready. I'll pick you up then."

In the end, this sweet stranger drove one hundred miles: from work to the hospital, to our campsite for the bikes, to the pharmacy for pain medication, and then to his home in Carmel, where his wife, Bobbie, greeted us like long-lost cousins.

"You need time to heal," she said. "Stay as long as you like."

Over our three-day stay, we heard about their son's bike trip. Strangers helped him out of a tough jam. Our hosts were paying it forward.

With the help of Vicodin and Ibuprofen, David slept fifteen hours. He had cracked his helmet, but the MRI showed no body breaks. His ribs, spine, and kidneys were all intact. He had internal bruises and was in shock. The emergency room doctor said he couldn't ride for at least two weeks and recommended further diagnosis. When David awoke, we made a new plan: We'd leave bikes and luggage in Carmel. David would fly home and see his doctor. I'd take the train to New York City and stay with Emily. If David's doctor thought the injuries were prohibitive, I'd return home later. But if David got the green light to continue our journey, he would fly back to New York, and we'd return to Carmel to pick up the bikes.

BOBBIE'S BOLIVIAN MOTHER, RUTH, was visiting. We spent the afternoon talking to her in Spanish. Her late husband was Jewish. He had escaped Poland in 1939 and ended up in Bolivia. My father's family had fled

Nazi Germany for Cuba; then Miami, Florida; and finally New York, where my grandfather issued his mysterious deathbed warning about the state of Connecticut, which led us to this kitchen table in Carmel where we forged ties across decades and continents.

17

PREOCCUPATIONS

New York

I watched from a block away as Emily offered NYC farmers' market customers advice about garlic. "The supermarket sells one kind, but there are over three hundred varieties." Behind them, Hasidic women in wigs and black skirts fingered cabbages, while hipsters—also in black—argued the merits of butternut and acorn.

I knew parents who worried about their adult kids moving back home. Our child didn't have that option. When Emily graduated from college, there was no home to return to. In some ways the bike trip had reversed our roles. We called daily, and when we didn't, Emily let us know. "You could have texted," they would say. "Let me know you're OK." Now, watching them work—confident, happy—it seemed they had more reason to worry about us than vice versa.

The following morning, after Emily went to work, I sat at the kitchen table with their Greek housemate, Korina, a student at the New School in Manhattan. She told me about her summer participating in her country's anti-austerity movement. "Each night in Athens, thousands of us conducted a general assembly to discuss how to oppose the latest government action," Korina explained. "We'd project communications with protestors around the country on a white banner. Other parts of the world too. Today I'm going to a protest on Wall Street," she added. "You should come."

Flattered but hesitant, I asked, "What are the demands?"

"Like our assemblies in Greece, that will be decided by those who show up. The social movements of today are not like any you've seen before."

I thought of tortuous meetings I had attended to oppose war, fight education cuts, and support immigrant rights. Bypassing excruciating debates over a list of demands, power struggles over who would address the crowd, sounded great. However, I couldn't wrap my head around how I would know I supported this Wall Street demonstration.

"Well," I ventured, "will you be inciting arrest? A jail cell in New York City's not in my plans."

She shrugged.

KORINA CAME HOME WITH tempered enthusiasm about the day's action. New York wasn't Athens. A couple hundred people had participated. Tomorrow, however, her friends intended to occupy the Financial District.

THE NEXT DAY, AFTER Emily went to work and Korina to class, I took the subway to Wall Street. There were no protesters, but the NYPD had occupied the space, blocking traffic. I joined international tourists who filled the sidewalks along the roped-off street, trying to make sense of what was going on. The officers looked bored. One cop, whose short sleeves revealed tattooed arms, asked his comrades, "Got a Tums?"

I ducked into a café and was ordering tea when a parade filled the sidewalk. Young people and a few elders marched slowly, carrying musical instruments, children, US flags, and one large Industrial Workers of the World banner. Hand-drawn signs read "No More Wealth Care, Pay Your Fair Share," "Debt Is Slavery," and "Liberate the Planet."

A cop blocked the door to the café as the marchers honored the police barrier, circled twice, and disappeared. When the officer moved away from the café door, I returned to the sidewalk, crowded again with tourists.

I heard a woman from London ask a policeman to snap her photo. His response was curt.

"Lady, it's not a good day for that."

DAVID RETURNED FROM MINNEAPOLIS with a prescription to rest another week and begin slowly. We went together to Zuccotti Park, a small triangle of public land a few blocks from the Financial District where the Wall Street activists were now encamped. They had designated the center of the park as a food pantry. Sleeping bags were heaped along the sides. A quilt of cardboard placards—each one unique—abutted the sidewalk.

The activists gathered in the remaining space, conducting a general assembly. Instead of using microphones, the first rows repeated the speaker, creating a group mantra. They used a simple sign language: shake hands to show approval, rotate wrists when someone was going on too long. The proceedings were livestreamed—a funny combination of low- and high-tech communication. Someone had donated $10,000. A budget committee considered how to spend it. A labor organizer solicited support for a cheese factory strike in New Jersey. Several spoke in solidarity with Troy Davis, a death row inmate scheduled to be executed in Georgia that night. Women were encouraged to speak.

Nearby, school children rallied, identical shirts and banners making it clear they opposed cuts to education. The occupiers made no such effort to present a united message. They were still working on a statement of purpose. One focus they all agreed on: the 1 percent elite was screwing the rest of us. There was no way of knowing the movement would spread, just a hint on a young man's sign.

I'm jobless. I have all the time in the world.

18

NEVER AGAIN

New York, New Jersey, and Pennsylvania

Returning to Carmel, New York, by train to pick up our bikes, we stayed one more night, and then returned to New York City in three short days, determined to follow David's doctor's orders to "take it slow for three weeks."

Our Ossining, New York, bed was a pull-out couch in an art studio filled with clay bowls and earrings. Around our hosts' kitchen table, our conversation moved from the Mideast to Montana and stretched into the night. It wasn't until the next morning, when we were about to leave, that Loren said,

"Life has changed since our son became our daughter."

I didn't know then that Emily was nonbinary. I said, "My daughter's love is a girl," happy to see how my words caused her shoulders to relax.

She hugged me. "Our vacations these days are mostly to camps for families of transgender children."

"Way to support your kid!" I said.

ON FORDHAM ROAD IN the Bronx, amidst a crush of humanity and concrete, stalks of corn grew on a median strip. We walked west to 205th Street, then rode the Hudson River Greenway to the bottom of Manhattan. Our

loaded bikes did not turn heads until we reached tourists at the 9/11 Memorial construction site.

As we biked, NYPD officers arrested occupiers in Zuccotti Park en masse. Mayor Bloomberg said he feared "riots like Cairo and Madrid" if Congress did not implement a jobs program. At Pier 11, where we waited to catch our ferry, cops armed with submachine guns policed the waterfront, while tourists took photos of the Statue of Liberty.

On the ferry, Miss Liberty loomed and then shrank. Within minutes, we disembarked and took the Henry Hudson Trail through woods and meadows. It seemed a world away from New York City, but our destination—Middletown, New Jersey—was inextricably tied to Manhattan. The bedroom community had lost the most people per capita when the Twin Towers fell. Our host, Dan, worked in the Chase Manhattan Bank building. "In the days after, I went to the office and tried to keep systems going," he told us, over dinner. "I watched paper fly. The sky was black. Searchlights made it look like a movie set."

"He hasn't spoken about this for years!" his wife, Toby, said softly.

Toby took us to the town's 9/11 memorial park. Young faces etched in stone told thirty-seven stories. In one, there was also a fishing net, and a homemade picture book titled *Going Crabbing with My Favorite Uncle*. On the last page of the book, a young boy held a phone and cried. To me, this Middletown memorial created intimacy, tore hearts, said "Never again!" I wondered, however, if another eye would see justification for revenge.

Toby must have read my thoughts. "The day after 9/11," she said, "I saw a Muslim woman in the grocery store and glared at her. The woman cried. I vowed never to do that again. I saw a man at a gas station, baseball cap jammed over his turban. I said, 'God bless you.' He looked surprised, grateful. A look passed between us: two humans caught in dangerous times."

I told Toby, "When I was twenty-four, my father and I visited Auschwitz. In the guest book, many wrote, 'Never Again.' It was the early 1980s and the US government was funding Salvadoran death squad leader Roberto D'Aubuisson, who considered Hitler his mentor.[33] Dad and I debated whether 'Never Again' means anything if we only apply it to 'our' people."

"There's a mosque a mile from our house," Toby responded. "A few days after 9/11, we drove by it. Congregants walked the street frightened, like Jews for centuries in Europe. No one attacked them, yet there was enough silent animosity to make them feel afraid in their town. In the years since, Muslims in our area seem to feel comfortable. I have not witnessed any bad behavior toward them. Everyone is capable of hatred of the other. I have given up trying to be noble. I have settled for trying to be decent."

Cycling out of Middletown, we passed more bedroom communities, each with its own 9/11 memorial. Some were makeshift: a cross, some flowers, messages on paper. Others were granite and marble. We stopped at them all.

BEFORE WE LEFT MIDDLETOWN, Toby warned us: "A young couple who stayed with us quit touring after bicycling New Brunswick." But we had a place to stay, so off we went. Pushing our bikes through the thorny brush on the edge of a freeway to get into town, we wished we had heeded her warning. Leaving the next morning was worse. We rode circles on streets not made for bicycles until, weary and hungry, we stopped at a café on Hamilton Street.

The walls of the café were bare and dirty. Patrons talked the morning away. No one looked like they could afford a cup of coffee. The proprietor, like her surroundings, appeared to hold on to life by a thread. We ordered second breakfast. She brought a pretty pitcher of milk and two bowls of oatmeal, with a center of fresh blueberries and banana slices arranged like the petals of

33 D'Aubuisson ordered the murder of Salvadoran Archbishop Óscar Romero.

a flower. When I brought my cash to the register, she refused payment. "Have a great trip," she said. "I wish I could do it."

IN A NORTHERN SUBURB of Philadelphia, we joined the Jewish New Year celebration of my high school friend, Todd, and his large and boisterous family. I overfilled myself on gefilte fish, matzo ball soup, challah, horseradish, and cut apples, only to discover we'd just finished appetizers. Vegetable kugel, prunes and olives, Bundt cake, fruit salad—we ate to make up for bad meals past and got drunk on conversation in anticipation of lonely days ahead.

19

BRIDGING THE GAPS

Pennsylvania, Delaware, Maryland, Washington, DC, and Virginia

To get from New Jersey into Pennsylvania, we crossed the Delaware River where high winds had nearly capsized George Washington's flotilla in 1776. Unlike Washington, we took a bridge. Like him, we crossed in a rainstorm. Washington's goal was to attack German and British troops. Ours was to find a bathroom. The historic site on the Pennsylvania side had public restrooms. They were locked. The tyranny of a repressed bladder might not be hell, but when it becomes a state of being, it has crippling consequences.

COMING INTO PHILADELPHIA, WE found one of the city's thirty-nine McDonald's restaurants on 79th Street and Ogontz Avenue, ordered two decafs, and dripped dry. The patrons—older Black men—talked across tables. They helped us find the one plug in the room, atop the trash can. We and the phone recharged until the sun came out.

We rode toward the Schuylkill River, passing neat row houses, watching homes get bigger and neighborhoods whiter. On the River Trail, another short burst of rain resoaked us. Like the first storm, it stopped abruptly, and blue skies resumed. Lured by the sun and the luxury of a paved bikeway, we willfully ignored our turnoff to Wilmington, Delaware. Instead, we rode to Valley Forge, where Washington and 10,000 troops spent the winter of 1777 and 1778.

I stood dumbfounded at the base of the statue of "Mad Anthony" Wayne, the infamous general we encountered in Ohio who had massacred Indigenous villagers during the Battle of Fallen Timbers. The Park brochure noted that Washington considered Wayne a loose cannon but found his "rashness" useful in getting men who were not eager to fight "riled up" to do battle. Nearby was the Patriots of African Descent Monument. I was trying to fathom the life of a Black soldier in an integrated army under the leadership of a general who owned slaves, when a phone call from a host expecting us in Wilmington brought me back to 2011 and the depth of our dislocation.

We'd spent the day riding northwest to get southeast, and now it appeared we'd double-booked ourselves. David called back to explain to the host why we wouldn't be showing up, then called the second host to tell them we'd be late. The second host had never heard of us but agreed to take us in.

We rode the twenty-five miles back to Philadelphia and boarded the train to Wilmington, where a group of commuting college students gathered to hear our story. David's hands drew the rectangle with a Floridian tail as he recited, "Minnesota to Maine, tip-of-the-Keys, west to San Diego, north to Canada, across the Cascades . . ."

"Lost my job," I chimed in.

"You are the most exciting people I've met on this train," one young man exclaimed. He paused, adding weight to his judgment. "And I've met some real wack jobs!"

FOR TWO DAYS IN Wilmington, we tried to un-wack. We frequented Walgreens as though it were a temple and we were spiritually deprived, seeking flu shots, vitamins, and a cure for infected urinary tracts mangled by bike seats and a dearth of private places to pee. Despite different anatomies, our symptoms were identical: one body, accustomed to leaking, urgency, and pain.

Wilmington, like Cleveland, was an in-between place. In Trolley Square, a confused Civil War monument had Union symbols and the inscription *Rebellion of 1861–65*. Our host, a local historian named Sally, explained, "We were a slave state that remained in the Union. Delaware soldiers fought on both sides. The Mason-Dixon line is the Maryland border, but the Chesapeake Canal divides north and south in Delaware."

Sally told us a story of Wilmington that was now achingly familiar: boom and bust, white flight, Black impoverishment. Like Rochester, New York, city boosters were betting on waterfront development. Commercial prospectors, eager to exploit the confluence of the Brandywine and Delaware River despite environmental concerns, were promising prosperity to this former "chemical capital of the world."

WHEN FREDERICK DOUGLASS BEGAN his escape from slavery, he boarded a train in Baltimore. A harrowing moment during his journey was in Havre de Grace, Maryland, where passengers had to get off the train, take a ferry across the Chesapeake Bay, and reboard on the north bank.

In 2011, there was a train bridge across the Chesapeake. Cars had the Hatem Bridge. Bicyclists and pedestrians, however, were prohibited from crossing of their own volition. Walter, the owner of Biller's Bikes in Havre de Grace, transported cyclists for a fee. We waited for him at the Dunkin' Donuts a block from the bridge.

Loading the bikes, he seemed distracted. David suggested he tighten the rack ties. Walter brushed him aside. We climbed into his car, me in back, David in the passenger seat. Walter started across the bridge, talking like a tour guide.

"Havre de Grace was a gambling mecca. A scene in *The Sting* took place here. Town's been depressed since the racetracks disappeared in the sixties, but it's coming back. A military base in Aberdeen will bring eighteen thousand jobs to the area. Should boost my business. They're into fitn—"

He veered to the side and cranked his head. I turned to see what he was looking at, in time to see David's bike bounce down the freeway under the car behind us. My mind's eye, so used to seeing bike and man together, saw David under the vehicle. I swirled around to check the front seat. David was there, hands over mouth, suppressing a sob.

The car behind us skidded. The vehicle behind it stopped. Walter climbed out, grabbed the mangled bike from under the car, and rejoined it to the rack.

"Don't worry," he said. "I own a bike shop. I'll make it good as new."

The rest of the afternoon, we listened to Walter's stories while he repaired the bike. When he finished, it was dark, and we had ten miles to our destination. Walter drove us halfway. When he left, we rode a quarter mile before it became clear the repair was faulty. We walked the remaining five miles, our anger mitigated by hosts who welcomed us with, "Stay as long as it takes to fix your bike."

The next afternoon, David monitored repair session number two. I spent the hours at Java By the Bay, writing and eavesdropping on two women gossiping.

"What got into him?"

"He was separated from his wife, laid off, about to lose his home. He thought he could bridge the gap."

"I know, but robbing a bank?"

"Not very good at it, either. He pretended to have a weapon. Only asked the teller for a thousand dollars."

"His bail is one hundred thousand dollars, I heard."

WHEN I RETURNED TO the bike store, Walter and David were laughing. Walter had replaced David's crank with one from a Bianchi hybrid.

"Now your bike is part-Italian."

While I was in the coffee shop, it seemed that the two men had formed a brotherhood, bonding over a problem they were convinced they had solved.

They had also planned how we would get to Baltimore by nightfall. It was too late in the day to ride the whole way. Walter and his partner, Mara, would drive us to the Torrey C. Brown Rail Trail in Monkton, thirty miles from the city.

This time, Walter let Mara provide the commentary. A native of DC, she quipped, "I moved north and ended up south. John Wilkes Booth is from northern Maryland. Locals say he murdered Lincoln because he was bipolar. They've refurbished his mansion like he's someone to be proud of."

IN BALTIMORE, JOSIE, NATE, and their toddler hosted us on the third floor of their skinny row house. Josie, who taught kindergarten, excused herself.

"Gotta write a lesson plan for thirty-two students."

While Josie worked a second shift, we played with the little one, devoured Nate's mushroom dish, and listened to his stories of urban organizing. He showed us paper money adorned with the face of Frederick Douglass. "It's a BNote, our local currency. We're fighting Walmartization. The transactional velocity of BNotes is high. No reason to save them—though it feels better to have a Douglass in your pocket than a Washington."

Leaving town, we saw a picket line of carpenters in front of a half-built structure at Johns Hopkins University. A union rep explained their grievances: "They changed our titles and made 85 percent of us laborers instead of carpenters to exempt us from union representation."

I nodded empathetically. "I'm an adjunct instructor. In my business, those with lower-paid titles are too busy trying to make it into the elite group to think about organizing. You are smarter."

The union rep was a community organizer with fingers in many progressive causes, including a new Baltimore action: the Inner Harbor's Occupy Baltimore encampment. "You should check them out," he directed.

On our way to the waterfront district to look for the occupiers, we circled east of Green Mount Cemetery, past hulls of boarded and burned-out row houses. On bright green grass along Inner Harbor, we shared a breakfast burrito and took in the cruise ships. Water taxis and sailboats glistened in the sun, surrounded by luxury hotels. *Here is the waterfront development Rochester, New York, and Wilmington, Delaware, seek,* I thought. I wanted to ask the occupiers if all this glitz was building prosperity for the city's poorest residents or sucking it away, but we couldn't find them.

From Baltimore to the nation's capital, we searched in vain for the bike route our iPhones advised. Amenities for cyclists and pedestrians seemed to disappear at the metropolitan borders. Five miles from DC, we faced a river of cars too vast to cross or join. Michael Trueheart, our DC host, had offered, "Call if you need a ride when you get close." We called.

Michael described himself as tall; a top hat accentuated his pencil profile. His shirt drooped like a blouse on a hanger. We wanted to take him out. He shook his head.

"I don't eat."

Driving, he careened across lanes like a man whose life was invincible, or not preservable. We were close to his home, not far from the White House, when he told us of his pancreatic cancer.

Michael had a sharp wit and tongue. He was doing all he could to stay positive. He kept up with friends in his Tall Club, joined a prayer group, met regularly with a man in remission from the deadly disease. Still, as the evening progressed, we watched despair clutch him. The newspaper headline that day—*Apple Founder Steve Jobs, Age 56, Dies of Pancreatic Cancer*—didn't help. I didn't either. It seemed my femaleness filling his living space irritated him. The sarcastic barbs came fast, and they stung. No one should have to be pleasant or take care of others when they are dying. I assumed the disease was talking and tried to be invisible. David, who extends gentleness to men in crisis without compromising their masculinity, sat with him late into the night.

Michael was impressed we were spending our day in DC at an anti-war demonstration. A decorated Vietnam veteran who provided technical assistance and computers for soldiers returning from Iraq and Afghanistan, he was disgusted with the recent wars and those who perpetrated them.

We stayed with Michael for two nights. On the last morning, he pulled out a journal and handed me a pen. I wrote that praying did not come naturally, but since it made a difference to him, I would. And I did, for the true heart who rescued us from the freeway and put us up when he was down and out.[34]

WASHINGTON, DC'S NEWSEUM HAD a window display of October 7's front pages. The Occupy movement headlined in Boise, Philadelphia, Burlington, San Diego, Richmond, and Minneapolis. At the demonstration to mark the ten years of war in Afghanistan, peace activists incorporated Occupy demands. Gold star families with larger-than-life photos of those they'd lost lined one side of the plaza. There was a strong contingent from Minnesota. The rest were mainly from the East Coast, including a full contingent of Baltimore Occupiers.

Leaving DC at dawn, we floated down the National Mall, past the Washington Monument to the new Martin Luther King Jr. Memorial, where quotes set in stone, shouting truth in this seat of power, were bathed in yellow morning light.

On the bridge into Virginia, we passed hundreds of young lobbyists and political aides cycling north, dressed to impress. The Potomac Heritage Trail

---

34 Michael Trueheart died on May 3, 2012.

was a treat of fall colors with awe-inspiring views of DC and the river. Bliss ended fifteen miles later, at Mount Vernon, the plantation of George and Martha Washington, where we sought food and shade. Privately owned, the Mount Vernon Ladies' Association controlled the history presented to tourists. Photos of twentieth-century presidential visitors gave the place an air of officialdom. Displays erased or sentimentalized Black people, whose forced labor made George and Martha one of the richest couples in US history, propagating a myth of wealth unconnected to suffering. At the restaurant, a smiling white woman dressed as an eighteenth-century servant handed us a brochure that crowed, "Here you will learn about the *real* George Washington."

We don't remember concentration camps from the perspective of Nazis, I thought. Centering enslaved people at plantations is especially important when the enslaver is the designated father of your country.[35]

35 Since our visit, and especially since 2020 uprisings, the conversations and exhibits at Mount Vernon have gotten more complex and truthful. https://dcist.com/story/20/08/06/in-reopened-exhibition-mount-vernon-tells-the-stories-of-people-george-washington-enslaved/.

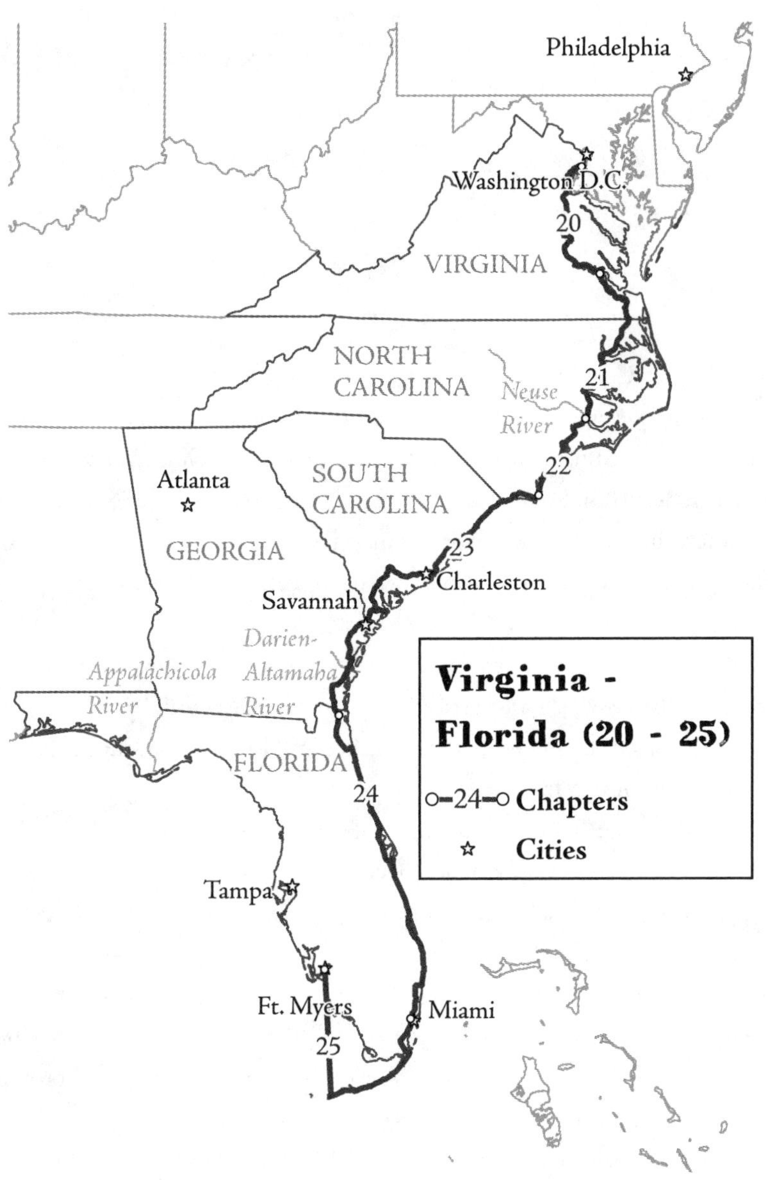

Philadelphia
Washington D.C.
20
VIRGINIA
NORTH
CAROLINA
21
Neuse
River
22
SOUTH
CAROLINA
Atlanta
GEORGIA
23
Charleston
Savannah
Darien-
Altamaha
River
Appalachicola
River
FLORIDA
24
Tampa
Ft. Myers
25
Miami
Virginia -
Florida (20 - 25)
24 Chapters
Cities

20

NO PLACE FOR A BICYCLE

Virginia

The East Coast Greenway bike map directed us to pass through three northern Virginia military bases. In Maryland, a woman who had lived on one when her husband was fighting in the Persian Gulf War said I would find them beautiful. I doubted it. To me, they were manifestations of a public investment in war instead of community. For her, the bases *were* community. I thought about her perspective as we neared the first one and saw a lovely, wooded path with a happy *Bicycle Route* sign.

The sign was imprisoned behind barbed wire and guarded by a placard that read *Watched by Military Guard Dogs*. Before we could decide what to do, a baby-faced, gun-toting soldier approached us. "Bikeway's off-limits," he said. "Been closed since 9/11."

I showed him the Greenway bike map. He shrugged.

"Ma'am, northern Virginia's no place for a bicycle."

We added fifteen suburban miles to get around the first two bases. Our only alternative to the third was Route 1—under construction—one lane, no shoulder. Semis and afternoon rush-hour traffic converged on the tiny strip of asphalt. As we entered the highway, a truck scraped my pannier. My heart jumped, and my body went after it, over to the gate of the third military base. I no longer feared the armed guard who held our safety hostage. Calibrating my tone to hit the right combination of helpless woman and commanding mother, I pointed at Route 1.

"You send us there, we die."

He let us through.

We camped in a regional park outside of Dale City. Two sweet children on bikes came to watch us unload. Four young adults in the site next to ours were having a fun evening. In the middle of the night, however, they began to fight. I heard a woman sobbing, a man swearing. Someone screamed, "You're gonna kill her!" I tried to rouse David. Sleeping bag over ears, he insisted I misheard. I called 911. The police circled the campground. When they left, the fight began again, muted now.

After a sleepless night monitoring with my ears as though my vigilance would keep someone alive, I dreaded Route 1. This stretch of road was named after the president of the Confederacy, highlighting its evil character.[36] We made it one mile on the Jefferson Davis Highway before seeking refuge at a Mexican café, where men congregated by a road sign, *Against City Ordinance to Pick Up Passengers on This Corner*. As we locked the bikes, a small blond woman pulled up in an SUV and shouted out her window: "Who wants to build a patio?" Five Latino men climbed in her van.

We took our time eating huevos rancheros, unsure of our next step. We had two choices: walk five miles on the verge of the Jefferson Davis or take a twenty-mile detour. We decided to take the detour, adding a suburban parkway and a pretty segment through Prince William Forest where we had to walk soft gravel. We rejoined the Jefferson Davis at the juncture of the National Museum of the Marine Corps and the FBI Academy, a triangle of death and deception I'd be eager to escape at any other time, but we were desperate to get out of the sun. We stepped our weary bodies inside the first

36 After a decade of Black Lives Matter protesting and organizing, the Virginia legislature voted in February of 2021 that localities must rename the Jefferson Davis Highway by 2022, or the state will impose the name "Emancipation Memorial Highway." Emancipation Highway. That almost tempts me to take a ride on it.

open establishment—the military and law enforcement-themed Globe and Laurel Restaurant.

On the side of the dark entrance were signed photographs. I found myself face-to-face with Ronald Reagan, and beside him George Bushes, one and two. Next to the presidents was Oliver North, the National Security Council staff member who sold arms to Iran in violation of a US embargo and secretly funneled the profits to Nicaraguan counterrevolutionaries. Squinting at male silhouettes in the plush interior, I wondered, *Was this where they masterminded the Iran/Contra Scandal?*

A petite woman with 1960s bouffant interrupted my thoughts. "Kitchen's closed," she said, wincing and blocking our way.

IN 1935, A MILK truck killed my mother's father in Fredericksburg, Virginia. The fatal accident was on my mind as we rode curving roads, seeking, unsuccessfully, a way out of town that avoided Jefferson Davis Highway. Not sure of our next step, we returned to downtown Fredericksburg, with its appealing stores, sidewalk musicians, and friendly folk my mood couldn't appreciate.

A woman at a Chinese restaurant picked up none of my angst. "I so envy your togetherness," she sighed. "Me and the husband are going to the lawyer." Her daughter called while we were talking, and I heard her gush into the cell phone, "I just met two bicyclists. They have the *cutest* accents."

Still avoiding Jefferson Davis, we wandered past a museum with an imposing name. Though it was hot, and we were aimless, I did not want to stop at the Battlefield Visitor Center at Fredericksburg & Spotsylvania National Military Park. We rode back to the Amtrak station, thinking we might catch a train to Ashland, but they wouldn't take bikes. Drifting without a destination, we found ourselves on a freeway. Off at the exit, we returned, like a boomerang, to the Battlefield Visitors Center.

"Fredericksburg is the bloodiest piece of ground in the country," the military park guide said, laying out gruesome details of the 1862 battle. Union troops, unable to cross the Rappahannock River because the bridge was out, stayed put while their engineers built a temporary crossing. As they waited, more Union soldiers amassed on the riverbank. Confederates watched the human arms buildup, matching numbers on the other side.

"When the battle began," the guide concluded, "regiments rose and fell, a thousand an hour."

"Whoa!" said a youth on the tour, lifting his Confederate cap in the air.

WE GOT A CHEAP hotel on the Jefferson Davis Highway. Through thin walls, trucks rumbled an overture of tomorrow's terror, drowning out the inner voice telling me to push on. As the thought of quitting surfaced, continuing suddenly seemed absurd.

"I'm done."

I was surprised to hear David respond, "OK."

We considered our options: a bus or train to Richmond, a plane to Boston, stay with my mom awhile. Leave the bikes if we had to. We'd figure it out in the morning. The relief was physical. The steady rumble of trucks became a lullaby. I slept.

(Two years later, at Hosmer Library in Minneapolis, David handed me a *National Geographic* coffee-table book on the National Slavery Museum in Fredericksburg, Virginia. I admired the glossy photos and absorbed the gallery descriptions. "How did we miss this side of Fredericksburg?" I cried louder than library volume.

I Googled the museum. Douglas Wilder, first Black governor of Virginia, conceived the project in 2001, persuaded a private developer to donate land, hired architects, and began collecting artifacts. He asked the Fredericksburg

City Council to make the museum tax exempt. They refused. Four years later, they increased the property's taxes twentyfold. In 2008, museum boosters published the *National Geographic* book, hopeful they could use it to raise the funds. By 2011, the only part of the museum completed—a freedom garden—went to seed. The project filed for bankruptcy two weeks before we biked into Fredericksburg. In October 2013, the city claimed the land and sold it to a baseball stadium developer for one dollar.)

WHEN WE OPENED THE door of the Fredericksburg motel to hunt for breakfast and execute the end of our trip, a van-taxi big enough for two loaded bikes sat in the parking lot. It seemed like a sign, a message to keep going. We didn't talk about it, just paid the driver eighty dollars to drive us twenty-eight miles, into the rural south—out of no-place-for-a-bicycle northern Virginia.

South of Ashland, we traded traffic for desolation. I dared not complain. I concocted a game I called Rope, Reptile, or Rubber: Is that coil on the roadside a snake, twine, or the outer piece of a truck tire?

It was fifteen miles before we encountered a sign of humanity. The owners of Studley General Store were wary of us until we praised their crab cakes and sweet potato pie. Compliments won us use of the bathroom. In the store's interior, next to a poster of a naked woman making love to a beer bottle, was a photograph labeled *Confederate Generals circa 1862*. Studley's sold reproductions for twenty-five dollars. A woman visiting the general store invited us to use her hot tub. We declined when she warned, "Stay out of Hopewell. It's where the Blacks are." The blunt racism shocked, though we had heard similar warnings from white people up north, in coded language.

After we got back on the bikes, it began to rain. A lone truck lost its balance, tipping in front of us, unloading an entire tire tread like a snake shedding skin. If we'd been a few feet further ahead, we surely would not have survived. Heart in my throat, I argued with David about the safest plan: move quickly to get off the road (David's idea) or walk in the weeds for a mile until we turned onto a road with a shoulder (mine). Usually I won these arguments, but rain is wetter and colder when you walk. I agreed to a little of both.

The rain was frigid. Business signs in the distance raised our hopes of indoor respite, only to lead us to an abandoned restaurant or gas station. Our ride came to an end in Williamsburg, Virginia, where most tourists reenacted battles and visited outlet malls. We skipped the carnival history at the Jamestown Settlement Museum, and instead spent two hours in their café, eating overpriced bread pudding with raisin sauce, taking turns warming up under bathroom hand dryers.

Our Williamsburg host was a metalworker who played a colonial version of herself for a living. The pay was awful, but she had teenagers who needed the health insurance. In the morning, after her girls left for school, she put out cereal for us, then swished out the door in her floor-length skirt, off to the seventeenth century.

Leaving Williamsburg, we wheeled our bikes onto the bow of the James River ferry. Dark clouds jumped across the sky, erupting on us. Other passengers, dry in their cars, watched us drip. Facing north on the wet deck, we had the privileged view of the *Susan Constant*, a sixteenth-century vessel they called a flyboat.

The rain stopped on land, and we dried quickly. We rode past soybean and cotton fields. I knew soy. I had never seen cotton up close. My associations—from books and folk songs—were all about struggle: slavery, sharecropping, boll weevils, textile factories, sweatshops. The plants themselves, white cotton balls glistening with new rain and occasional pink flowers accented with brown and green, were surprisingly beautiful.

WE READ OUR WHITE host's bumper sticker—*American by Birth, Southern by the Grace of God*—and thought we might not share worldviews. David found a safe male space comparing bicycles. I sat inside with his fiancée, a woman in her forties with big hair who exuded warmth and sadness. Our conversation crossed Mason-Dixon lines, aided by wine and female intimacy. I told her I studied history. "I *love* history!" she responded. "I'm an army brat. Took a class on the Vietnam War at the base. First, I was the only one who wouldn't want my child fighting that war. By the end of the class, the rest of the students agreed with me."

She had lived in Charleston, South Carolina.

"Y'all are gonna *love* it!"

She slid off the couch and out of the room, returning with a billow of white and wire. "I used to wear this for Civil War reenactments."

I must not have reacted as she hoped. She shrugged. "Black people volunteered to be Union soldiers." Then, without missing a beat, she said, "Stand up." I obeyed. She put the hoop skirt made for someone a half-foot taller, over my head.

"I'm gonna give it to you."

We drank more wine and laughed, imagining the white puff sailing atop my bike.

21

HIGH WINDS, LOW RAILINGS

North Carolina

North Carolina hit like a sweet, acrid liquor: visceral memories inspired by red clay, lilting tongues, and the sugar-grease smell of hush puppies. Though I had only lived in the state three years, in the context of my roaming childhood, it was as much home as anywhere.

My family moved from Boston to Durham, North Carolina, in July 1966, during the same week 1,500 Ku Klux Klan members were gathering to confront Martin Luther King Jr., at a rally in Raleigh. At the extended-stay motel that was our home while my parents looked for a place to live, my first North Carolina playmate showed me her tiny white hood. She wanted to know, "Are you a Yankee or a Rebel?"

I was nine when King was assassinated. That evening, picking up on the stress of adults, I began to cry, hard enough that I hyperventilated. I wasn't crying for the murdered civil rights leader. This was a habit I had gotten into that year. I feared that my parents would leave me. I had no reason for this. I wasn't an abused child. But there it was. I used the power of my lungs to assure myself they did not have a chance to get away. Dad would show up by my bedside with a paper bag and put it over my head until I breathed normally. Then my reward would come. He would take me outside. Barefoot and in my pajamas, we'd hold hands and walk along the park across the street. He would talk to me like an adult.

The evening after King was assassinated, Dad came quickly with the paper bag. When my breathing slowed, he pulled up a chair.

"We can't go for a walk," he said. "There is a curfew."

"What is a curfew?"

He told me it was like when he was a child in Nazi Germany, and they had to stay inside.

"Why did Martin Luther King die?" I asked.

"The best people die young. The worst are hard to kill. Resisters tried to kill Hitler. His supporters died instead, drinking the poison, hit by the bomb under his desk."

"Hitler had supporters?"

"Yes. He convinced German people that loving the fatherland meant following him."

"But you were German."

"Not according to Hitler."

This conversation continued between us for as long as Dad lived. It set the trajectory for my adult life and turned me into the internationalist I called myself when I had the language to articulate it. It motivated my activism and study. I wanted to understand how nationalism overtakes people, replaces empathy, makes way for hell on earth.

All this was on my mind as I bicycled the North Carolina coast, devouring collards with hot pepper vinegar, black-eyed peas, fried okra, and fresh catfish. I loved hearing the word *reckon* roll off people's lips. Black and white dialects were mellifluous and familiar, though some were incomprehensible to my now-Midwestern ear. When a farmer offered to "carry us" in his truck, I understood but asked again. I had not heard this turn of phrase since 1969.

This surge of emotional attachment to a land of my childhood surprised me. *Is this how an allegiance to "Fatherland" or "Confederacy" happens?* I wondered. The connections we make to places are sensual. How easy it would be to attach myths to smells, tastes, and sights. Myths of "blood and soil." *Perhaps land attachment is a natural human trait,* I thought, but so is the generosity strangers offer us. How do we nurture that kind of hospitality, so it is strong enough to overcome nationalist bigotry?

ENTERING EDENTON, NORTH CAROLINA, on a Sunday morning, churches hummed with gospel sounds. The towering Chowan County Confederate Dead monument, ringed with US and North Carolina flags, affronted us.[37] Colonial Park, with its prehistoric-looking cypress trees standing in the water and its public bathrooms, wooed us. There was an invitation on the water's edge for boaters to dock overnight. "We could have camped here and saved on a motel," I sighed, thinking of that night in Newark, New York, when we docked with the boats.

David shook his head. "Socialism for the rich."

He pointed at an ordinance tacked to the bathroom door. I sighed, reading words custom-made for selective enforcement: *No Boisterous Conduct, Indecent Language, or Loud Music.*

"And white," I added.

The only open café was across from the Confederate monument. Civil War and other military photos decorated the walls. Two men in their fifties sat at the next table. One was complaining about "Northern retirees invading Edenton, seeking cheap housing and warm winters." He glanced our way before finishing his thought. "I sold my house to one of those damn Yankees. Got a good price for it."

---

37 On June 9, 2020, two weeks after the murder of George Floyd, Edenton's mayor issued a statement condemning racism and acknowledging calls to remove the Confederate statue. https://www.dailyadvance.com/chowan/news/local/edenton-town-council-oks-statement-denouncing-racism/article_7106b43a-9732-505b-a907-bd6ad2848fd8.html.

After breakfast, we visited the Penelope Barker House, a mansion on the waterfront advertising a "special display" on Native Americans. The docent was excited as she showed us the faux Indian dolls, a children's timeline, a few arrowheads. I was embarrassed for her, proudly offered this infantilizing mythology; ashamed of myself for not telling her so. The primary Barker House exhibit honored the colonial Edenton women who broke gender rules, signing their names to a petition protesting British taxes on tea.

I combed the website of this majority Black town, looking in vain for a museum honoring Harriet Jacobs, another Edenton feminist icon. Jacobs escaped a plantation, lived as a fugitive, worked as an abolitionist, and wrote and self-published *Incidents in the Life of a Slave Girl*. Edenton's visitor center wasn't open on Sundays, so we were unable to take their walking tour of sites mentioned in Jacobs's autobiography. Jacobs told the world that plantation owners systematically raped the women they enslaved. As of this writing, Edenton's website does not mention this primary contribution to our understanding of the slave economy. The cover-up Jacob risked so much to expose continues.[38]

Someday, the Confederate monument's regal base will be the pedestal on which the likeness of Harriet Jacob stands, I thought. *A Jacobs Museum will host exhibits on slavery and rape culture with the goal of* Never Again! What right do I have to make such a hopeful prediction? None, to those who see me as a damn Yankee. I could tell them I have roots in North Carolina and it is forever in my heart, but that's not the point. Heroes who liberate belong to us all.

THE SPAN OUTSIDE OF Edenton, across the Albemarle Sound, was hardly a bridge—just a road crossing water, no land in sight. It had a warning

38 https://www.visitedenton.com/sites.php#site-statehistoric.

sign for bicyclists: *Caution: High Winds and Low Railings*. We hit land just as congregants were leaving storefront churches. I was a trespasser with my bicycle, white skin, and skimpy bike shorts on a road that belonged to Black women in dresses and hats of brilliant colors.

An herb farmer invited us to stay in Washington, North Carolina. In the clear dark night, we stood in her driveway and admired the Milky Way, until a gunshot disturbed the serenity. Our host was sanguine. "This is hunting country. October to January, you put up a sign if you don't want people shooting deer, black bear, raccoon, possum, or birds on your land. Sometimes they do anyway. Cities declare themselves sanctuaries to prohibit shooting birds in town."

THE FREEWAY BRIDGE OVER the Neuse River into New Bern was three miles. We dodged rush-hour traffic, glass, nails, tire treads, and a dead possum.

Our New Bern hosts, three women educators at Craven Community College, drew me in with their contagious laughter. They had just completed the mountain-to-coast ride across North Carolina. "It was soooo much fun," one woman said. "Except for those Porta Potties."

Her friend nodded. "I'd love to do a longer adventure, but I can't live without bathrooms."

"And what about makeup?" the first one added. "I couldn't live without makeup."

I considered my response. At home I struggled to keep my hair combed, glasses cleaned, and shoes tied. Living without the usual embarrassment about my lack of female finesse was one of the pleasures of the bike tour. Not that I didn't care about my looks. I had hoped the trip would transform me into a slim young beauty. It hadn't happened yet. In fact, I was a mess. Bike shorts highlighted unsightly bulges. I had raccoon eyes, a peeling face, legs covered in bruises and cuts. The helmet obliterated my thin hair, producing a bald look. Filthy most waking hours, I wet my shorts at least once a day.

I dodged the makeup question, didn't mention bladder infections, and omitted the story about seeking shelter in a smelly biffy on the Massachusetts-New Hampshire border during a thunderstorm. Their sweet laughter bathed me as I quipped, "I've come to worship Porta Potties."

My new friends were eager to show off their region, boasting, "North Carolina has a fantastic community college system," and advising, "Don't miss our plantations." I engaged them on the community colleges, demurred on the Confederate nostalgia. Beyond the immorality of celebrating the locus of human bondage, visiting dolled-up mansions during a recession felt like endorsing a façade meant to distract us from depleted economies.

They weren't the first white southerners we disappointed with our lack of interest in plantations. Eastern North Carolina had an economic hurricane to overcome. Municipalities were refurbishing them specifically to attract *us*, the white tourists. Timed to coincide with the Civil War sesquicentennial, made-over plantations were the South's version of the North's waterfront developments—false tickets out of bad times.

22

SMOKE AND MIRRORS

North Carolina

The way a town dies reflects regional cultures. In Wisconsin, taverns remained open when all else closed. In the Northeast, nail salons were the last to go. In foreclosed North Carolina towns, only God and guns were still in business. Gun shops had nothing to offer us. Churches were our saving grace. We helped ourselves to their outdoor spigots and shaded front steps.

North Carolina coastal farmsteads had their own cemetery plots, barely distinguishable from elaborate Halloween gravestones adorning people's yards. Seasonal decorations and short days reminded us it was October, even as rising temperatures told us we were moving south. My now-Midwestern eye wondered at cotton fields the size of a Minnesota ditch next to boarded-up farmhouses. Roads were flat and quiet, but sun, high winds, and bugs provided drama. Hurricane Irene had created perfect mosquito conditions. Bonfires of storm debris warded off some bugs. David loved the smell; it reminded him of childhood autumns when you could still legally burn leaves in Wisconsin.

"ARE YOU MORMON MISSIONARIES?"

The questioner, in his fifties and with a skull patch on his jacket, stopped us in front of Saigon Sam's Military Surplus in Jacksonville, North Carolina. He knew we didn't belong.

In Jacksonville, each restaurant, tattoo parlor, payday loan center, and sports bar marquee proclaimed support for the troops in deals and homilies. The Super 8 where we spent the night courted military clientele with free ribs and beer. The motel staff watched indulgently as young men with crew cuts climbed in and out of motel windows, grabbing twice their share. I had a couple of beers on Super 8 and sat down with a free Corps paper and the *Daily News*, available in the lobby. I read about US Marines building hospitals in Latin America, an MRI machine headed to Helmand Province in Afghanistan, a soccer game between soldiers and locals, Halloween preparations, and a fundraiser to fight muscular dystrophy. An advice column suggested to parents, "It is never too early to teach children violence is not an acceptable problem-solving method."[39] Human interest stories mixed with alcohol gave me a warm buzz. The *Daily News* front page sobered me up:

"Camp Lejeune's new infantry immersion trainer is like a visit to an elaborate theme park—albeit one set in Afghanistan, with piped-in smells of rotting flesh and burning wood, booby-trapped with black powder explosive. An authentic Afghan village from the dirt covering the floors to the prayer call sounding overhead, the $20 million, 3,200-square-foot facility is a jaw-dropping novelty. . . ."[40]

Riding out of Jacksonville, head down, I fought a headwind and a brain stuck on phrases that should never be paired:

rotting flesh—jaw-dropping novelty

prayer call—black powder explosive

"KABOOM!" The deafening blast was followed by a blinding haze. I braked.

When the air cleared, I read the sign: *Military Exercise When Lights Flashing: Watch for Thick Smoke, Low Visibility on Freeway.*

---

39 "Ask the Expert," *Rotovue*, October 12, 2011. *Rotovue* is the Camp Lejeune Marine Corps Base's weekly periodical.

40 "Surviving on the Battlefield," The *Daily News* (Jacksonville, North Carolina), October 21, 2011.

IN SURF CITY ON Topsail Island, we booked two nights and walked, silent, on the beach. A soldier and his lover passed. I slipped polished rocks into my pocket—little weights for my front bag. We had just made plans to meet Emily in Austin over Christmas. I was collecting treasures to give to my child. In the evening, we watched a public television documentary on North Carolina's Civilian Conservation Corps. Elderly CCC veterans expressed pride in their service "defending the nation against the dust bowl."

Off the island before dawn, we joined one hundred people at the local IHOP for weekend brunch. Wilmington, North Carolina, had Spanish moss–covered trees, tall narrow churches, and competing historical markers. Older plaques celebrated Confederate generals. A marker erected in 1998 at the home of Black newspaper editor Alexander Manly read, "A mob burned his office in 1898, leading to a race riot and restrictions of Black voting in North Carolina."

"*Race riot?!*" I exclaimed to my audience of one. "That white mob assassinated Black leaders, killed sixty people. It was a *coup*, unseating an elected biracial government with a white supremacist regime."[41]

The Cape Fear Museum of History and Science—a warm place to spend a surprisingly cold afternoon—did not explore the Coup. It had a display of

41 The story of the Wilmington biracial government, massacre and coup has entered public consciousness since 2011. It is important North Carolina history that uncovers both a white supremacist atrocity, and a hidden history of multiracial solidarity. A marker telling a more accurate story was erected in 2019. The 1898 Memorial Park, erected in 2008, remembers the victims. We missed it. You shouldn't.

local hero Michael Jordan's report card, a gallery on North Carolina Jews, and an exhibit on Wilmington's origin as an international seaport. Though Africans, in bondage and free, produced the tar, cotton, and tobacco that made the city a global market player, and Wilmington was the only port on North Carolina's island-filled coast large enough for slave ships, the exhibit's world trade route map omitted West Africa.

WAITING FOR THE FERRY to Southport, North Carolina, we stopped at Fort Fisher, a Civil War landmark. A docent dressed as a Confederate soldier tried to sell us a raffle ticket for a "real Confederate musket!"

"Y'all carry this on your bicycle, and no one will bother you."

23

SLAVE RELICS

South Carolina and Georgia

Mother: "You covered the whole neighborhood and came home with five candies?"
Girl: "Home foreclosures."[42]

In North Carolina, cabbage palms looked forced and fake in condo gardens. In South Carolina, palmettos were plump and happy—where they belonged. Evergreen live oaks spread their branches to make a canopy. Dressed in Spanish moss, they caught the late-day sun in ribbons. Shrimpers with license plates from every state on the eastern seaboard fished inlets, nets enveloping like jellyfish. Their slogan: *Friends don't let friends eat imported shrimp*. We watched a flock of early-morning birders with their giant lenses stalk a salt marsh, then huddle, exchanging battle stories. "Caught the blue heron. Short-billed dowitcher got away."

The circle of brush surrounding our Huntington Beach State Park campsite, deep in the Francis Marion National Forest, seemed perfect for witches toiling and troubling. We awoke to the sound of someone rustling. Unzipping the tent door, we saw two raccoons standing on their hind legs, heads peeking above the picnic table. In the morning, our childproof glucosamine bottle lay on the ground, gnarled with tooth marks, pills gone.[43]

---

42 From an editorial cartoon in the October 27, 2011, issue of *The Charleston Chronicle*.

43 For the rest of the trip, David loved to tell people about our encounter with arthritic and determined giant raccoons. The animals got taller and more adept with each telling.

NORTHERN ACCENTS—NEW YORK, BOSTON, Cleveland—overlapped at the Thomas Café on Front Street in Georgetown, South Carolina, where white customers in their sixties enjoyed coffee and a shared copy of *South Strand News*. A tiny elite had once reaped fabulous profits here, enslaving people on rice plantations. Timber, steel, and tourism had replaced rice, and today the predominantly Black working class and the Northern, white, retired class lived in separate spheres. The Thomas Café faced a picturesque harbor at the confluence of four rivers. We added two more "damn Yankees" to the white Café crowd.

I picked up the *South Strand* editorial page. The political cartoon showed a tattooed, pierced Wall Street Occupier saying, "Why won't anyone give me a job?"

"Ha!" I said, showing it to David.

"Why are you laughing?" he said. "It's ignorant."

"I know. I'm thinking about a tattooed New York cop I saw occupying Wall Street."

We left Thomas Café, passing Front Street's other built-to-look-old shops and its overly quaint watchtower. On the outskirts of town, we passed a steel factory.

BETWEEN GEORGETOWN AND CHARLESTON, US Highway 17 became Sweetgrass Basket Makers Highway, abutted with pine forests and marshes purpled with flowering sweetgrass. African American women sold their wares in huts on the shoulder. We stopped at one woman's stall and appreciated her artistry—woven vessels accented with bulrush and palmetto fronds. What she needed was a sale.

AFTER MANY EDGE-OF-THE-EARTH-BRIDGES-TO-NOWHERE WITH drains the size of bike tires, strewn with spikes, dead possums, and truck retreads, the Ravenel Bridge into Charleston was a delight. Its fortified arches created shapes and shadows as awesome as their famous Brooklyn and San Francisco cousins. A concrete safety wall separated bike and pedestrian paths from cars. Built in 2005, the bridge is named after a politician known for racist epithets and support of the Confederate flag. In segregated Charleston, the bridge was a singular multiracial space. Cyclists, runners, strollers, and people in wheelchairs joined us on the three-mile span along the Cooper River.[44]

Most of Charleston's French Quarter was boarded up. Tropical vines softened the ugliness of plywood. Curlicues, lions, balconies, stained glass, bright colors, and our ears told us this wasn't Utica, New York, or Waterbury, Connecticut. But plywood is plywood, and poverty is poverty.

The Gullah Geechee culture was evident in Charleston. Language, architecture, religion, food, and plants reminded me of the island of Barbados, which I visited on a research trip. The Barbadian tourist industry had tried to herd us to beaches and away from inland plantations where people still harvested sugar in oppressive conditions. Likewise, here in Charleston a tourist magazine recommended we eat at a glitzy "authentic" Gullah restaurant, then hightail it to the countryside to visit a plantation, walk in a tropical garden, and bask in pervading nostalgia for the Confederacy.

44 On May 7, 2015, activists stopped traffic on the bridge to protest racially targeted police violence. On June 21, 2015, a massive chain of people marched in solidarity and sorrow across the bridge after a white supremacist killed nine African American parishioners at Charleston's historic AME Church.

THE CHARLESTON WOMAN OF the house was out of town. The man—a cyclist—left the door open, encouraging us to make ourselves at home. Two beds in the guest room were covered with purposeful piles, craft projects awaiting their makers. Gingerly moving each stack, we crawled into each other until we were one egg, remaining attached until morning when we unraveled and carefully replaced each pile on the bed.

Exhausted, I insisted on another night in Charleston. We found a hotel on the southern edge of the city. The young clerk finagled a fancy room for us for a deep discount. She wanted to talk. After we unpacked, I came down with my notebook, looking for her. She wasn't at her desk. Outside the open door, I saw her crouched on the ground. I watched as three women ran to her side.

"What happened?" I asked the clerk at the desk.

"Someone murdered her fiancé."

THE TOUTED "GREENWAY" BIKE path out of Charleston wasn't smooth. The first two miles were difficult but bikeable. After that, the aspiring rail trail deteriorated into rocks and sand. Instead of turning around, we kept going, walking aside what looked like an abandoned railway track. For once, David was OK with going slow. He enjoyed birdwatching, and he knew I needed to walk. The hotel clerk in Charleston was on my mind, and I was in no state to concentrate on safely maneuvering Highway 17.

After five miles, we encountered a ravine and the remains of a railroad bridge. Its gaps didn't look big enough to fall through but were large enough to assure us the bridge was in disuse. On the other side was a quiet road. We weighed the choices: backtrack seven miles, spend another night in Charleston and take Highway 17 tomorrow, or . . .

We lifted the bicycles onto the trestle. The gaps were bigger than they appeared. I kept my downward glances shallow, avoiding holes, blurring the chasm below. The track vibrated, sending a shock up my legs. As we pulled off the trestle, the low horn and clack grew deafening.

Why didn't our trip end there, with two foolish cyclists crushed by a train, falling to their deaths? Was this God? Were we watched over? My mind flashed back to the young woman at the hotel in Charleston. What kind of higher power would speed us over the bridge yet refuse to deflect a bullet to save a young man and the dreams of a young woman?

Walterboro, South Carolina, was playing a community Halloween murder mystery game, like Clue, with Main Street as the game board. Players interviewed costumed suspects in downtown stores, collecting evidence. David took photos of himself with the costumed ladies. I couldn't play. Murder mysteries are not fun when murder is close.

WALTERBORO'S SLAVE RELICS MUSEUM was on a side street in an old Victorian home. There was a note on the door: "Knock. The doorbell does not work." We knocked. No one answered. I noticed the official post:

This building is condemned.[45]

IN RIDGELAND, SOUTH CAROLINA, we sat on the edge of the motel bed, watching TV. David wanted an escape. I insisted we "stay in Ridgeland." We tuned in to a public station showing a local library board meeting. The deadpan financial officer droned his report. His live audience struggled to stay

---

45 Henry Louis Gates Jr. is shown examining artifacts from the Slave Relics Museum in his 2013 PBS series *The African Americans: Many Rivers to Cross*. The museum had reopened in 2012, but by 2016 it was permanently closed.

awake, but for his virtual audience, physical exhaustion turned the mundane into high comedy. I started to laugh. Soon, David joined in. We laughed so hard we nearly missed the moment the meeting got interesting.

The city had allocated one pot of money for two projects: to build a new library and refurbish a local plantation. A white woman offered to donate her antebellum heirlooms to the plantation to save money for the library. Other white members began describing cherished ancestral items they could contribute. The board chair—a Black woman—brought the meeting back to order.

THE TALMADGE MEMORIAL BRIDGE into Savannah, Georgia, was as daunting as Charleston's Ravenel Bridge had been inviting. Approaching it on a narrow, trash-filled span, we passed the sign, *Welcome. We're Glad Georgia's on Your Mind.* Neither of us could stomach the bridge. David put his thumb out, hoping to flag a pickup to carry us across. I zoomed in on my iPhone map, hoping for a miracle.

And there it was: a small, dotted line—a pedestrian ferry.

We veered off the cluttered highway and entered an antiseptic world of giant palms and deserted Romanesque, postmodern buildings—an exclusive oasis for international traders, corporate conveners, and speed racers. Porsches on a racetrack whirred in the distance. At the ferry dock was a Westin hotel. I sensed free food: apples for me, ginger cookies for David, lemon iced tea for us both.

On the ferry, we met a young Black couple from Atlanta on a romantic adventure, visiting Savannah for the first time. We absorbed their excitement. Disembarking at the historic riverfront with its cobblestone streets, ancient trees, statues, fountains, and perfectly restored three-hundred-year-old row houses, the four of us did what tourists do in Savannah: take pictures.

But David and I were tired, unable to appreciate "the most beautiful streets in the South." We began to argue about directions to our host's home. A young man brooding on a park bench interrupted, asking questions we heard a dozen times a day: "Where are you going? How many miles a day?" And an unusual one:

"How did you two meet?"

"Doing Central America solidarity work," I answered.

His look told me my answer did not make sense. Still, I continued. "In the 1980s, our country waged covert wars, supporting brutal dictators. We wanted to stop it."

He looked confused and frustrated. I relented. "We shared interests. Why do you want to know?"

"I watched you biking around town. You are clearly in love. I didn't think such a thing was possible anymore."

Leaving the glow of the young man's eyes, we walked a whole block before we resumed our argument. However, it was not long before we were interrupted again, this time by the sight of protest signs.

War Is Not the Answer! Labor Unite! Human Needs, Not Corporate Greed!

We Are Pissed Because We Are Getting Pissed On by the White House, Congress, and Wall Street!

We walked toward the sign holders and into Forsyth Park. I introduced myself to a woman named Kelly, in her early twenties, wearing a homemade *Occupy Savannah* tee. Her sign read, *I can't afford to buy my own Senator.* For four weeks, she and her friends had commandeered this park, a few blocks from the city's tourist center.

"We are a legal, daytime occupation," she explained. "The police ride by and give us the thumbs-up. Once a day, we march to the financial district and tourist area. The rest of the time, we stand on this busy road next to the square, making our presence known. Today, representatives from eight unions and a few politicians are here. We've got an election on Tuesday."

She introduced me to James, a veteran, also in his mid-twenties. "I was proud to serve my country, but I'm prouder to serve here," he told me. "After my tour, I pledged I'd never get up at dawn again, but I'm here every morning to put up the tent."

Kelly invited everyone to make a circle. A Black preacher gave a rousing speech. Kelly asked him to bring his constituents next time: "religious folks, Black people." When the preacher came over to "shake the cyclist's hand," he shook his head. "These people think I can work miracles."

MOST TOURISTS TAKE THE freeway into Savannah's cobblestone core and never glance at the sea of foreclosed homes we passed when we left the waterfront region of million-dollar restored colonial row houses. At the Burger King on Martin Luther King Jr. Boulevard, we stopped to use the bathroom—two white, middle-aged people in spandex, entering a young Black space. I wondered if this was *the* Savannah Burger King where Troy Anthony Davis was accused of killing a police officer in 1989. The state of Georgia had just electrocuted him despite an outcry from human rights groups who pointed out that the jury had convicted him based on recanted testimony.

AT A STRIP MALL in Richmond Hill, Georgia, where we sought dinner, little Halloween zombies and superheroes collected treats. The Dixie Outfitters Southern Heritage Store sold Confederate flag bikinis and child-size rebel soldier outfits. Cute kids, white supremacist commerce, and a conversation at the Fuji Sushi with a Japanese/Black family mixing homework and tempura, jolted an impolite mix of emotions. With a mouth full of edamame, I forced down the lump in my throat.

Turning off Highway 17 at Eulonia, we rode Route 99 through depopulated southern Georgia coastal communities. Majestic pines and oaks covered in Spanish moss partially concealed crumbling structures, and salty ocean breezes softened the edges of a subsistence economy. At the foot of the Darien River bridge, we turned a corner and entered another world: wine shops, B&Bs, pricey dockside dining, and suave tour guides eager to plan our evening.

Exhausted, we succumbed to this budget-breaking spot. Sitting on a porch overlooking the water, I swallowed a book of Georgia state history. Tom Watson, a Reconstruction-era agrarian activist, organized white and Black sharecroppers here in the 1890s. By the 1900s, however, he was blaming Blacks, Catholics, and Jews instead of landlords and banks for the woes of white textile workers and itinerant farmers. *The devolution of Tom Watson is the real lost cause for the South's 99 percent,* I thought.

While David readied our bags for the next day, I lay on my luxury bed continuing my local history immersion. Georgia Public TV was showing a documentary on cotton textile factories that bemoaned "traditional values" lost when cotton towns died. Nostalgia for a time when workers' lives were controlled by employers seemed outrageous to me, but, I thought, *if you can be sentimental about plantations, I guess you can get dewy-eyed about sweatshops and company towns.*

I did not have the emotional experience of growing up in one place, developing cultural attachments to a place, an industry, a life. Empathy for that longing could only be intellectual. What I did know was that a sliver of the cotton profits stayed in Georgia, making fortunes for a tiny elite. Northern cities siphoned the rest. Black and white labor histories were getting a whitewash and blackout in Georgia.

24

IMAGINED SECURITY

Florida

No Security.
—Florida wayside sign

At the Crossroads Diner in Yulee, outside of Jacksonville, Florida, I was eating breakfast and idly skimming a newspaper when a local story caught my attention: *Militia members caught with homemade biotoxin!*[46] Chemical weapons had not been on my list of fears. My gut flipped grits and eggs, imagining domestic terrorists shouting, "Bonus points!" as they unleashed their ricin poison on collateral bicyclists. The militia members reportedly believed they were under government siege. Though their weapons were aimed at random passersby, their ideological targets were the IRS, the Department of Justice, and the Bureau of Alcohol, Tobacco, Firearms and Explosives.

JACKSONVILLE, FLORIDA, THE LONGEST city in the continental US, stretched down the coast for fifty miles. The north side was rural and industrial, with farms, tropical brush, and mammoth Budweiser and Bacardi factories. We passed a crumbling brick school with a dusty yard. Hungrily, I devoured cabbage and pigeon peas at a Caribbean deli before catching the eye of a woman eating off an abandoned plate. On the south side, we rested at an

46 "Militia members plotted to kill federal officials, prosecutors say." CNN, November 1, 2011, http://security.blogs.cnn.com/2011/11/01/breaking-four-in-georgia-arrested-for-plotting-ricin-attack/.

outdoor smoothie café on a palm-lined street. Children pouring out of a shiny school, all glass and new paint, joined us for a snack.

A short, tough ride against a headwind took us to St. Augustine, a town on the edge of the aqua Matanzas River. At the Lightner Museum, we locked our dusty bicycles in the Victorian courtyard and escaped the sun, wandering through hallways of arrowheads, stuffed alligators, and coats of armor. Later, pulled by the sound of a drum circle, we rode past the gleaming columns of the Bridge of Lions and the seventeenth-century Spanish fort where, in the 1830s, the US Army imprisoned Seminoles who resisted Indian removal. Around the corner from the fort, a young blond man in full camouflage sold "authentic Native American artifacts." On his cassette player, Indigenous voices rose high above their drums.

A few blocks away, rhythm and blues music drowned out the Native singers. Musicians, surrounded by cotton candy booths and hot dog stands, celebrated two proud chapters in the city's Black history. When Florida was a Spanish colony, people fled slavery on an underground path south to freedom in St. Augustine.[47] During the Jim Crow era, when most Florida beaches were off limits to Black people, activists struggled to make the city a vacation haven for African Americans.

We sailed out of St. Augustine on an enormous tailwind. Speeds topped thirty miles an hour without pedaling. On Ormond Beach, we splurged on a plate of mussels and read about the Florida Tea Party, which was convening close by. The *Daytona Beach News-Journal* reported participants were "32% women, 37% men." I wondered if it was a typo, or if 31 percent of Tea Partiers rejected binary gender categories.

It was hot again, and a sidewind made balance difficult on traffic-filled Route 1 by Cape Canaveral and the Kennedy Space Center. Crossing a bridge toward AIA and the ocean, we rode through our first barrier island. Two

47 Harriet Jacobs's grandmother was caught fleeing to St. Augustine. (Harriet A. Jacobs, *Incidents in the Life of a Slave Girl*, Cambridge, Massachusetts: Harvard University Press, 2009, p.6.)

loggerhead turtles lumbered across the road. We camped at Sebastian Inlet State Park, where wood storks, egrets, pelicans, osprey, and humans gathered to fish. Birds as tall as me landed in front of our picnic table. We met Sierra Club volunteers, cleaning latrines at the Pelican Island National Wildlife Refuge for the thrill of "experiencing the greatest biodiversity in the world." They welcomed us to the century-old sanctuary, surrounded by hotels, military installations, and retirement condos.

IN 1981, DAVID SPENT six months as a community organizer in Liberty City, a Black working-class neighborhood of Miami, where poverty was pervasive and jobs scarce. Afterward, he got a job canvassing on the million-dollar strip on the A1A between Jupiter and Boca Raton. He went to three homes. At each, a butler ushered him to the owner on his yacht. After the third house, David threw up in the canal.

Cycling the strip where David once lost his lunch, we saw gardeners shaping shrubs that hid the mansions David had canvassed. Moving inland, we skirted potholes on Martin Luther King Boulevard. Children and parents playing T-ball in a vacant lot lined with police tape ran over to greet us.

Our white Boca Raton host did not live in a mansion. He lived in a development of townhomes, one-car garages, and gates like the one in Sanford, Florida where, three months later, vigilante George Zimmerman would kill Trayvon Martin, a Black teenager carrying Skittles and iced tea.

Our host had just lost his job as a home security installer after twenty-five years with the company—no severance, no notice. "Right-to-work means right-to-be-fired-without-notice," he scoffed. He expressed an indignation at Florida's anti-union climate that was righteous and an anger at everyone who wasn't white and male that was not. I wanted to leave, but I was exhausted. He offered us a bed. *Learn from him,* I told myself.

He took us out to eat. At the restaurant, a car pulled into a parking space he wanted. When a Black couple emerged from the vehicle, he was triumphant, his race theories reinforced. He was lonely and troubled, and he wanted to talk. David lent his trained ear. I receded to his teenager's bedroom, not wanting silence to signal agreement. When we rolled out of his driveway the next day, he offered a bag of granola bars and some racially offensive advice about Miami drivers, then wished us Godspeed.

MY AUNT MAJA LIVED in Miami Springs. David and I put our sleeping bags on her porch, where we could smell the grapefruit trees. In the afternoon, we sat together: Maja in her wheelchair, me on the couch. My aunt's lilting German accent and authoritative personality reminded me of my grandmother. I took the opportunity to ask her about Grandma.

"Mutti was a nurse during World War I," Maja reminded me. "The radiologist she worked with was killed. Your grandma took his place; eighteen years old and no medical schooling! She was a loyal German citizen, yet she knew before many of her Jewish neighbors that the country she loved would kill her if she did not leave. She sent your grandpa away, so when the Gestapo came looking, he was already gone."

Maja was ten years older than Dad. I thought about that age difference as I compared her stories, to those I had heard from him. Dad's memory of Nazis tearing through their apartment was that of a five-year-old. He could not understand why they upset dresser drawers. Didn't they know his father was too big to fit in there?

When Dad talked about the ship to the Americas, he most remembered hiding under his mother's skirts, afraid of the Orthodox ladies in the women's room when they took off their wigs, revealing bald heads. Now Maja told me, "I was sixteen on the boat. The two-week crossing was fun. I flirted with the young men. That's where I met my husband, Frank."

Dad had told me that at the refugee camp in Havana, he had followed his mother as she completed her camp job, pulling heads off live chickens. Maja was old enough to go places on her own in Cuba. She remembered witnessing an infamous injustice.

"When the MS *St. Louis* came into Havana harbor, I stood with a crowd to welcome the newcomers. The boat was so close I could touch the outstretched hands of excited children hanging on the railing. I watched in horror as Cuban authorities turned the ship of German Jewish refugees away."[48]

In Havana, Grandma went to the US embassy daily to see if her name was on the list of people accepted. One day another woman did not show up, and Grandma claimed to be her. She sold her jewelry to the Havana synagogue to pay for passage to Miami.[49]

When the family reached Florida, Dad and his other sister, Helga, started school. There, Dad remembered the sting of child laughter when he proudly recited, "H is for *hatpins*," pronouncing "pins" with two syllables so it sounded like "penis." By that time, Maja was working, sacrificing her education to help provide for her siblings.

Like many of us—refugees and their children—Maja put distance between herself and the people who came to Miami afterward. Cubans, Haitians, Dominicans—people with legal papers, and those, like our family, who came without. But Maja also stayed. When her parents moved the family to New

---

48 The United States and Canada also refused them safe harbor; and the boat sailed back to Europe, sending passengers back to battlefields and concentration camps.

49 In 1987, I visited that Havana synagogue and saw their display case of items refugees exchanged for passage.

York City, she married Frank and they bought the home where, seventy years later, Maja and I sat, trading memories.

WE SPENT A DAY in Miami, fulfilling David's desire for a Cuban breakfast and my need for a haircut. David wanted black beans. He got huevos revueltos con white bread and an earful from the Cuban men in the café, complaining about Nicaraguan newcomers. My hairstylist was a bubbly Nicaraguan woman. When she heard about the bike trip, she told me this story.

"I have six brothers. When I was ten years old, they put me on a bike without brakes and sent me down a hill. I fell, got all bruised up, and never got on a bike again. To teach me how to swim, they put a belt around me and threw me in the water. I nearly drowned. I understand, a little, the trauma of people who survive rape or war. When I get near water, the whole event comes back, like it happened yesterday."

25

KEY BRIDGES

Florida

One Human Family
—Key West motto

Before we'd left Minneapolis, I read in *Adventure Cyclist* about a woman who toured the Keys. Etched in my mind was a picture of her looking fabulous, sipping some key lime elixir out of a coconut, sitting under a grass hut with the blue sea in the background. That was going to be me. I could feel the breeze, imagine the triumph. I'd buy a yellow sundress, lie on the sand, rejuvenate in all my splendor before the long trek across the southwest.

It seemed sensible to ride through the noonday sun. It was only eighty-six degrees. Even at this latitude, mid-November days were short. David noticed first. I swerved into traffic. He shouted for me to stop. I parked on the side of the road and collapsed onto the pavement. My head pounded and my eyelids burned. I threw up my breakfast.

We got the nearest room, paying for a beach we never saw. Instead of snorkeling with angelfish while his woman with the yellow sundress dug her toes in the sand, David laundered soiled bike clothes and made me sip water every ten minutes. When I managed to sit outside for a short while in the evening, we—and everyone else at the resort—watched surreptitiously as a couple of Swedish tourists—young, beautiful, naked—stood on the pool's edge. The sight of them fed a corrosive spot in my belly. There was a deep ocean between me and those sentries of tropical pleasure.

I was still not up to par when we took off in the morning calm. At a café of blue tile and kitsch, I didn't want to leave. Only a rain burst, leaving cooler air and mercifully bike-friendly clouds, nudged me out of my seat. We needed those optimum conditions for our ride across the Seven Mile Bridge.

By this time my fear of biking bridges was acute. I wasn't afraid they would collapse like the I-35W Mississippi River Bridge in Minneapolis had in 2007. It was the no-way-out that got me. Eyes glued to my strip of concrete, I imagined a boat-hauling pickup losing control of its backside, catapulting me into the sea. Behind me, David practiced his colors: "turquoise water, white fishing boats, pink shrimp, green iguanas, brown pelicans." I did my best to tune him out.

Arnold Schwarzenegger blew up the Seven Mile Bridge in the movie *True Lies*. Now I thought, *the bridge is a lying truth*. It violated my law of expectations. At the seventh mile we paused on land for a mere moment, before crossing water again. [50]

AS WE STOOD IN line behind a group from Connecticut to take our pictures next to a cement cone painted *Southernmost Point*, a steady stream of drivers paused, sticking cameras out the window. Guides in open-air tour buses shouted, "We are ninety miles from Havana, one hundred sixty miles from Miami, eighty miles from Walmart!"

It was a heady moment. "Tipadakeys" had become a single word we

---

50 As we pedaled the Seven Mile, activists in Milwaukee, New York, Miami, and a dozen other cities occupied bridges, calling for a public works program to repair the nation's infrastructure. In Minneapolis, eleven were arrested on the 10th Avenue Bridge, demanding an end to the racial employment gap.

chanted several times a day, whenever anyone asked where we were going. But the marker itself was not nearly as interesting as other southern-most landmarks that attracted little attention. There were no crowds at the city's AIDS Memorial. Key West lost the most people per capita to that pandemic. No one was taking their photo next to the plaque celebrating locals who had liberated a nineteenth-century slave ship. We stood alone at the *Colored Beach* historical marker, where, during World War II, the US Navy seized the sand, leaving Black people without a place to swim until the 1960s.

We skipped the Ernest Hemingway Home and Museum. The novelist once lived and drank on Key West, but it seemed you didn't have to be famous to find your way here. We saw rich and poor, gay and straight, tourist and resident relishing the slow pace, often finding common ground over alcohol.

It took me until our last day on the Keys to figure out how one is *supposed* to enjoy this slice of Caribbean tropics: under a palm or tiki hut, sipping an icy drink, letting crosswinds blow your skirt. We walked slowly that morning, kicking coconuts. At midday sun we were sitting inside the Sugar Apple Market, drinking fresh carrot juice. Toward evening, we ambled toward the turtle museum at the ferry dock. The nearly extinct green turtle was an icon—the moniker of hotels, cafés, and bars, painted on walls and tees. Key green turtle soup was a global delicacy until 1970, when Key canneries closed due to overharvesting. The museum curator pointed to the kraal outside the building. "If you're lucky, ya might see our leatherback." We stood over the water cage waiting, until the turtle emerged.

The sea was rough on the night ferry from Key West to Fort Myers. People on the upper deck lost their liquor. We huddled on the lower level and watched the antics of eleven white-bearded, ruddy-faced, turtleneck-sweatered Ernest Hemingways returning from a look-alike contest. We disembarked, green as turtles, grateful to have new friends who met us at the boat and provided two days of comfort and manatee-watching in Fort Myers.

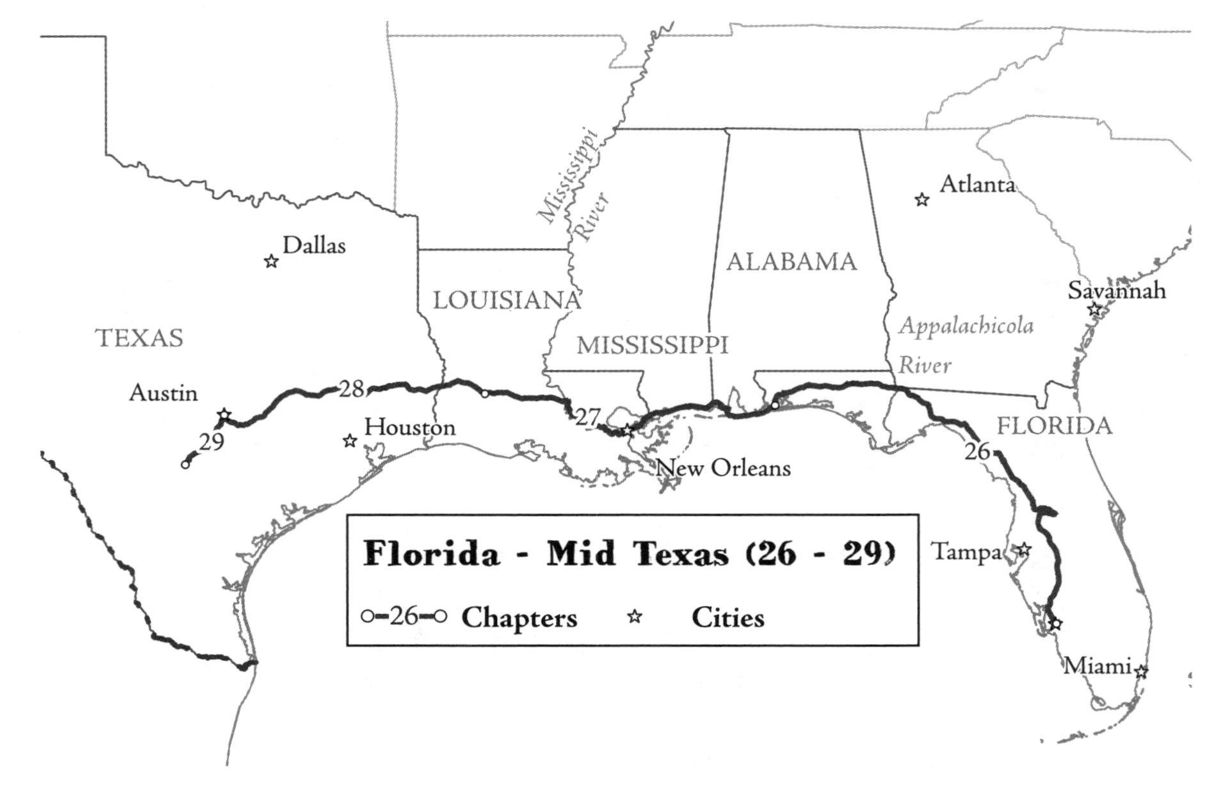
Florida - Mid Texas (26 - 29)
○–26–○ Chapters
☆ Cities
TEXAS
LOUISIANA
MISSISSIPPI
ALABAMA
FLORIDA
Mississippi River
Appalachicola River
Dallas
Austin
Houston
New Orleans
Atlanta
Savannah
Tampa
Miami
26
27
28
29

26

SEGREGATED SUNSHINE

Florida

Thou shalt not bear false witness.
—Ninth Commandment, Exodus 20:16

Biking inland from Fort Myers, we entered a region of Florida hidden from tourists and wealthy residents. The first stretch north on Highway 17 seemed unpeopled: just us, tropical swamp, and unforgiving sun. The landscape transformed abruptly. My Midwestern eye struggled to make sense of cattle ranches with Wyoming-style gates married to lush orange groves, and skinny, two-dimensional bovines that looked more like emaciated Central American cattle than hefty, corn-fed Minnesota cows.

After fifty-two miles, depleted and dehydrated, we sought shade on a bench, under the awning of a mini-mart outside Arcadia—the first establishment since we'd left Fort Myers. We dripped popsicles, munched on plantain chips, and watched as migrant farmworkers filed out of buses, vans, and cars and stood in line to buy provisions, filling the air with Spanish banter.

Next to us on the bench was a young man. David passed our plantain chips to him, introducing himself in Spanish. Alvaro had walked six hundred miles from South Carolina to find work in the Florida citrus groves. "I've never done farm work before," he said. "Been washing dishes for years, but work dried up this summer." He'd been sitting on this bench since 5:00 a.m. "A farmer found me eating his fruit yesterday," he explained. "Asked if I wanted a job picking. He told me to wait for him here."

THE PEACE RIVER CAMPGROUND in Arcadia had a dusty kiddie carnival and petting zoo. Children rode go-karts by our tent site, kicking a brown cloud into our lungs. Sitting at a picnic table, I wrote, *I don't want to be here.* I glanced up. A giant turtle was coming toward me, with a woman in a pink tee trailing behind. "This is Michelle," the woman said, introducing me to the turtle. "Get it? Miss Shell? She's an African tortoise. She likes to greet the new campers. I have to follow her and watch what she eats. Florida's not her native territory."

"Not mine either," I said.

WE BEGAN THE NEXT day reluctantly, letting a cooler hour slip away at a Mexican café. The previous day's toll of breakless sun and ten miles too many still weighed on us. It was thirty miles before first relief, at a tienda outside of Wauchula, where a folding chair in the cool darkness was my salvation. We sucked coconut popsicles and listened to a Spanish call-in radio show. Most of the calls went something like this: "My cousin left home a week ago to work in the citrus fields. We haven't heard from him since."

White people—a table of cops, a table of teachers—packed the Java Café on Wauchula's Main Street. A Latina cooked behind the kitchen door. Outside, five Black men put up a town Christmas display. The cashier pointed at them.

"I feel sorry for 'em. Been working in this heat forever."

I looked out the window again, this time noticing prison uniforms and a watchful foreman I had somehow not seen before.

"I don't," the cashier's boss replied. "They're criminals. Work's good for 'em."

THREE HOURS LATER, WE were still in Wauchula, fixing flat tires. While David bought tubes at Walmart, I sat on the sidewalk, working on my flat. An old white man—skinny, John Wayne-type, driving a 1950s Cadillac—pulled up in front of me, dangling a Snickers bar. He crooned, "I'm the Candy Man, come here and get a piece." He skidded away when David showed up.

By the time we fixed the tires, it was dark. I wasn't eager to spend the night in Wauchula, but the forty-five-dollar room at the Tropicana Motel had pretty marble floors. No stinky carpets. I needed something nice. Later, we ate tofu and peapods and watched a Chinese American boy show off his drawing of a manatee to an appreciative white trucker ordering sweet-and-sour chicken; a slice of beauty in a town showing us its ugly.

FROM WAUCHULA, WE FOLLOWED the Peace River up a series of diverting hills. We hadn't seen a hill since northern Virginia. We pieced together the puzzle of these gentle undulations in Fort Meade, an old town with stately churches and historical buildings. It looked like an economic neutron bomb had hit Fort Meade's commercial strip, removing people, leaving structures standing. The Boardwalk Café was the only business open. We doubled the customers. The waitress greeted us, saying, "We're closing in twenty minutes."

"Why?" I asked, pointing to the hours sign.

"Not enough customers."

"Looks like a lot of places closed for good in this town," I ventured.

"Environmentalists shut the phosphate mine," she said. "Some say Legoland will bring us back, but those jobs don't pay like mining."[51]

David nudged me as we left: "So miners made those mysterious hills."

"Yeah," I replied. "And made some corporation a killing. Now the community's paying for their environmental crimes."

On the bike path between Fort Meade and Lakeland were plaques celebrating the *Florida Cracker Heritage* of these miners and their forbearers.

OUR HOST IN LAKELAND had a *Rick Scott for Governor* bumper sticker. She turned the living space in her three-room house into our bedroom. The smell of cinnamon and the gentle licks of Dr. Seuss, her giant dog, woke us. We devoured the sweet rolls she had perfected as master volunteer, feeding Katrina cleanup crews in New Orleans.

She sent us off on Thanksgiving Day with a sack of lentils and pita bread. We ate her sandwiches on the Van Fleet State Trail, watching an alligator slither in the mud. Despite the perfect picnic lunch, we were hungry again by midafternoon. We joined customers at a gas station, purchasing candy, chips, pop, beer, and cigarettes, talking about not having a place to go for Thanksgiving. We too had no place to go on this gather-together day; and we too scraped a snack in this junk food emporium. Nothing new, but suddenly the lack of real food in this only-place-open enraged me. Forgetting the purpose of gasoline, I grumbled, "Why be open if you can't feed the people?"

On the outskirts of Groveland, Florida, cars clogged driveways. Kids played on lawns. Adults laughed and drank cold ones. A feeling of deprivation grew, though we both denied it. I had a headache and was going slower than

51 The mine had employed 200 people, and those workers supported this town of 5,000. In 2010, People for Protecting Peace River and the Sierra Club argued in court that the expansion of the phosphate mine would pollute the main fresh water source for West Florida. The lawsuit was settled three months after we passed through Fort Meade. The mining company donated land for a state park and the company was able to resume mining for another ten years—until 2022.

my usual glacial pace. We arrived in town just as a corner café closed its doors. It occurred to us we might not eat *anything* for Thanksgiving dinner.

We checked in at the Groveland Motel and checked out Rubio's Tienda across the street. It was open. They had a deli and a couple of tables. We ate tamales, pollo, frijoles, and ensalada washed down with cans of unsweetened tea. For dessert, we bought tomatoes and lemon. Later, we took the avocado from Aunt Maja's tree, ripening in my bike bag since Miami, and made guacamole.

Back at the motel parking lot, a middle-aged Black man with a high school–age son in the passenger seat pulled up beside us. He was a minister from eastern Florida, beginning to bike distances, seeking advice. He gave us his card. "Too bad you're going *west*," he said. "I would love to have you stay with me and meet my congregation."

"Now we can't say we didn't get an invitation on Thanksgiving," David said when he drove away.

MOST OF THE GROVELAND guests were farmworkers, paying $200 a week for one room with a kitchenette. We did our laundry with Miguel, a thin man—shorter than my five feet, two inches—who answered our intrusive questions in Spanish. "The citrus factories pay nine dollars an hour," he said. "Fieldwork pays by the bushel. If you are fast, you can make ten dollars."

Before dawn, we heard vehicle motors. Watching from our window, we saw Miguel climb into a van. We climbed back into bed.

BLACK FRIDAY BEGAN BLISSFULLY. We rode the paved Withlacoochee State Trail, serviced with bathrooms and shaded benches. Two whooping cranes—five feet tall, silvery white—showed off their seven-foot wingspans. We found comfort and sustenance at the Odd Cuples Café in Bushnell, where a delightful collection of coffee mugs was displayed on a high shelf. The waitress was tired but triumphant. "I was up all night, in line at Walmart. But it was worth it. I got Let's Rock! Elmo and *Angry Birds* for my four children."

In the afternoon we stopped in Floral City, an oasis on the Withlacoochee Trail filled with cycle shops and cafés. At the town museum we learned that in the 1890s, ten thousand Black miners had dug phosphate rock there. Soon after, prison labor replaced wage work at the mine, but it was unclear from the museum display who the prisoners were or where the Black people of the town went.

About forty miles from Floral City is the former town of Rosewood. It had been a thriving Black timber town with an independent Black business district until a white mob burned the town to the ground on New Year's Day, 1923. Estimates of the number of people massacred range from eight to 150. Today Rosewood is a sign and a plaque. In the 1980s, a reporter uncovered the story. In the 1990s, in response to public pressure, survivors and their kin began receiving small reparations from the state of Florida.[52]

Today, Floral City is 96 percent white, half the size it was in 1890, mine long gone. Squinting at 1920s school photos, I asked the docent, "Where are the Black children?" He seemed to change the subject, but maybe his response was a segue: "I'm *Old* Florida. I used to live in Fort Lauderdale, but then the Northerners came and turned it into New York. I came to Floral City to find old Florida again."

The bike path ended. Trucks hauling logs from the Goethe State Forest rode our shoulder, dropping debris for us to dodge. We sought relief at a general store near Otter Creek, where a bumper sticker over the cash register read, *I'm a Florida Cracker: an Endangered Species.*

---

52 See Michael D'Orso, *Like Judgment Day: The Ruin and Redemption of a Town Called Rosewood* (Putnam, 1996). Not far from Floral City is Ocoee, where whites carried out a similar massacre in 1920.

"What's this?" I asked, pointing at white mush in Styrofoam containers in a cooler on the cashier's counter.

"Mullet dip," the woman said. "It's homemade."

I sampled the smoky fish paste, David changed a tire, and my new friend talked. "This was once a teaming timber town. The lumber mill closed fifty-one years ago, the year before I was born."

As we left, she shot me a wistful look. "Don't forget about this chapter of your book."

Riding out of Otter Creek, I took my mind off timber trucks, thinking about her admonition, struggling to understand the rise of "Old Florida" and "Cracker" nostalgia. In this region, timber, phosphate, orange, and tomato bosses viewed labor as expendable cogs. Western Florida segregated workers racially, and animosities appeared intense. Histories of white violence against Black and Indigenous people haunted all corners. Embracing the term "Cracker"—considered a slur up north—might elevate some bygone European ethnic identity and reclaim working-class pride. It also might be a clever divide-and-conquer ruse, keeping forgotten white workers from uniting with Black and Latinx neighbors who shared their economic interests. People seemed to be yearning for a self-sufficient white homeland of yore that never existed in this region of stolen Indigenous land, destroyed Black towns, and dying mines and mills.

TWELVE MILES UP THE road in Chiefland, we talked with a frail, joyful couple at the Yum Yum Shoppe. They looked too small to eat the creamy mounds in front of them—the whole whipped-cream-cherry deal. "We've been together since we were teenagers," the man explained, handing me photos he kept in his wallet: he and his wife as young lovers; his wife in a bikini, holding a fish as big as she was. "We grew up outside of Harrisburg, Pennsylvania. Moved here in 1958. We are *not* Old Florida."

There it was again, a reference to a Florida exclusive, revered, and past.

White Minnesotans didn't use that term, but there was an Old Minnesota myth too, in which Indigenous land was virgin territory, the 1862 US/Dakota war a tale of Dakota savagery, the hanging of thirty-nine Dakota men justified, and the forced removal of Dakota people from Mni Sota Makoce erased.

When I moved to Minneapolis, the Scandinavians and Christian Germans who established Old Minnesota culture ways made it clear to me I was a foreigner in my adopted home. People let me know I stood too close for their comfort. The way I touched people was not acceptable. Folks had stopped telling me to keep my distance, so I must have learned to do so. Or maybe those who had moved to the state since 1976 had warmed the place up. Still, at home, I rarely felt local. On the road, however, I was Minnesotan. Here in Florida, we met snowbirds from Michigan's Upper Peninsula and greeted them like long-lost cousins. From this southern distance my homeland had expanded to include the entire upper Midwest.

Our host in Fanning Springs wasn't Old Florida, but close. He grew up during the '60s in Atlanta, a native of the white working-class South. He had recently attended an all-school reunion at his alma mater. "Well, half-school," he clarified. "With integration, the high school went from white to Black. The alumni don't mix. Our reunion organizers keep us separate."

His home in the woods was an easy ride to Cross City. We arrived during church hour on Sunday morning. Sitting in the outdoor lunchroom of a Cross City elementary school, David did bike maintenance while I read the *Dixie County Times*. The paper's masthead was arresting: *Join the Historical Fight for Our Community's Voice. Stand for America. Attend the Ten Commandments Rally at the Courthouse, 4p.m. Today.*

A businessman had placed a six-ton Ten Commandments tablet on Cross City's courthouse grounds. The national Liberty Counsel and the American

Civil Liberties Union were descending on the tiny town to support and protest. I knew we should stick around to see what happened, but I needed a break.

So instead, we detoured east, to the fishing village of Steinhatchee, and rented a trailer outfitted for fishers. I sat on the water's edge and watched giant pelicans soar, skitter, and dive. As the sun set, they became prehistoric shadows. Rain came in, tide went out. Droplets slid to the end of a palm frond and fell.

The next morning, our break from Old Florida was elongated by bike repairs. David worked on a tire determined not to inflate, while I eavesdropped on three Northern fishermen avoiding the rain, comparing Vietnam draft evasion stories.

"I listened to the draft counselor," one of them said. "Carried a purse, swallowed tin foil, and still passed. They asked about my dad, who died in World War II. I was his only survivor. They deferred me. Funny, the draft counselors never asked me that question."

"I leaned forward six inches and said, 'Far as I can bend,'" the second one said. "Sergeant followed me into a liquor store, accused me of faking it, but it was too late. I had my deferment papers."

Not to be outdone, the third one took his turn. "Three of my buddies decided to get an arrest record. They gave me the bail money. Their heist was uncovered, and they all shipped out, but I was convicted of conspiracy and prohibited from service."

The rest of the day was miserable: late start, intermittent rain, cold headwind, and a defective tire. Timber trucks dropped whole branches on the road in front of us. David rode a flat for eight miles. We'd rest every four miles, then will ourselves to do another four.

One mile from Perry, we made a U-turn, following an intriguing sign: *Cracker Farmstead and Museum*. The docent was happy to have visitors. She pointed at an exhibit on timber. "Builders prefer Florida pine trees," she asserted. "It's the unique fibers. Florida Crackers have worked lumber and hunted game here for over a century." *Still partly true*, I thought. For the last 150 miles, nearly everyone we'd met was dressed and armed for the hunt.

"Where are the timber mills today?" I asked. "We saw two in Cross City, but they were empty. All the timber traffic seemed to follow us to Perry."

She shook her head. "They just closed those mills in Cross City."

IN ONE DAY, WE moved from summer to winter. We escaped the twenty-degree freeze on a desolate stretch of pine forest at a gas station with seven different trade union decals on the window. Inside, we rubbed frozen fingers at a table next to a display of bumper stickers: *NOBAMA*; *You Are in America, Be American*; and *NRA—God and Country*.

WE SPENT TWO DAYS with a Tallahassee couple we did not know, yet so much about them felt familiar: the books, the political art, the jigsaw puzzle finished over Thanksgiving with their grown daughter, still on the table. Even their Christmas cactus bloomed in November like ours. Katya began her career as a radical journalist in the 1960s, working for Liberation News Service. "Now, I lead writing workshops in a women's prison and a nursing home," she said. "Places where people might not communicate if not forced together." She and I agreed: sharing stories breaks barriers. "That's what our bicycles do," I said, but I wondered. The easy intimacy with Katya illuminated the distance between us and the rest of western Florida. Were we connecting, or just voyeurs?

ON DECEMBER 1, WE turned west onto the Florida Panhandle. Incarcerated men laid tar on the side of the road as we entered Chattahoochee. We stopped to admire church spires, the Apalachicola River dam, and fall colors cascading into the valley. It reminded me of Northfield, Minnesota, in late September. Northfield has two colleges nestled in its hills. Chattahoochee also had two campuses: a mental hospital, and a prison workhouse.

We parked the bikes in front of Whitney's Seafood Restaurant. I ordered catfish with okra, collards, and cornbread. We were far enough north to be south again. The place was half-full, customers Black, owner white. Everyone knew each other. An elderly woman sitting near me counted her dimes. She ordered the soup and asked where I hailed from. I asked if Chattahoochee was her home.

"Been here most of my life," she said. "Worked at the state hospital for thirty-two years. I retired last year to take care of my mother. She passed two months later."

"Did the hospital give you a good retirement package?" I asked.

Her face hardened. "*No*," then swiftly, softly, "but I'm grateful for what I get." She changed the subject. "How old are you?"

"Fifty-three."

"My daughter's age. She lives in the next town. My son . . ." She frowned. "He's dead."

As we got up to leave, the woman squeezed my hand. "Have yourself a sweet journey."

AT THE HOLIDAY RESTAURANT in Bonifay, the conversation went from comments like "I'd shoot anybody who crossed my property" to jokes about a bus that burned, carrying the rival football team. The kids had gotten out without physical harm, but listening to people laugh about children in danger was bad for digestion. We left our plates half eaten. David, who feels with his gut, was nauseous the rest of the evening.

The next morning, after twelve cold miles, we were famished when we glimpsed the Whistle Stop Café, hidden a block from Westville's main road. We wolfed down omelets, surprised at how delicious they were. The cook came out to accept our compliment, and we ordered pancakes.

Lacey, the young waitress, had an open face and an easy smile—a teenager without apparent angst. Her cousin, Sam, a seventh grader and the cook's son, peppered David with questions about strange places and funny people. David told him about raccoons opening vitamin bottles, seven-mile bridges, riding across New York City. Sam drank it all in. Finally, David said, "All right, now tell us about you."

"I have two jobs," Sam said proudly. "I give kiddie train rides. Plus, my neighbor pays me to clean up from the fire that burned his house."

"Tell us about this town," I prodded when he petered out.

A man and woman in their fifties with matching chunky good looks stopped eating. A woman sitting alone, stressing over her laptop, looked up. Sam's mom and another woman emerged from the kitchen.

The man took a breath. "We have a story to tell, but you don't want to hear it."

Before we could assure him that we did, the woman with the computer shook her fist at the laptop. "Damn! Can't figure out how this reservation system works. I had a ticket to Manhattan, and now it's gone."

"Maybe I can help," I offered. "My kid lives in New York City. I've flown there many times."

"Manhattan, Kansas. My son's stationed there."

"Oh, sure."

I felt a desire to belong—to make a connection, to not be the clueless Yankee cyclist. I returned to my table as Lacey brought out pancakes. They were as good as the omelets. Everyone else turned their attention to assisting with the flight. The woman had never booked online before. Neither she nor anyone else in the room had ever been on a commercial airplane. I tried to imagine her son returning after a tour in Afghanistan. He'd have some stories to tell.

"What about that story?"

The chunky man surveyed the room for affirmation. He pointed out the window at the bare field and mass of trees beyond. "Used to be a lot of giant oak trees here."

He paused. We nodded for him to continue.

"Not too many of them left." He paused again.

"Used to hang people from those trees. Through the 1960s. From the oak in front of the post office—for coming into town. The older generation of Blacks still don't come here."

I stopped eating. The pancake flipped in my gut. I tried to telepath David to keep quiet. My mind raced. From Chattahoochee to Crestview, the area was full of prisons. I wanted to ask: Did the lynchers get the electric chair? Were they doing life? Is this the Old Florida everyone is nostalgic for? Were they proud of this story? Ashamed? Not either, it seemed. Just the cross they had to bear; an unalterable part of their identity. I wanted to suggest a reconciliation conference, reparations, a way to move on, to make room for positive stories for kids like Sam and Lacey to build on. But I didn't. Instead, I mumbled something about how these were hard times and people were hurting.

The man took the bait. "Everybody here is poor," he said. "They farm, sell firewood and scrap metal to get by. Timber's our industry, but illegal trade provides the main income. Used to be moonshine, then marijuana. Now it's meth."

WE RODE SIXTY MILES of Florida Panhandle that day, entering Crestview just as excited families were dragging lawn chairs to watch the Christmas parade. Joining them, we watched the exhilarating intensity of young musicians marching with their bands. Fire and police brigades blew their sirens. Ron Paul was the only presidential candidate represented, but every Republican in the county was propped on a convertible, tossing candy. The idea of a city-sponsored Christmas celebration affronted my northern Jewish agnostic sensibility. Still, I was enjoying the parade, until Junior ROTC Marines marched by in fatigues, adults barking orders. I asked David, my expert on all things Christian: "Wasn't Jesus the Prince of Peace?"

THE NEXT DAY, WE skimmed and soared like pelicans along Bob Pitts Road and Blackwater Heritage State Trail, through primordial swamps and tropical farms. David was ecstatic. "Roads like this skew your perspective," he said. "Makes you think biking is fun."

On this day we also enjoyed meeting a man at a Chinese buffet in Milton who traded in horses. "We're the only nation in the world that doesn't eat horse," he said. "It's good meat—tasty, red, and full of protein." He paused. "I had a dream like yours: to ride a horse across the Rockies. But we had that problem with the Russians, so I joined the Navy. That took twenty years." He rubbed his giant stomach. "Now I have this."

But the magic wore off by evening—another sixty-mile day, ten miles too many. Entering Pensacola frantic to be done, I led us on a shortcut through backyards, turning back only when confronted with barbed wire. When we arrived at our hosts' home, I sent David to wine and opine with our new friends, begging for rest.

In a dark room, under a woven rendition of Buddha, I closed my eyes. My body became one with the couch. I tried to empty my mind, but Old Florida crowded in, imploring me to understand. I thought of Lacey at the Whistle Stop, inheriting an atrocity; of the woman who worked a lifetime at Florida State Hospital, scraping for a bowl of soup; of Alvaro, walking two states to pick oranges; of the men in the chain gang; of the gas station owner displaying pro-union and socially reactionary politics; of the wealthy businessman erecting a Ten Commandments monument; of the Liberty Counsel and the ACLU, who stole a foreclosed town's economic outrage when their timber mill closed; of the cashier in Otter Creek with her Cracker Pride bumper sticker who made me promise not to forget; of the thousands who filled prisons and mental institutions, ran stills and meth labs when the timber, phosphate, citrus, and tomato enterprises took the money and ran.

Florida's western geography was fantastically diverse. Its timber had unusual qualities. But the financial devastation in Old Florida wasn't unique—US poverty during this Great Recession was as ubiquitous as pine trees, growing in all corners. Nor were the racism and historical amnesia that stunted the collective power of this region's working class.

I peeled my recovered body and restless mind from the couch and joined the party. Our Pensacola hosts, Bob and Gerry Eddy, were scraping eighty years. They had been cycle-touring for half a century. Bob, a Unitarian minister, admired the philosopher Epicurus. "From him, we get the idea about pursuing happiness," he mused. "Epicurus said hunger is the best spice. He was about enjoying, not hoarding."

"Hunger, yes," I agreed. "And exhaustion, weather, mental dislocation, and the itch of unresolved questions. Relief from these are delights we pursue daily."

27

CATEGORY 5 DENIAL

Alabama, Mississippi, and Louisiana

Down in Louisiana, we are suffering from category 5 storms . . . and the folks on Pennsylvania Avenue . . . from category 5 denial.
—Jerome Ringo[53]

Ignorance on fire is no worse than knowledge on ice.
—My cookie fortune, Hello Tokyo, Gonzales, Louisiana

Lead Belly's song had been in my head for days. *And if this train don't turn around/I'm Alabama bound.* Now, crossing the bridge into Orange Beach, Alabama, during a storm, we nearly did turn around. Rain fell in stinging pellets. A gust of wind jerked us backward. Across the bridge, visibility dropped to zero. We stopped. When the fog lifted, we saw the sign ringed with high rises: *Welcome to Alabama the Beautiful.*

The RV Park manager in Alabama Port did not want to let us camp. But it was cold and dark, and she knew we weren't going anywhere. She wasn't unfriendly, just tired. "Me and the husband retired, sold the house, bought an RV, came to the Gulf to fish," she told me as she walked me to the shower building. "Then the husband got terminal cancer. After he died, I was stuck here, working to pay the doctors."

53 Kevin Danaher and Alisa Gravitz, eds., *The Green Festival Reader: Fresh Ideas from Agents of Change* (Boulder, Colorado: Paradigm Publishers, 2008), 88.

"We'll leave early," I promised, as if our quick exit might bring back her husband or pay her medical bills.

She smiled weakly. "I shouldn't complain. Having a job makes me lucky in these parts. The oil spill destroyed the Alabama coast." She pointed at a nearby RV. "Woman who lives there was working temp, cleaning up BP's mess. Now she's sick. BP temps don't get no health care."

A GANG OF FERAL cats at the RV park invited themselves to share our can of tuna. Predawn, it was our turn to stalk the Alabama Port gas station, scavenging a convenience store meal. While we waited in line, a bony young woman wearing a dirty white hoodie that hid her face tacked a notecard to the bulletin board:

"I need work. Land or sea. Good at many things."

Under her notice was a leaflet put out by Project Rebound: *Experiencing mental difficulties related to the oil spill? Stress, financial crises, depression? We can help.*

Riding Route 188 out of Alabama Port and into an icy headwind, we passed Hurricane Boulevard, the abandoned offices of Oil Spill Law Group, the ruins of Rebel Motel, and the First Baptist Church of Bayou La Batre, whose marquee advertised Servicios en Español. The wind slowed our speed to seven miles an hour, prolonging our frigid agony.

At the Blue Heron Café in Bayou La Batre, a blast of warm air, a chair, and a lukewarm mug of Lipton tea were epicurean delights. The December 4 edition of *USA Today* was lying on our café table. Mike Hubbard, Alabama's Speaker of the House, had an editorial lauding the state's new immigration law requiring employers, landlords, and teachers to report on undocumented workers, tenants, and students. Alabama tomatoes were rotting on the vine as immigrant farmworkers fled the state. Hubbard argued the entire country should follow Alabama's lead.

WIND CHILLS IN THE twenties—a good day to sleep inside, we thought. In retrospect, a tent would have been a better choice. I had a bad feeling about the Imperial Motel in Ocean Springs, Mississippi, as we rode into the parking lot, but forty dollars—"cash only"—seemed like a good deal. It was exorbitant for what we got. The walls of our room were oily, the floor slanted. The stink of mold, dust, stale sweat, and smoke did not offend less with time. There was no heat. I shivered under dank covers while the owner, who wore the same perfume as the room, stood above me, uselessly thrusting a screwdriver into the thermostat.

The bathroom floor had the topography of a pit mine. Climbing into the slippery tub, David fell and slashed his hand along the splintery wall. A hospital was a mile away. We walked our bikes, David elevating his hand. A doctor from St. Paul gave him ten stitches and a story.

"When I was a kid, we'd cross the river chanting *M-I-S-S-I-S-S-I-P-P-I* as fast as we could. I never thought I'd live in the state! I got a job in Chalmette, Louisiana. When Katrina destroyed the hospital, I transferred here."

At a Vietnamese café, blocks from the hospital, the TV replayed a slick anti-immigrant ad between updates on a "second Virginia Tech shooting." Halfway through my rant about borders, guns, health care, and how the Imperial Motels treated the homeless people who lived there like fleas, I looked up. Left hand limp, David picked at food with his right, eyes glazed, in a pain-medicated twilight zone.

Demonstrating he could steer with his bandaged hand, David insisted on a fifteen-mile ride. We found a thirty-five-dollar room in a new hotel between Biloxi and Gulfport, checked in at 2:00 p.m., and spent the afternoon eating whole-grain IHOP pancakes, but stress about getting behind made it difficult to relax. Since Fort Myers, Florida, we'd been riding hard to meet Emily in

Austin, Texas, for Christmas. I dreaded calling our hosts, Esther and Harley, in New Orleans, to say we'd be a day late. Esther focused the conversation on our needs, offering to pick us up twenty miles out of town. Her gift kept us on schedule and lifted our spirits immensely.

At a wayside fruit stand in Waveland, a predominately white town on Mississippi's Gulf Coast, a woman with shaky hands took our coins. All the folks staffing the stand looked sickly except a man who introduced himself as Pastor Ben. He told us of his effort to beat the town's drug and alcohol Goliath.

"Katrina, recession, and the oil spill demolished our fish and tourism industries," he explained. "The city laid off all its workers—police, fire—a few months ago. Without jobs, addiction is rampant. Fast food companies stopped giving drug tests—not enough sober workers to fill positions." He handed us a bag of satsumas. "Lord willing, the jobs will come, but addicts won't hold 'em when they do."

IN PEARLINGTON, MISSISSIPPI, ON the Louisiana border, we stopped at a gas station to use the bathroom. A spare, toothless Black man selling collard greens and garage sale items offered us chocolates and peppermints. We'd learned to take offerings from strangers graciously. In Lakeland, Florida, at a gas station adjacent to a homeless encampment, a skinny man with stringy blond hair, clutching a twenty-ounce can of beer, gave David two dollars and got angry when he tried to refuse the gift. The collard vendor guessed our thoughts: "You can't always be asking. Sometimes you gotta give."

At the *Welcome to Louisiana/Bienvenue en Louisiane* sign, we ate chocolates and peppermints. Across the state border, wetland foliage crept onto the shoulderless road. No cars or people, just a small billboard advertising *Cajun Swamp Tours*.

THE GULF COAST MEASURED time as BK or PK—before or post-Katrina. From Biloxi, Mississippi, to Fort Pike, Louisiana, we enjoyed PK bridges, one with a separate bike/pedestrian path and iron distance markers embossed with local animals and birds. The one into Fort Pike was tall and grand, with a long, gradual ascent. From the highest point, New Orleans looked like a submerged alligator in a giant lake.

IN A FEW SHORT hours, with New Orleans hosts Esther and Harley, we covered all the forbidden topics: politics, religion, money, how to support our LGBTQ children. They prepared a delicate fish—the most delicious I had ever tasted. When Harley filled the hot tub, I made the social mistake of refusing. Instead, I sat in our guest room, reading.

"You're freaking out. What's going on?" David asked me when he returned from the steam bath.

"I want to do the impossible," I replied. "I have twenty-four hours to understand what lies beneath this ocean-level city."

I did not succeed, of course. We had just enough time to see that New Orleans had an exquisite and unique culture and geography. But we'd learned to find singular beauty in less iconic places. It was the typical that struck me:

parts of town had it all; others denied housing, grocery stores, trees, buses, streetcars.

Esther dropped us off on the banks of the Mississippi. I waited until she left before dissolving. Sobs rose from some home-longing place. We watched barges that could have passed through the Twin Cities. The winding river looked familiar, but its embankments were foreign. In Minneapolis, it sits in a deep ravine. In New Orleans, a levee separates water from land. At the top of the levee was our bike path, going north.

A Christmas parade progressed down a road abutting the river. The children tossed plastic beads instead of candy, as they had in Crestview, Florida. Republicans and junior Marines were also absent. So was the live music. Dance teams did basic moves, disco trucks providing rhythm. A child handed me a white plastic flower. I wound its wire stem around my handlebar, next to the smiley-face horn from the woman in Cleveland.

BATON ROUGE WASN'T BICYCLE-FRIENDLY. That didn't stop our host, Nicko, a thirty-four-year-old cyclist who lived car free. He had turned his garage into a studio where he twisted glass into multicolored, uniquely shaped miniature bongs to sell in New Orleans head shops.

Nicko grew up in New Orleans. After Katrina, he left his demolished house and hit the road with a brigade of hurricane-homeless youth armed with Red Cross lodging tokens. "Only expensive hotels took the vouchers," he explained. "We stayed in some fancy places." The young itinerants passed rescued pets back and forth. Nicko had two cats traveling with him. "I made a splash walking down Castro Street in San Francisco with two felines on leashes. I've never gotten that much attention from *girls*."

From Nicko's perspective, Katrina had some positive effects on New

Orleans. "Now, people are living in better places. A new neighborhood in midtown is mixed: young people, Mexican immigrants. That's a good thing." I told him about the Christmas parade without school bands, an anathema in a region famous for its live music. Did post-Katrina charter schools cut music programs out of the curriculum? He didn't know, but he argued, "Before Katrina, there was more live music where my mother lives in Jackson, Mississippi, than in New Orleans. Now, creative young people have come to be part of the post-hurricane recovery, and they are changing it for the good."

We drank Nicko's hot tea and white wine and went back for heaping seconds of his homemade turkey gumbo, consuming a pot he had planned to eat all week. Nicko gave us his bed and mapped us a route out of town, sending us across the Huey Long Bridge.

"It used to be a railroad bridge. The ascent was so steep, they had to add extra engines to pull the trains. Huey Long named it after himself when he was governor," Nicko explained.

He grinned, adding, "I've sent many cyclists over it. None of them have ever come back."

We took Nicko's route through the Louisiana State University campus, past the Honeywell chemical plant, down Scenic Highway where the ExxonMobil refinery stood, to the Huey Long Bridge. At its base was Mr. Lucky's Truck Stop, where guys with pickups filled with scrap metal stopped to buy lottery tickets and fortify themselves with quarts of Bud before crossing.

The Bridge had no shoulder. It rose sharply, followed by a long gradual decline—a bicycle kill zone. Trucks going full speed had no way to see us in time to slow down. Seeing the terror on David's face as he looked up at the vertical span had a strangely calming effect on me. Let him carry the fear for once.

It was worse than it looked. The pavement on the edge was oily and strewn with industrial waste, giving us no choice but to take the lane.

Back on land, standing in the ditch, watching trucks fly down the bridge, we wondered why we were alive. David—who thinks he can change reality with positive thinking—proclaimed, "Should be the last bridge until we get to California. We are west of the Mississippi, leaving the coast, about to enter the desert." I, who believe him when it suits me, breathed relief.

If you look on a map, you can see that the Mississippi River in Louisiana does not move quickly to the sea. It twists and turns like a giant boa constrictor, flowing as much east and west as south. Human beings have added to the twists, constructing waterways to push stormwater away from towns toward the ocean.

A man in a pickup in Livonia stopped us. "Morganza Spillway ahead," he said. "Three miles, no shoulder. Would you like me to drive you across?"

We had already gotten a room for the night, so we refused the kind offer, giving us a whole evening to anticipate the mysterious Morganza Spillway.

THE SIDE RAILS OF the spillway were low, the land below dry. David used his mirror to keep an eye on vehicles not moving to the other lane on the shoulderless span. I failed to understand what we would do if they refused. Go over the side?

Over shrimp po'boys and catfish burgers, the whole room at Billy's Café in Morganza, Louisiana, discussed what the foolhardy bicyclists had done. A small man with a red bandana covering his bald head, wearing a motorcycle jacket with Confederate flags on each shoulder and Rebel Rider stitched on the back, took command of the conversation.

"You're not allowed to bike the spillway without a police escort," he said. "It's too dangerous. I know. I'm a police officer."

If he saw me gasp, he didn't let on. A Confederate cop was scarier to me than a spillway. He continued, providing an engineering lesson: "The Morganza is a ravine, built to take the Mississippi River overflow during a flood. We opened it for the second time in sixty years in May. Some wildlife swam to safety. Lots died." Then, without pause, he asked, "What do you carry for protection?"

I deferred to David, who offered, "A dog whistle."

The Confederate cop looked disgusted.

David added, "We've traveled six thousand miles without incident."

The Confederate cop teared up! He recovered quickly, seemed to change the subject, telling us about a trip he took after returning from Vietnam. "I saw a deer in Wyoming, nibbling in someone's front yard," he said. "Wouldn't happen here. We'd shoot it. The deer'd know and stay away."

It sounded like a non sequitur, but I knew it wasn't. He was acknowledging that we came from a place with different customs. In Michigan we snuck into a schoolyard to sleep, and in Massachusetts we tented in a parking lot, but since we'd crossed into Virginia, we'd become cautious about bending the law. The South had rules we didn't know.

I didn't eat at Billy's. The Japanese restaurant in Gonzales, Louisiana, was a welcome surprise, and the waitress Shirley Huang as warm as the Confederate cop had been disconcerting. Shirley pointed out the tall, handsome hibachi chef wowing teenagers at another table.

"My husband works here too."

"Who cooks at home?" I asked.

She smiled. "I cooked in China, but now, when we aren't eating at the restaurant, he cooks."

The couple had left China in 2004, for Chinatown in Brooklyn, New York. "How did you end up at a Japanese restaurant in Louisiana?" I asked.

"In August 2011, Hello Tokyo came to New York and recruited us. It's been hard to get used to the heat."

TANTE SUE LOOKED LIKE a socialite, a Southern dame, lunching on the other side of the café. Her unladylike voice boomed at us from across the room. "People will think you're crazy if you come to Mamou, Louisiana, and don't see Fred's. We are what makes Mamou the world capital of Cajun music."

David and I dutifully followed the eighty-year-old proprietor across the street to an unassuming windowless building. "In 1985, *National Geographic* did a spread on us. Since then, we get visitors from all over the world," she explained. "We're only open Saturday mornings. We begin at 8:00 a.m. with Cajun music, drinking, dancing, and eating. The bar closes at 2:00 p.m."

Inside the dim room, Huey Long photographs created a shrine in one corner. "My hero!" Tanta Sue enthused. "They don't make them like that anymore."

I WISHED I HAD asked Tante Sue to elaborate. In the 1930s, Senator Huey Long peddled a "Share Our Wealth" and "Every Man a King" platform. From what I could see, the current Louisiana motto was *Let the 99 Percent be Paupers*. After riding through impoverished communities suffering the demise of one-product economies, it was strange to see poverty and economic vitality go together. Louisiana statistics corroborated what I saw. The state was a robust producer of sugarcane, sweet potatoes, rice, cotton, pecans, grain, seafood, and timber. It had the most oil refineries, natural gas processing plants, and petrochemical facilities in the Western Hemisphere—and the South's highest poverty rate. In Louisiana, industry did not mean employment, and having a job did not mean making a living.

"THE BEST PLACE TO get food in Oberlin is the casino," said the motel owner, so we took the free shuttle. We were twenty-eight miles from Mamou. We thought we'd hear some Cajun music, but the only tune playing was the hum and ring of a thousand slot machines. Bleary-eyed gamblers of all ages and races chain-smoked, eyes glued to screens, spending what they owed.

FOR BREAKFAST, I ORDERED gumbo at Oberlin's Keith's Place Café and Grocery. The woman who set a bowl of broth before me was angry.

"I'm tired of school secretaries saying Happy Holidays to me. My son fought and died in Iraq for my right to say Merry Christmas."

She looked at me, waiting for a response. My mind raced, social science brain making deadly connections—the Exxon Mobil refinery in Baton Rouge and Exxon's massive oil fields in Iraq. My activist soul held a *No Blood for Oil* picket sign. My mother's heart thought about Emily. I stirred my bowl, struggling to offer something that would comfort. I looked into her hard-pain eyes.

"Merry Christmas," I said.

LOUISIANA WAS HARD ON my psyche, but Cajun country crept under my skin. At the crack of the early winter dawn, we passed fields of purple-gray soil, spring-green shoots, yellow blossoms, flooded rice paddies, majestic horses. A funny group of cows ran alongside us. On the sharp corner of a windy road littered with sugar cane stalks, we found a perfect spot to watch hundreds of tiny sparrows swarm, drawing shapes across the skyline. On Highway 61, along the Maurepas Swamp, a blue heron and a snowy egret followed us for miles—or did we follow them?

28

HOGS AND ANGELS

Texas

Never go into the Big Thicket without a compass.
—Rick, in Coldspring, Texas

East Texas was a surprise: the place to be in December for fall colors. The tangled Big Thicket was good for hiding cyclists in neon, relieving themselves. Inspired by the loveliness, I found myself singing. "Oh, What a Beautiful Mornin' . . ."

David sang too. "All My Exes Live in Texas . . ."

KEN IN KIRBYVILLE, TEXAS, knew Minneapolis. Nine months of the year, he trucked goods up Highway 35 to Minnesota. In his kitchen, he displayed a photo of his grandfather with a prize-winning bull and a framed Farmers Union membership, circa 1920.[54]

Ken had five daughters. We met one: a bright-eyed young woman, training

54 The National Farmers Union originated in Point, Texas in 1902. In 2011, Point was building a monument to commemorate the group and attract tourists. Ken's grandfather was a member of a Mississippi chapter of dairy farmers and farm workers that advocated for cooperative economics and votes for women. It began as a biracial organization but did not stay that way.

to meet the weight requirements for Basic Training. Ken showed off two bobcats mounted in the living room, shot by another daughter. "I told her when she shot the first, it would be a once-in-a-lifetime experience," her father said, beaming. "Then she went and bagged a second one!"

Ken hunted for food. "Venison is central to our diet," he said. For two thousand miles, we had been riding through communities of food deserts and hard times, where hunting was central to survival. When David told someone selling satsumas on the side of the road about raccoons opening our vitamin bottles, the fruit seller smacked his lips. "Cook 'em with sweet potatoes. They're delicious."

Hunting was also cultural and a source of local lore.

At Bubba's Restaurant in Coldspring, Texas, three men situated themselves close to us. They reminded David of his dad and uncles in rural Wisconsin, regaling the same stories each time they gathered. They lured him to their table with a hunter's tale filled with elongated flourishes. As it progressed, one hunter found himself alone with a four-hundred-pound feral hog.

"My first shot hit behind the ear. The hog winked and walked off."

The hunter kept shooting; each shot a pregnant story. The hog remained impervious until . . . "He charged! I faced a wounded wild animal with twelve-inch tusks, sharp as steel."

"Luckily," the second man interrupted, "I keep a loaded 300 Mag elephant gun in the back of my pickup, just in case. I put a bullet behind his ear at point-blank range. This time, Hogzilla did not blink."

The third man, who introduced himself as Rick, brought the story to an end. "When we removed the head, it weighed one hundred and five pounds. The rest of the body we soaked in salt-and-sugar brine for days."

These men owned vast tracts in East Texas—Spanish land grants that Anglo ancestors obtained in manner fair or foul, after the Mexican-American War. "Most of the acreage is only good for hunting," Rick told us. Rick knew Governor Rick Perry personally. Sensing that we weren't fans, he teased, "How do you like the roads Perry fixed for you?"

"Some surfaces are coarse," David countered. "Cuts our speed."

Rick gave David his card. "Tell me which ones, and I'll let him know. While you're in Texas, call me if you need anything. I've got friends everywhere."[55]

LUNCH WITH THE HUNTERS had me pining for a feminine oasis in this cowboy world. The sign as we entered tiny Shiro, Texas—*All Citizens Are Armed*—did not make me feel more at home. The ruffles on the windows of Let's Break Bread looked hopeful, but the inside decor sent mixed messages: crosses, scripture quotes, and portraits of John Wayne. The other customers—all men—were trading tales of woe.

"I planted a garden and bought chickens, getting ready for hard times," one man said. "But I don't like vegetables, and I'm not crazy about eggs, either."

"I was putting in fence posts in Oregon when a tree fell on me," another said. "Broke my back. Came here to see if there's any work I could still do."

The café owner saw me eyeing the message card on the table: "Jesus is my savior." Perhaps my discomfort showed. "I was an unbeliever once," she said, pulling up a chair to tell me a story of faith-based recovery from ovarian cancer, complete with angels, and chemotherapy thrown in to fend off the doubters.

Her language was so different from the hunters' tale. Words like *menstruation* and *cervix* flowed as she looked into my eyes and squeezed my hand. The heroine of her story had "long red hair that fell out in one piece." The two women had worked together at Oceaneering, a company whose tagline read *Global provider of deepwater products for the offshore oil and gas industry.*[56]

55 Rick checked on us several times, and sent his blessings. Rick Perry was governor until 2015, when he ran for president. He became Donald Trump's secretary of energy in 2017.

56 In 2021, Oceaneering's motto changed.

AFTER A WET FIFTY-FIVE-MILE day, we arrived in Huntsville, Texas, soaked and worn, and got a room at a truck stop. Hungry, we headed for the nearest cantina, but the Bandera Grill was pricey. We didn't order much. In the Valero gas station, searching for a semi-healthy snack, we saw a Black man standing in front of a sign that read "12 oz cans of pop, 2 for $8."

"Can I get one for four dollars?" he asked the white saleswoman.

"No," she said. "Then it wouldn't be a sale."

They went back and forth that way until the man pulled something out of his waistband. He put the harmonica to his lips and began playing "Jingle Bells"—simple at first, then jazzed. He left the Christmas tune and began a lilting blues riff. A young cowboy trying to buy a pack of Marlboros leaned on a cooler filled with Budweiser, jaw dropping into a silly open-mouth grin.

A white man walked in, paused, walked out. Perhaps—like the hunter with the loaded elephant gun—he kept an assembled flute in his truck, just in case. He returned with the instrument. The two musicians filled the air with a serenade, turning the Valero gas station into a holy, sweet, get-down kind of place.

FOR MONTHS WE HAD raced the ever-encroaching dusk, maneuvering unfamiliar streets in darkness, tired and cranky, feeling it a miracle to be alive. On the winter solstice, our timing was perfect, though we took our time, pausing at the top of a ridge, to watch five weather systems— five theaters of East Texas sky. I even had a staring contest with a longhorn cow.

At 4:06 p.m., we entered the gates of the Acres Alegres Ranch, our home for the night. Our host was petite, tough, and handsome. She once had cattle. Now she farmed walleye. Part of her ranch was a sanctuary for skunks, deer, wild hogs, and copperhead snakes. She made furniture and wooden toys. A row of handmade miniature logging trucks sat in her shed, ready for some lucky child. She played the dulcimer, sang in a choir, and was bilingual, in charge of welcoming Spanish-speaking newcomers to her church. She and her shiny black Model A car were the same age.

She showed us our bed—a barn loft overlooking meadow and forest—before leaving for a church Christmas party. As her car disappeared over the horizon, the electricity went out. David searched in vain for candles and a fuse box.

I gave in to darkness. Sitting on the porch, I watched until the last bit of sun left the sky. There was still a streak of light over the horizon at 8:00 p.m., enough to create monsters out of tree trunks. When it was gone, the winter moon glowed.

A revelation on the darkest day of the year.

29

THE MANSION AND THE SHED

Texas

There's a war against the homeless in this city.
—Claire in Austin, Texas

David had developed the ability to find anything on the side of the road—wrenches, hats, bungee cords—just when we needed them. As we neared Austin, he found a Christmas stocking in perfect condition. "For Emily!" he said. He would fill it with candy. I would add the polished rocks I carried from Surf City, North Carolina. A little later, he found a new pair of size-nine cowboy boots that might fit our lanky child. I stopped him from strapping them on the back of his bike.

"They are too perfect. Someone will be back to look for them."

Getting to Austin's city limits wasn't difficult, but getting to the hotel David's family had reserved for us as a Christmas present was something else. Arriving in an airport taxi, Emily looked up at the tangle of freeway.

"How did you get here?"

"Powered by love."

IT WAS A COLD Christmas Day in Austin. The bus smelled of homelessness. A man in his twenties got on and began a conversation with an older man sitting a few seats away. They looked alike—not just their rumpled clothing, missing teeth, and sallow skin, but also their sandy hair, soft chin, and blue eyes. The younger one told the elder about a Christmas giveaway and how to turn it into cash for liquor. They exchanged a smile. The elder pulled the cord. The young one waved and said, "See you, Dad."

We bumped into Occupy Austin at City Hall. As we approached, young men exchanged notes about a guy circling town, giving away $100 bills. Others played touch football in the plaza. Claire, in her sixties, was the only one who wasn't young or destitute. "Occupiers with homes aren't here today," she explained, reading my thoughts.

I asked about the large number of people living on Austin's streets.

"A few months ago, Houston gave homeless people a bus ticket to Austin," she explained. "The population quadrupled. Austin responded by passing a no-sitting law: get caught with your butt on the ground, and they bar you from that area for two years. The ordinance is illegal, but before the court throws it out, people are racking up criminal charges."

A young man pulled David over to show him his Occupy Austin tattoo. Claire continued, addressing Emily and me. "A few years ago, they removed a bench in Zilker Park used by transient people. They promised to replace it with a volleyball court. But, of course, no court. Now the city has hired 'bush-beaters' to search parks and throw away people's possessions."

She pointed at the pyramid of City Hall stairs, strewn with sleeping bags. "They treat Occupy the same way, changing the rules on us: where we can sit, stand, sleep. Every three days, they hydro-blast our encampment. Such a waste of water."

AT JEANIE'S JAVA ON Austin's Congress Avenue, we searched the internet, looking for a bike for Emily to ride with us to San Antonio. Emily got into a conversation with the woman sitting at the next table. When she heard about our quest, she exclaimed, "I have a bike on my porch I would be happy to donate to the cause."

Our sophisticated New York progeny looked like a kid at Christmas. "You really *can* find anything you need on the road!"

I-35, THE MAIN ARTERY between Austin and San Antonio, also traverses the Twin Cities in Minnesota. We took three days on back roads, doubling the miles from one city to the other, aided by an overly generous young widow whose late husband had bicycled. She put us up in her two homes perfectly situated for us in San Marcos and New Braunfels, treating us to her sublime vegan cooking and a hot tub in a rock garden.

San Antonio was no easier to enter than Austin. Safe at the stately Antonia Inn, Emily considered the vagaries of our new existence. "You guys have such a weird combination of freedom and lack of freedom. For over six months, you have not cooked a meal or washed a floor."

"Or worried about what outfit to wear, or raked a lawn, or invited friends over for dinner, or thrown out junk mail," I said.

"Don't you get tired of biting your tongue?"

"You learn things," David said.

"That's why I write," I added.

The Antonia Inn was blocks from Fort Sam Houston. In the breakfast room, I took notes as a Marine stated his facts: "Corps's the strongest, tightest family in the world."

"War fucks you up permanently."

"Best decision I ever made, enlisting in the Marine Corps."

TEN YEARS EARLIER, THE Christmas after 9/11, we traveled to San Antonio and visited the Alamo. Our tour guide—hired by the Daughters of the American Revolution who run the historic site—transformed the failed 1836 battle in a war for territory into a valiant multicultural struggle: European-American heroes, assisted by an African American man, a Native American woman, and a Mexican man, fought an autocratic foe. Even a child played a heroic role. The story fit the political needs of 2001, when the Bush administration was rallying Americans of all races to support an invasion of Afghanistan. Like Ripley's carnival across the street, you could believe it or not. A few years back, a group of Chicano scholars said, "Or not." They staged a teach-in, pointing out that Crockett, Bowie, Austin, and Houston were interlopers on Mexican and Indigenous territory, wedded to a Texas economy dependent on slavery.

This time, we skipped the Alamo but couldn't escape its presence. We passed Alamo Optical, Alamo Motors, Alamo Heights Junior High School, Alamo Drafthouse Cinema, Alamo Pizza & Wings, Alamo Quarry Market, Pie Alamode, and the Alamodome.[57]

We did participate in the city's other tourist draw, the San Antonio River Walk. The WPA had erected San Antonio's river walls as an anti-erosion project in the 1930s. The city's poorest residents lived along its banks until the 1970s, when hotels replaced neighborhoods. We walked out of the flashy tourist district, through an underpass decorated with neon fish. On the outskirts of downtown, we passed barrios not benefiting from the river glitz. The contrast wasn't as stark as in Baltimore, but close.

We had lunch with Enrique, a childhood friend who had been elected

57 In truth, Pie Alamode doesn't exist—yet. When it opens, specializing in Texas pecan pie with Texas grapefruit ice cream, give us credit.

South Texas Water Protector. "Before the River Walk," he told us, "if you wanted to party, you headed to an underground casino. At the end of the night, owners would shove their earnings under the bank's basement door. The next day, the teller would deposit the cash. Today, downtown shops are empty."

I told Enrique about other communities eager to follow San Antonio's waterfront development example—Rochester, New York, considering moving the Erie Canal, and Wilmington, Delaware, planning to commercialize the Brandywine River, without thought to the environmental costs. Enrique nodded emphatically. "For drought-stricken Texas, careful water use is even more essential. Sometimes this city operates as though they were British Petroleum before the Gulf oil spill. Proceed without caution."

WE SPENT A WEEK with Emily in San Antonio. In the mornings, we hung out with Ramon, the breakfast chef at the Antonia Inn, and listened to his stories. He realized we weren't typical tourists. When we asked about public transportation, he told us, "I could send you on the express bus, but I don't want you to miss the mansion and the shed."

Ramon had been a police officer in Albuquerque, New Mexico. Thirty years earlier, he'd had an accident and received a settlement of $375,000. "I told my lawyer, 'Put this in an account and don't let me touch it until I'm sixty-two. If I come crying and begging, don't give in.' I cried and begged several times over the years. I've worked many low-wage jobs since then: the Dollar General store, hotels—usually two jobs to make ends meet.

"A few years ago, I took a trip to Mexico, fell in love with this little town sixty miles outside of the capital that was raising funds to fix their church. I called my lawyer. This time I didn't beg. I told him, 'It's not for me.'

"I handed the priest an envelope. The next morning, I heard a commotion outside my hotel window. The entire town stood outside, cheering. I gave the church fifty thousand dollars. Recently, the Archbishop of San Antonio visited the town. He told me they changed the church's name to San Ramon. They have a picture of me in the hallway.

"In May, when I turn sixty-two, I'll retire and get the rest of my money. My friends in Albuquerque, who thought I was crazy thirty years ago, now say I was smart. They're not going to be able to retire."

IN THE HOTEL LAUNDRY room, Emily and I met Trimel, a thirty-year-old who wore his emotions on his face. "Happy New Year," I said.

"Happier than last year, I hope," he said.

"Why's that?"

As Trimel folded and refolded a blue shirt, the story of a young life that began on the upcycle but spun out of control tumbled out.

"I came to San Antonio from Georgia to study business administration and play basketball," he said. "I became an accountant, got married, bought a house, had four children. January 2009, I got a pink slip. By April, the bank foreclosed on my house. We were homeless for five months. My wife—we separated."

He cried. I kept my eyes on him. Emily stuck quarters in the washer, both of us wanting to let him know his show of emotion was OK. But Trimel showed no embarrassment. "My favorite Bible scripture is 'Jesus wept.' As a child, I learned men are not supposed to cry. It's good to know Jesus wept too."

I leaned against the washing machine, nodding.

"I'm going back to school to study green business," Trimel continued. "With global warming, I figure there's a need." He placed folded pants on top of the blue shirt. "And I started an anti-violence organization. Homelessness can lead to depression and violence quickly."

I pulled items out of the dryer. Emily sorted. Trimel talked about the devil. "He throws roadblocks in front of those who turn to God," he said. "God gives double for your trouble."

I learned a similar theology from my dad, I thought. "Hitler survived assassination attempts," he would say. "Not Martin Luther King." The good were punished, evil protected. I wanted to say to Trimel that when people with so much to offer get pink-slipped and lose their homes, that devil is corporate, earthly, and defeatable if we act together. But I knew that first we must pick ourselves up. I understood the devastation of job loss. I couldn't imagine losing my home and family as well. Trimel had found a way to move forward.

Emily and I put our folded laundry into a bike pannier. We were about to leave when Trimel said, "I believe our conversation was no coincidence. I don't believe in proselytizing. The people who helped me told me their stories instead of telling me what to believe."

"Yes," I agreed. "Stories heal."

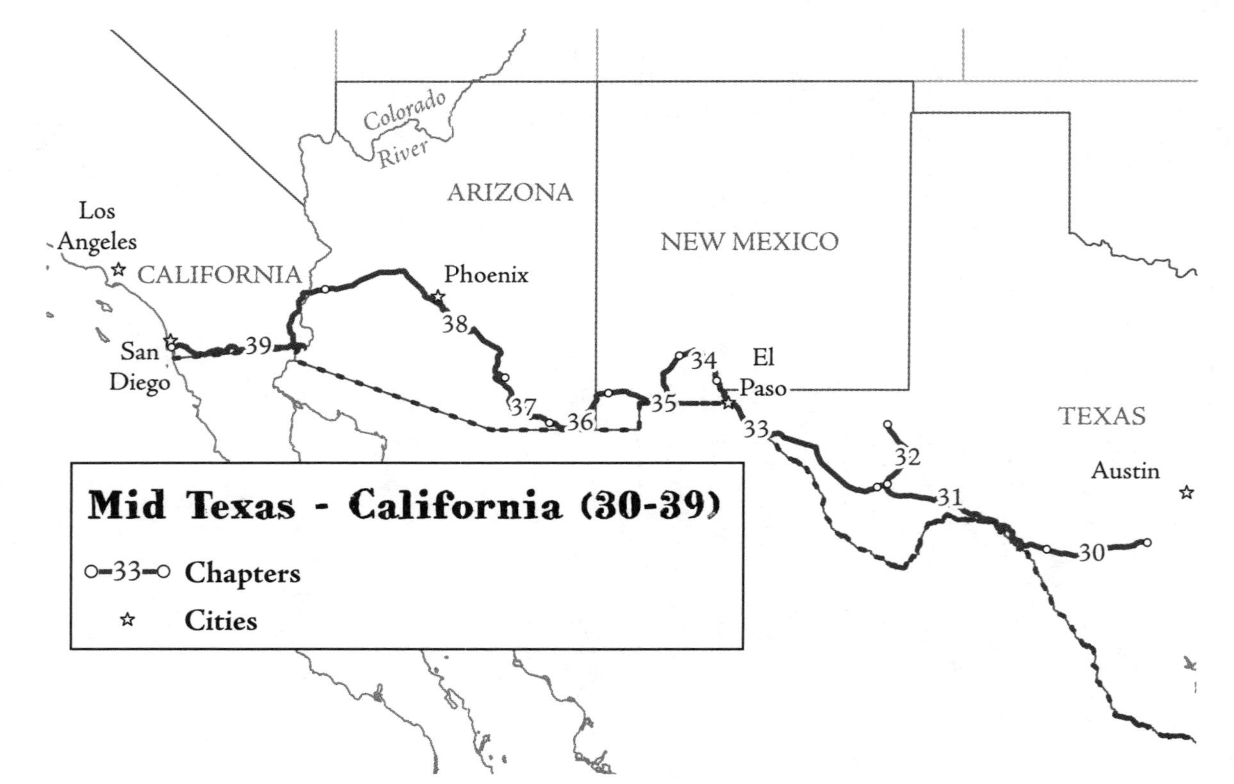
Colorado River
ARIZONA
NEW MEXICO
TEXAS
CALIFORNIA
Los Angeles
San Diego
Phoenix
El Paso
Austin
39
38
37
36
35
34
33
32
31
30
Mid Texas - California (30-39)
33 Chapters
Cities

30

A MATTER OF PERSPECTIVE

Texas

The next day, Emily left. After the taxi pulled away, David and I wept. We were both apt to display that kind of emotion when our child was taking off, but this was different. It's one thing for a couple to engage in a dangerous adventure together, but quite another to increase the chance a young adult will be rendered parentless by such nihilism. These weren't scenarios we talked about, but those fears—held dormant during our days as a threesome—rose to the surface as the taxi drove out of sight. We argued our way out of town, walking most of the way, spending an interminable hour figuring out how to take a bus through a frightening underpass. Once we left the city, however, US 90 was empty and vast as the cavern in my heart.

We did not go far. Twenty miles west was Castroville—not Tejano, not cowboy, but a yuppie oasis from both. The Texas State Historical Society's Landmark Inn on the edge of town had rolling green grounds, lush pecan trees, and a book-lined breakfast room. As the sun rose, I settled into an easy chair with my cup of tea and read an entry in the guest journal written on Mother's Day:

A Beautiful Day! Mom and I are headed out to Hondo to see my eldest son at the State Prison. He is 26, working on his Bachelor's. He helps others prepare for their GED. He's interested in working in a rehab program with adolescents—what we are all praying for. We had a two-hour visit. My mom was so glad she came.

I sipped my tea and added my entry to the journal: *Emily landed safely in New York. On our way to Hondo. A Beautiful Day!*

By afternoon, I forgot to be grateful and began ruminating on the treacheries ahead. Even drivers found West Texas frightening. Our hog-hunting buddies in Cold Spring had tried to assure us: "Go far as you can, then stick out your thumb." I questioned their advice when we passed a sign at the Hondo exit: *Hitchhikers May Be Escaping Inmates.* We rode on, to a motel in Uvalde, where worry became terror. David tried to calm me, taking trips to the grocery store, filling our bags with extra water, food, and toilet paper. But he could not change the facts. The next day's ride to Brackettville was forty miles of desert without a place to rest—a practice test for the sixty-five- and ninety-mile stretches without services to come.

THE TEXAS DESERT SUN could still parch in January, and then seep away by late afternoon, sapping the earth of all warmth. Leaving town, we said goodbye to grocery stores, cafés, motels, color, water, and bathrooms, and entered the land of scrub brush, thorns, dust, and decay. I carried a stone in my stomach, imagining accidents, snake bites, and waterless camping in a place God had forsaken.

At mile five, physical exertion and the monotony of the task allowed my mind to wander, the hardness in my gut beginning to dissolve. At mile ten, I had to pee. I began searching for a culvert or a bigger bush, not for privacy—there was no one to hide from—but for shade.

At mile twelve, a dark object emerged in the distance. By mile thirteen, it had taken on the shape of a structure.

A mirage?

No, it was clearly a building. I did not question it. I imagined entering, resting in the cool dark, on a real toilet.

Cars stalled on the other side of the road as we approached. The only vehicle we'd seen since Uvalde was a green and white Border Patrol truck. And here it was. Three men in uniform came toward us. Border guards. Looking at their young faces, I made my request, donning a sweet smile.

"We don't have a public bathroom," one said. "This is an immigration checkpoint."

My smile got less sweet, more desperate. The officer exchanged glances with his partners. He pointed to the open door of a tiny room.

"You can use that."

David went into the men's holding cell, closing the door. I propped the women's door open with my handlebar bag, peeing in partial sight of young men in uniform.

DURING THE EMPTY MILES left in the day, I mulled over my reaction. Fear that I would be locked in a detention room wasn't rational. I did not fit the profile. And my fear of the desert was overblown too. If we got in an accident or ran out of water, those ever-present green and white patrol vans would be a resource. A woman walking across the border, however, faced real life-threatening perils: dehydration, sexual assault, starvation, and a Border Patrol nightmare that might begin in the cell where I relieved my bladder.

31

DESERT APPARITIONS

Texas and Coahuila, Mexico

We didn't cross the border; the border crossed us.
—Chicano saying

The native language of Brackettville, Texas, was Spanglish, a seamless flow from one to the other. We embarrassed ourselves asking for a Mexican restaurant. Mexican food was just food here. Even the place advertising fried chicken and burgers served beans, rice, tortillas, and lime with every meal.

David had a cold. We booked two nights at Brackettville's Fort Clark, built to conquer Indigenous people and obtain dominion for white Texans. In the 1880s, the US Army had stationed African American recruits known as Buffalo Soldiers here. The fort museum brochure read, *Buffalo Soldiers Heritage and Outreach Program emphasizes Texans' shared Western heritage.* I thought about those brochure words as we ate breakfast at Julie's Place. At the next table were four Border Patrol officers: three Latinos and an Anglo, like us, seeking a hot meal and company on this cold January day. Shielding my notebook under the corner of my plate, I wrote:

If we tell ourselves formerly enslaved people dying to secure Native territory for white immigrants is "shared heritage," we are more likely to view a mixed group of border guards who prohibit newcomers from inhabiting stolen lands as racial harmony. Of course, Black soldiers were accomplished. The limited options open to them after Reconstruction, and the immorality of their assigned task, are the stories that need telling. Like the Buffalo Soldiers, I'm sure our Border Patrol breakfast mates are brave and diligent. That doesn't make their assigned task just.

I posted my observations on my blog, ending with: *Everyone has a right to move to seek a better life, especially in this region of stolen land*—not knowing the doors those words would open.

A LOADED BIKE LEANED outside Brackettville's Krazy Chicken Café. We sat down with John, a thirty-year-old man cycling east from Orange County, California. We expressed mutual distress at the number of dead towns and ghostly hulls littering the American landscape. We had different perspectives on what should be done.

"We need an Entrepreneur Corps, like AmeriCorps, to teach small business owners how to stay afloat in the new economy," John enthused.

"When the sawmill closes, Main Street closes," I countered. "Hitting the sweet price point or balance of service and product won't save them. They need life-giving renewable industries, dignified pay and conditions, and community investment to build diverse sustainable economies."

John shrugged.

David asked him about his destination for the night.

"I'm staying here another day," he replied.

"What is holding you?"

He smiled. "Online dating has progressed. There are two women in Brackettville I want to check out."

A YOUNG WOMAN WITH silky black hair sitting at the counter of River City Doughnut and Coffee in Del Rio, Texas, picked at her buttered muffin and flipped the page of her anatomy text. I caught her smile and asked if she knew of a bus to the border.

"Used to be border taxis," Carla said. "Not many people crossing now."

I asked about her studies. We exchanged intimacies about our children. Carla told me about her migration to Del Rio at age four. "This Christmas was the first time I took my three children across to visit my grandmother."

She assessed us. "I'll drive you to the border."

A quarter of a mile away, Carla stopped the car. "I'll turn around here," she said. "Stay in the tourist section. You'll be all right. It was more dangerous a few years ago, but it's gotten quieter."

There was little traffic on the border bridge, most of it trucks. A mother and son stood in the middle, embracing. Two cars, one with Coahuila and the other with Texas plates, were parked on an outlet. The central calle in Ciudad Acuña was dressed for visitors. In between bars and souvenir stands, a dozen dental offices beckoned with signs in English: *A healthy smile means so much.* We were the only extranjeros we saw, and we did not drink, buy trinkets, or get our teeth fixed. We did enjoy a delicate mushroom soup at Hostería Santa Martha. When we entered the café, they were playing the Beatles' *Sgt. Pepper's Lonely Hearts Club Band.* After a while, the place filled with lunchtime patrons and music switched to plaintive Mexican ballads.

Back on the border bridge, a woman stood, knitting the last rows of a long red and green scarf. We used our phone cameras. David captured a horse wading in the river, citizenship unclear. I took a shot of watchtowers that reminded me of crossing the East/West German border in 1982. We both took photos of the plaque on the side of the US Border station.

A US guard emerged from nowhere, demanding our phones. "It's illegal to take photos in the border crossing area," he said. "Why did you take a picture of that plaque?"

"It says George W. Bush is president and not Barack Obama," David answered truthfully.

The guard was defensive. "Bush was president then."

I looked at the date on the plaque: 2009.

After a few minutes, he returned our phones.

RIDING OUT OF DEL RIO, we passed the Amistad Reservoir. The United States and Mexico share management of this basin in the Rio Grande, with its miles of tentacles reaching into each nation. Not since the Louisiana bayous had we seen so much water. The brilliant blue surrounded by gray and red rock intensified the impact of the desiccated expanse that followed.

Comstock, Texas, had more Border Patrol vans than people. We stayed at the Comstock Motel, wedged in the middle of the Border Patrol headquarters. Across the road, US, Lone Star, and Confederate flags flew on the roof of Jim Holley's Place, next to a small store with this sign by the cash register: *Speak English. This Is America.*

We were in enemy territory, identities hidden under white skin.

THE NEXT MORNING, HUNGER and fear of the desert sent us into the café we'd managed to avoid the night before. Sitting at the only table was a brown man, shaking his head at a giant burrito. He wore a poncho, Indigenous belt, and Vietnam veteran's cap. Carlos had stopped for a glass of water to take his pills, ordered food he wasn't hungry for, and now was sharing a table and his life story with a couple of cyclists.

After Vietnam, he'd worked for Continental Airlines as a flight attendant. Now retired, Carlos flew free between homes in Dallas and El Salvador. "I'm learning Nahuatl from my Salvadoran neighbors," he said. "Do you know how Mexico got its name?"

"After the Mexica people," I said, giving the letter *x* a *sh* sound. "A Nahuatl word."

Carlos looked at me quizzically. "I used to teach Latin American history," I explained, gesturing for him to continue.

"When Mexicans say they're not Indian, that's like Apaches saying they're not Indian," Carlos said. "Of course, there's a problem with that word." After parsing about arrogant Europeans who misidentified the people of the Americas, he launched into a defense of "Malintzin," the Mayan translator and mistress of the Spanish conquistador Hernán Cortés.

I'm not sure which of us was more surprised to be conversing about Mexican conquest and identity politics in that dusty café with its racist displays. As the three of us left, we passed a sign on the wall: *Obama: Don't Re-Nig*. Outside, Carlos was happy to have his picture taken. He took off the veteran's cap before David snapped the shutter.

"I'm wearing the hat for the Buffalo Soldiers' dedication ceremony at the Seminole Canyon State Park," Carlos said. "You should come."

THE STATE PARK WAS hidden from the road. Without Carlos's invitation, we would never have guessed humans inhabited these barren canyons. Entering the park building, I saw Black and Indigenous men and women standing next to larger-than-life portraits of themselves, trading family stories. I drifted toward a display that told of enslaved people who escaped to Florida, joined Seminole tribes, migrated to Mexico, returned after the Civil War, and became Buffalo Soldiers.

The park ranger welcomed us like expected guests. "Saw you on the road!" he said. "So glad you made it! Help yourself to refreshments." But for once I was too busy devouring conversations to take advantage of free food. I helped myself to intermingled oral histories, thinking what an honor it was to witness this jam session, sharing a heritage, yes, but without the false glory, building alliances to liberate the future. In a region of walls and checkpoints, here was a gathering of bridge builders.

David talked with Larvell "Sugar Bear" Blanks, a major league baseball player from 1972 to 1980 and the grandson of a Buffalo Soldier. Larvell, who lived in Del Rio, had just returned from visiting family in Minneapolis. In this grand theater of open space, a small world.

IN LANGTRY, A TOWN of eighteen people twenty-nine miles from Comstock and a quarter mile from Mexico, a man offered his FEMA trailer to us, "if you use your sleeping bags and don't mess the bed."

He told us, "When I moved here in 2010, the sheriff stopped by and asked, 'Do you have guns?' I told him, 'Of course.' The sheriff replied, 'Well, good. Up here, you have to fend for yourself.'"

"Deputized by appearance," I responded. The white man seemed unaware that my comment was critical, which was good. I was getting David's cold. I needed the bed he so generously offered.

In the morning, I felt worse. I couldn't do sixty miles without services to Sanderson, but I didn't want to stay in Langtry another night. We paid our host to drive us twenty miles. In his car, we passed a bus. For a moment, I thought, *Good to know there's public transportation out here.*

"There go the Mexicans," he snickered from the driver's seat. Later, we passed Border Patrol trucks dragging tires along the dirt frontage road. I wondered, *Something useful to do?*

As if reading my mind, he corrected me:

"They're catching footprints."

INFINITESIMAL DRYDEN, TEXAS, HAD a tiny grocery store/post office. A scarecrow with a long white beard sat propped up on a rocking chair in front of the building. As we approached, he moved ever so slightly, acknowledging us, startling me with his humanness. Buying the store out of tomato juice, apples, and cheddar cheese, we got out multigrain tortillas carried from Del Rio and sat down with Scarecrow Man. He asked, "What's been the prettiest part of your trip?" We told him about New Hampshire villages, South Carolina forests, Florida bird sanctuaries.

I extended my arms. "This is lovely."

It was Scarecrow Man's turn to look startled.

The West Texas desert is a panorama of emptiness. In Dryden, the sky alone provided variance. I imagined it would lose its magic, staring from a chair until your beard grew into your lap, or patrolling from a truck dragging a tire, or dodging trucks looking for your footprints. But biking, watching singular changes in shape and color created by rock and sky, could be breathtaking.

IT WAS STILL DARK at 6:50 a.m. as we sat in the back room of the Sanderson gas station, eating ninety-nine-cent breakfast tacos and debating how much water to carry on our ride to Marathon, Texas. Around us, a constant stream of Border Patrol guards—young men and a few women, many of them Latinx—stopped for the only good food around, ordering fajitas, frijoles charros, homemade tortillas, mac and cheese, and fresh fruit. The attendant knew what each one wanted and cooked to order.

The water question had become a complicated math equation. How much water weight should two people add for a sixty-mile bike ride, without stops to refill, climbing the high desert on a windy day when they each have a cold? Overhearing our debate, a kind fellow interrupted and offered to carry a six-pack of twenty-ounce bottles up the road for us. "I'm leaving in a couple hours," he said.

He was odd-looking. Worn navy pants, faded shirt buttoned to his neck, cobbled shoes. His outfit shouted, "I don't belong in this era." If it were later in the day, when hours of sun and wind cause the brain to conjure illusions, I might have thought him an apparition.

We exchanged introductions. He wanted to know what sent two unlikely cyclists on the road. We wanted to know what he meant by "conservative Quaker" and how one ended up in a West Texas gas station.

"Quakers are few and far between in Texas, and conservative Quakers are few anywhere," he acknowledged. "We are followers of the old-time religion: no ministers, modest dress, simple lifestyle, silent worship."

Eyeing the Border Patrol truck in the driveway, I lowered my voice. "Are Texas Quakers involved in the immigration issue?" He nodded. "Some provide sanctuary, like our nineteenth-century brethren who harbored escaped slaves."

WHEN THE QUAKER DELIVERED the water, he offered a peeled pink Texas grapefruit with a small chunk out of it. "I thought you might want to share this with me," he said. We ate slowly, savoring the burst of sweet and sour.

We had two other human encounters on the road to Marathon. A couple from Traverse City, Michigan, parked their RV on the side of the road and refilled our bottles. A portly, bald New York reporter in a tiny red sports car sniffed us for a story before speeding away. We watched his car recede for an eon—a red dot in a sea of gray and beige.

From Sanderson to Marathon, the headwind was so strong and the landscape so empty that for ten hours we stared at the same bend in the road. The pedometer clocked in at six miles per hour, but the bend did not get closer.

Until it did. Fifty-nine miles, climbing 1,200 feet.

"OK, Texas," I shouted into the wind. "You can stop saying, 'You ain't seen nothing yet.'"

32

BORDER POLITICS

Texas

Unscheduled praise service if water gaps wash out.
—Sign on Big Bend Cowboy Church, Alpine, Texas

Marathon, Texas, was a great accomplishment. But ahead were unfathomable seventy-five- and ninety-mile stretches without water, exacerbated by mountains and wind. Still, we proceeded without a plan, hoping a solution would arise.

Liz Rogers arose. She was well over six feet tall, with a deep, gravelly voice and a John Wayne–like presence. She had read my blog and decided she wanted to meet me. "You wrote, 'Everyone has a right to move to seek a better life,'" she rasped. "Now, I'm not sure I agree. I'm not for tearing down the borders. But I'd never heard anyone say that before." She invited us to spend a night in her guest house in Marathon, two nights in her casita in Alpine, and secured us shelter in three more locations, breaking up those isolated stretches of West Texas.

Liz was a federal public defender. During our day in Alpine she took us with her to court, one hundred miles north, in Pecos, Texas. Driving ninety miles an hour through the parched heart of oil country, hands off the wheel, Liz talked nonstop. "Governor Perry's leading prayer services asking for rain. But as you can see"—she pointed at an oil rig, pumping in the distance—"our dwindling water supply has not halted fracking."

We passed one car, filled with Liz's law colleagues. They shook their heads as we left them in the dust. "Water politics are complicated," she continued. "Clayton Williams—he ran against Ann Richards for governor in 1990—wants to sell rights to the water under his ranch to the city of Midland, where George Bush lives. His neighbors are upset. The region's the driest it's been in sixty years."

The Pecos courthouse was massive, like it belonged in Saint Paul, not a town of eight thousand. Liz introduced us to the security guard and everyone else in the building as she led us to the courtroom. We took seats in the back row, hoping the suit coat Liz lent David and the black winter jacket I'd bought in Del Rio would cover our incongruity. We wanted to slip in unnoticed, but Liz approached the bench, booming, "Judge, I want you to meet my friends."

We stood awkwardly. The judge, behind his perch, talked animatedly about his favorite bike trails and gear. "He's a buddy of George Bush," Liz would tell us later. He was gloating about his last race when nine Mexican men in jumpsuits entered the room, shackled at ankles, wrists, and waist, like the legs of a giant orange caterpillar.

No longer engaged, the judge looked at his roster, called a name. A man stepped forward and said, "I apologize for breaking the laws of your country."

One by one, the other men faced the bench and recited the same sentence. Liz did her best to unchain them with her words. They weren't criminals, but people, seeking a better life across the border. Each had an individual story. Liz towered and commanded as she pleaded their cases. Her partner—in a wheelchair—methodically developed their arguments. Their combined efforts seemed unbeatable, but they faced a dehumanizing system too monstrous for dedicated lawyers to overcome.

"Eighty percent of my clients are immigrants," Liz told us as we ate lunch at a restaurant in Pecos. "A few years ago, most crossed to find work. Now, people come to escape the violence. They say, 'Get me a two-year sentence if need be. Just don't send me back. I'll get killed.' Recently, I've seen a new twist to the terror. They deport everyone to the same place. The drug cartels capture deportees and force them to return with backpacks of drugs."

Our food came. Liz counted the Weight Watcher points in her salad. "It's 1939, and I'm sending Jews back to Germany. We need a refugee program for Mexicans today, but we're moving in the opposite direction. They used to deport you. Now, you go to jail and court first. If you reenter, you have a criminal record." She paused. "I voted for Obama, but I'm deeply disappointed with his border policies: more detentions, more deportations, harsher sentences."

The whole experience at the courtroom was surreal. I didn't trust my memory of it. Sitting with my computer on the couch at the casita that night, I quizzed David. "Did they really have shackles? As if they were dangerous criminals?"

"Yes."

"Ankles, wrists, and waist, like something out of a concentration camp movie?"

"Yes."

"Did the judge brag to us across the courtroom about his cycling speeds?"

"Yes."

"Was Liz amazing?"

"Yes!"

LIZ HAD CONVINCED HER boyfriend, Mike, to put us up on his ranch in Marfa. It wasn't far but involved climbing a small mountain and surviving an enormous headwind. On the way, we met a big man who was biking to Alaska to "lose weight." He had put a sail on his tricycle and was headed east, away from Alaska, enjoying a free ride. "I'm going thirty miles an hour without pedaling," he said. "You should try it."

Even locals commented on the wind, wondering how we managed. They talked of "fifty-mile-an-hour gusts" and "vehicles veering off the road." One woman told us she saw a young cyclist with his thumb out. It made us feel tough.

Once we stopped moving, however, our bodies took in the measure of what we'd done. David put his head on the table next to a half-eaten artisanal spinach pizza and fell into a deep sleep. Too tired to eat, I sat comatose, listening to women discuss how to quarantine gluten-free dough from its wheat cousin.

Marfa is an artists' colony. Creative people from around the world come here, inspired by blood-red sunsets and mysterious skylights. They mollify the harsh emptiness with coffee shops, art galleries, and each other. Youth from Austin and San Antonio weather the six-hundred-mile drive in search of an alternative scene in gun-toting Texas. Exhaustion left us unable to explore its delights. We could have been in tiny Dryden, Texas, or Weedsport, New York.

Liz arrived at the pizza joint to pick us up. The whole room sprang to life when she walked in, like a crowd in a John Wayne movie when he swings open the bar door. Heads turned. People rose from their seats. Liz greeted her fans, then ushered us to her car. She was taking us to dine with her boyfriend, her law partner, the former mayor of El Paso, his chief of staff, and an El Paso state senator. I could barely walk from car to restaurant, too tired to wonder how we'd ended up with this esteemed company, eating fancy food, drinking quart cans of Budweiser, talking border politics. Senator Eliot Shapleigh took the floor: "Eleanor Roosevelt humanized the Jews and their plight during World War II. We need that kind of paradigm shift in the way Americans see Mexican immigrants."

In the morning, we had toast with Liz's boyfriend, Mike, while it was still dark. He shoved his NRA membership renewal notice aside to make room for us at the kitchen table. Mike was a Republican in the bluest town of the reddest state in the union. He and Liz reveled in their political differences. Mike took pride in conquering "the most difficult terrain in the world." He told us:

"I've been a rancher in the Chihuahua Desert all my life. I visited Arizona once. The Sonora Desert is different. You'll see."

33

THE CAVALRY AND THE DAM

Texas and New Mexico

. . . The first was the cavalry, the second was the dam.
—Alex Kuo[58]

Determined to beat the wind, we left Marfa before dawn, but it was freezing. We thawed out at a café on the edge of town. The owner set down our eggs, while arguing with the TV report: "Veteran unemployment is high, but employers and the military are turning the tide."

"They lie. Promise and don't deliver," she retorted. "My son was unemployed for four years, coming out of the Army. Now he's working for ICE."

THE RIDE OUT OF Marfa was one parched expanse. We arrived in Valentine—population 217—at 2:30 p.m., red, dirty, desperate to get inside. The Miller family—friends of Liz Rogers—let us stay in a home they were renovating. Without this invitation, we would have had seventy-five miles into heat and against the wind to the first water and shelter. We never met the Millers. They left us a note: "Taco soup is for you." Rich in ground beef, big enough for a ranching family, it became lunch, supper, and breakfast for two vegetarians. Over eighteen hours, we finished it all.

---

58 Alexander Kuo, *The Man Who Dammed the Yangtze: A Mathematical Novel* (Hong Kong: Haven Books, 2001) 141. See also Kuo's blog post: Damming the American West http://www.bluefish.org/damming.htm.

A MILE OUTSIDE OF Valentine, perched in the bare desert, was a glass and mortar structure. As we got close, we found ourselves staring into a Prada storefront window displaying high fashion heels. We captured our reflections in the glass, gawking at the absurdity, as the Berliners who created it hoped we would. The artists claimed they wanted the installation to fade "as everything does in the desert," but when offended locals sped its destruction with graffiti and rocks, they restored it.

I was still thinking about the art/storefront when we stopped for shade and a snack inside a culvert. At its edge was an empty water jug. Inside there was a bra. I sat down next to someone else's underwear and unwrapped my granola bar. My mind restocked the shoe store. I tossed out the heels. On the bottom shelf, I put a dust-cracked cowboy boot to represent ranchers like the Millers. On the top I put a faded pink tennis shoe, representing the woman who left her bra in this culvert.

BETWEEN VALENTINE AND SIERRA Blanca, we passed a sign depicting a trash can. A tiny smudge on the arid landscape grew until it became an over-large canister. We dug into our handlebar bags and made our contribution to the only public garbage receptacle for a hundred miles.

IN THE SOUTHWEST, YOU can tell if you are in a Mexican or Anglo establishment by the Pancho Villa or John Wayne depiction on the wall. At El Chubby's in Sierra Blanca, we fingered striped blankets, Mexican dolls, and photo reproductions of Villa and Emiliano Zapata sharing the president's chair at the Mexican National Palace in 1914.

Sierra Blanca was an unfolding mystery, a scavenger hunt with clues placed on signs:

Prison: Do Not Pick Up Hitchhikers.

You Are Entering Vaquero Country.

Horse Motel.

At a tiny Methodist church, a handwritten note on the front entrance read *Because of the Wind, Use the Back Door*. On Business 10, billboards promised "Historic Motels" and gift shops advertised "Indian Curios and Turquoise," but all were permanently closed. A sign for East Main Street directed us down a gravel path. West Main Street was a muddy flat, but the Border Patrol station had a paved parking lot.

From 1991 to 2001, Sierra Blanca was the dumping ground for all of New York City's toxic sludge. As a result, the Mexican American population suffered severe and unique health problems. A 650-person immigration detention center, built in 2004, was sold to the town as an alternative to an economy of garbage.[59]

In the center of town were two brick buildings grand enough to fill a New York City block: a center for law enforcement and the new detention center—two cathedrals to policing in this village of dust and mud. In front of the courthouse, a stone plaque read, "Here, 90,000 Texas troops served the South, guard[ing] . . . frontier and coastline from Union troops and savage Indians." A few feet away, Spanish-speaking, Indigenous-looking children played a pick-up game of basketball.

---

59 https://www.nytimes.com/2001/07/27/us/new-york-s-sewage-was-a-texas-town-s-gold.html.

WEST OF SIERRA BLANCA, we met two Austrian cyclists traveling the world. The four of us compared notes until a Border Patrol officer interrupted us. He did not demand that the cyclists with distinct foreign accents show their papers. Instead, he asked, "Have you seen a red van?"

Four heads shook. When the Border Patrol left, one of the Austrians said, "We wouldn't tell him if we did. We are on the Mexican side of this war."

ON A PARCHED STRIP of borderland between Sierra Blanca and Esperanza, I squatted, careful not to let my bare butt touch spiky barbs, watering a wilted prickly pear losing its war against the drought. As I pulled up my pants, my ears filled with wind. I closed my eyes and listened.

A thirty-species chorus sang the musical's overture. Ranchers, ranch hands, javelinas, and bobcats from both sides of the border lifted their voices to protect the water. Act I was long and discordant, as negotiations are—songs of thirst, hoarding, fear. The ensemble reached harmonic convergence in the last act, trilling and chirping their plan to save the earth's elixir for their grandchildren's grandchildren. What a glorious finale! Even the cacti crooned.

An emancipated wild horse sized me up from a short distance. I returned to my bike and took a long gulp of water.

A short, hard rain soaked us.

From a small Mexican café in Fort Hancock, we dried out and called Liz's sister-in-law, Malloy, to tell her we would arrive soon. The café owner gave us directions. As we turned into Malloy's ranch driveway, we could see a piece of the border wall. In front of her barn, a large flag flew, blue and white, with the Jewish star in the middle.

Malloy ushered us in. "I'm sorry you got caught in the rain, but we needed it," she said. "Hopefully, there's more where it came from." She pointed triumphantly at a white-topped range to the southeast, in Mexico. "Haven't seen snow in forever!"

I considered telling her I'd had a vision that brought the rain but thought better of it. I wanted to ask her about the Israeli flag, but I thought better of that too. We sat in her living room trading stories, revealing divergent perspectives.

Malloy was the only white girl in her Fort Hancock grade school class. She and her brothers cultivated her parents' cotton farm. On the other side of their property was Mexico. The wall, covering half the borderline on her property, was new. People walked around it. To me, this was proof the US did not want to halt the migration of low-wage workers, just deny them rights. Malloy thought the wall stemmed the flow, and she supported the statement it made.

We ate Malloy's food and slept in her guest bed. We talked about the risks people take, acknowledging the chance she took inviting us into her home. I begged her to visit Minnesota so we could provide what she gave us—shelter to those who oppose your worldview. As we left, I looked back at the piece of wall and the Israeli flag, wondering what message that sent to the immigrants crossing into the US.[60]

I WONDERED HOW COTTON grew in this desert. We found the answer on a historical marker in Torrino, west of Fort Hancock: "In 1909, the United States buil[t] a dam and reservoir on the Rio Grande." Cotton farmers arrived soon after. In 1944, the US and Mexico signed a treaty specifying how much of the river's bounty each country would get. In the 1990s, Mexico was in water

60 Some Evangelical Christians believe Israel will become the promised land for the faithful after the Second Coming.

debt to the United States. Mexico paid the debt off in 2005, but it got behind again as drought plagued the region. Texas politicians were outraged, but you can't redirect water that isn't there. Responding to this pressure, Mexico announced plans to build its first dams.

What a little water can do! We saw green pine trees, alfalfa, pecans, peppers, egrets, great blue herons, even seagulls. We paused by a reservoir. A piece of the border wall stopped at the water's edge, starting again on the other side. A train sped by. Where there was no wall, a Border Patrol officer hid behind a tree. Another squatted in a ditch.

"Trains, water, border patrol," David mused. "Three big government projects in Texas, where promises of small government win elections."

WE FOUND A CHEAP motel on El Paso's eastern side. To muffle an argument in the next room, we replayed a haunting ballad our friend Gilberto had emailed to us. Antonio Aguilar's "Paso del Norte" told of a time when Ciudad Juárez and El Paso were one. It gave us a sense of place, easily lost in a windowless room with concrete walls painted green.

The next day we wound our way, slowly, to west El Paso. From an elevated point on Cotton Street, we saw the whole valley—smokestacks and rows of houses clinging to the mountainside on both sides of the border—and in the middle, the river. Over a century ago, the US built a flood control ditch in El Paso, moving the Rio Grande south six miles. For decades, the US and Mexico disputed the sovereignty of the new shoreline, until John F. Kennedy ceded six miles of Mexican land to Mexico to show Latin America that the United States wasn't the evil empire Fidel Castro claimed. We stopped at the Chamizal National Memorial, one of the twin public parks on both sides of the border that celebrated the dispute's peaceful end.

In the evening, Michael Wyatt, assistant county attorney, and his wife, an artist named Karla, took us to a faculty art showing at the University of Texas. The pieces were political and border focused. A cartoon, captioned, "How many must die so you can get high?" exposed US culpability in the epidemic of drug-related murders in Mexico.

Over dinner we shared our planned route through New Mexico with Michael and Karla. Between bites of falafel, Michael told us, "It's too early in the season. You'll see the fields, but not the thirty thousand farmworkers who harvest peppers, onions, cilantro, pecans, and grapes between here and Las Cruces. They get paid by the bushel—the same wage as in the eighties: as low as two dollars an hour."

When Michael worked for Texas Legal Services, he'd learned how difficult it was to prosecute abusive employers. "A contractor recruits and transports workers from El Paso to a different field every day. Workers sleep on the bus and have no idea who they work for." He added, "Many New Mexico farmworkers live in shelters or on the street in El Paso."

I asked about unionization. Michael shook his head. "You have the right to organize unless you're a farmworker. In California, the United Farm Workers got a law passed to include them, but not here."

After dinner, Michael and Karla drove us up to the Franklin Mountains. From an overlook, in the dark, El Paso and Ciudad Juárez were one glowing Paso del Norte—one continental crossroad.

CROSSING THE BORDER INTO New Mexico, we saw a field of giant twigs poking out of dry ground. If not for the signs, I wouldn't have believed they were pecan orchards. At Stahmanns Pecans plantation in San Miguel, we bought caramelized nuts and sat in a dark room with folding chairs, watching their promotional video describing the pecan production process. A robotic arm shook ripe trees. Machines sorted and shelled.

In the 1930s, pecans were shelled by hand. Then, labor leader Emma Tenayuca organized a powerful union of twelve thousand Latina pecan shellers. Southwest pecan farmers retaliated by mechanizing the process. The video didn't talk about workers or labor conditions, though people were visible, planting, watering, sweeping behind machines, and packaging Stahmanns's pies and caramel candies.

The orchards were lush in the video, not sticks on desiccated soil. When the Rio Grande is dry, farmers pump underground, accessing the Hueco-Mesilla Bolson Aquifer that stretches from Elephant Butte, New Mexico, through El Paso, into Chihuahua, Mexico. Acquiring that water is a political feat.

Border Patrol, like the cavalry of old, police the workers. What happens underground makes the pecans grow. Control water and labor, and you control the borderlands.

34

MIDDLE OF NOWHERE

New Mexico

Between Las Cruces and Hatch, New Mexico, sixty miles from the border, we went through a checkpoint. The patrolman waved us through. Above him was a Border Patrol billboard, a silhouette of three men in cowboy hats on horses and the words "We Are Hiring!" I wondered if the young man standing in the box, breathing exhaust, was having a cowboy day.

Hatch had Sparky's, a hamburger joint. I filled my plate with sides: pinto beans, grilled onion, corn, green chilies, and pineapple coleslaw, enjoying food, noise, human contact. Tom Hermann, a retiree from Wisconsin, sat with his wife at the next table. He leaned over and smirked. "You know what they call a bicyclist at Yellowstone?"

Leaving Hatch, Hermann's joke didn't seem so funny. If a cougar or a pack of coyotes attacked us in this desert, we'd be "meals on wheels" before anyone found us.

It was difficult riding—twenty miles of elevation on Route 26, followed by thirty of wind. At the turning point between up and wind was Nutt, population two. We met the whole town. Susan and Thomas, managers of the Middle of Nowhere Bar, refilled our water bottles and let us use the bathroom. The couple was from Tucson. They came to Nutt on a fishing trip a year earlier and decided to stay.

"What was the attraction?" I asked.

The town of Nutt answered in unison, "The people."

An hour later, sitting in the middle of the road eating our lunch, I laughed. I knew Susan and Thomas meant it. They managed a bar; their customers must be good folk. The joke was on us.

Whenever anyone asked us, "What's the best part of your trip?" we'd say, "The people."

For the last two days, we had one minute of interaction with another person: Tom Hermann at Sparky's in Hatch. We had no phone service, no reassuring calls to mothers and child. We'd barely spoken to each other. The wind obliterated any ability to communicate on bikes and left us too tired to talk in the evening. We'd been living in our heads.

Sometimes the gusts shut out my inner voices. The only one speaking was the wind.

35

COLONIZING SPACE

New Mexico

You know what it means to be born in space? Starting life in a mining town that is now an abandoned pit.
—Park ranger, Columbus, New Mexico

"Have you been to the museum? You can't come to Deming and not see our Mimbres pottery."

The inquirer was a short, wiry General Motors retiree with an artist's heart and a political mind who volunteered at the Deming Arts Center. "You're a historian, huh?" he asked me. "You know about Pancho Villa's raid?"

"Yeah," I said. "President Wilson sent ten thousand troops into Mexico to try to capture him. Weren't they stationed in Deming?"

He nodded. "And Wilson used the Villa raid to mobilize another 150,000 National Guardsmen here. When he was ready to enter World War I, he had an army.

"Nothing has changed," he went on. "George Bush put his Homeland Security training center here; called it Operation Border Wolf." He paused. "Mining comes and goes. Mimbres pottery and the Villa story attract visitors, but art and history don't sustain Deming. War's the constant."

WITH A GROUP OF Iowa snowbirds, we admired the black-and-white geometrical designs, human figures, animals, and birds on the Mimbres pots.

The priceless ancient artifacts were displayed alongside military uniforms and John Wayne commemorative saucers and plates.

WE STAYED AN EXTRA day in Deming, huddling over our computer at the McDonald's on Pine Street, debating three hard choices: 1. Go north on Route 180, up nine thousand feet, where it was winter in late January. 2. Ride the interstate—legal in New Mexico—sharing the road with trucks going eighty miles an hour. 3. Head south to Columbus and west on Route 9, where Hachita—a ghost town—was the only stop for one hundred miles.

I asked for advice online. An octogenarian in Hachita had provided water and camping space to two Michigan cyclists. We'd go the desert route.

DOWNTOWN COLUMBUS, NEW MEXICO, looked like a movie set. We walked empty streets, reading plaques describing which Americans died, and who saved who, on this exact spot when Villa's men galloped across the border and raided the town on March 9, 1916. The city museum retold each of the 110 minutes of the raid, in lurid detail. The Pancho Villa State Park exhibit—a "Latino Heritage site"—provided a bit more context. Still, the role US mining companies, railroads, and agribusiness played in fomenting the Mexican revolution, was reduced to a cryptic sentence: "U.S. investment made U.S. intervention inevitable."[61]

The current political drama in Columbus was as extraordinary as the historical scene it was dressed up to remember. For seven months, the town had been without a mayor, town council, or police force, after a gun-smuggling ring

61 President Donald Trump sent troops to the United States-Mexico border in November 2018 to stop a caravan of asylum seekers. Defense Secretary James Mattis defended the deployment, citing the US invasion of Mexico following Pancho Villa's Columbus raid as precedent.

made up of city officials was uncovered. *Wouldn't that be something,* I mused, *if the anarcho-syndicalist dream of some Mexican revolutionaries—a society run by workers—was realized in the town Villa raided.*

A white bus filled with day laborers pulled me out of *that* fantasy.

We stayed an extra day in Columbus, hoping the wind might change. I'm glad we did. I got to witness a border-fluid ordinariness below the historical pageantry, gunrunning, and government corruption. At the Patio Café, we talked to a Border Partners volunteer, "working to end poverty on both sides." A retired couple, nation-crossing for cheap pharmaceuticals, stopped for burgers with green chili sauce. Later, I saw children leave a Columbus school and get on a bus, riding home to Puerto Palomas, across the border.

IN THE DESERT, THE wind usually rises in late morning and dies in the evening. But on this morning, it was already roaring at 8:00 a.m. The force was so strong we expended energy just to keep the bikes upright. Dust swirled, filling our lungs. By late afternoon, the math was against us. We wouldn't make it to Hachita.

Stealth camping in the desert. My nightmare.

But then, the wind abruptly stopped, like a factory worker done with her shift!

At the sign to Hachita, we turned onto a dirt road, passing a dozen houses of tin, wood, and concrete, and a few RVs scattered along a four-block grid. A stately stone church with manicured yard told us that, though there might be ghosts, for a handful of living households, this was home. There was even a post office, and a person there to ask directions to Sam Hughes's house.

A layer of dust covered the four small rooms of the stucco home. Sam was recovering from pneumonia. His nostrils were too narrow for an oxygen tube, so he had one for his mouth. Most of the time, it dangled to make room for a Marlboro. Photos of three generations lined the walls. Sam noticed me admiring one of a woman sitting, hands folded. "We were married fifty-three years. She was Native American and deaf-mute. We met because I could speak her Native sign language."

He invited us to use his kitchen. Following my gaze to the onions and potatoes sprouting on his floor, he smiled. "My garden."

His pantry shelves were nearly empty. "I'm fifty miles from a grocery store," he explained. "I shop once a month. If the cost of gas keeps rising, it'll be once a year." From the look of his emaciated frame, I guessed he was living on tobacco. We made our oatmeal and tried to get him to join us. He refused.

In the morning, we returned to his smoke-filled home to warm up. Sam saw I was shivering and patted the seat next to him, instructing, "Put your feet next to the heater." His furry little dog placed himself on Sam's feet. Canine slippers.

We talked about the border war at his doorstep. Sam said, "If I hire someone illegal to weed my yard, I get a ten-thousand-dollar fine, but the farmer who hires forty won't be touched. Those workers pay into Social Security, workers' comp, without receiving the benefits. They keep this country afloat."

The TV filled a lull in our conversation. Donald Trump was endorsing Mitt Romney for president. "I support Romney," Sam asserted. "We need a hard head, not a soft soap." He grimaced at the wagging orange fop. "But what I've seen of him, there's nothing I like."

When the newscaster said that Israel might attack Iran, Sam shook his head. "Two people, two religions." He paused. "I loved the Iranians."

My face betrayed me.

"Surprised you, huh?" Sam said. "As an ironworker, I had jobs all over the world: Caribbean sugar plantations, Middle East oil rigs. In Tehran, we used to sit on the scaffold, watch the traffic and bet on when the next accident was going to happen."

Sam had traveled the world. Now the world came to him. Showing me a photo of young guests who stayed with him when they unicycled from Canada to Mexico, Sam gave me a cigarette-wobble grin.

"You think *you're* something."

FIVE MILES WEST OF Hachita, a thousand sandhill cranes hovered above a rancher's irrigated hayfield.

AT THE PANTHER TRACKS Café in Animas, New Mexico, a Latina Border Patrol officer came in for a sandwich to go. A man with a plate of chicken-fried steak asked her, "How's business?"

"Been pretty slow," she said. "But it's picking up in Arizona. The asparagus harvest has begun."

36

KING COPPER

Arizona and Sonora, Mexico

Cattle, cotton, citrus, copper. Arizona's southern neighbor provides workers to sustain these industries.[62]

The first change was color: red and purple hues on leaves and rocks, tiny yellow flowers, green shoots. The knee-high spiky willow bushes of the Chihuahua Desert became six-foot Sonora trees. Even rock formations seemed to grow, as if preparing for the Grand Canyon. Riding south to Douglas, Arizona, a coyote scampered across the flowering plain. We had a tailwind and some long gradual descents. Even the ups were a blast. After weeks of brown and beige, the rainbow of hues at the ridgetop fed our souls.

WE ENTERED THE GADSDEN Hotel through a side door. The dark hallway emptied into a cavernous lobby with a vaulted ceiling. To the left, a white marble staircase led to a Tiffany-stained-glass mural depicting the Sonoran Desert. The mural spoke of past opulence. The budget price reflected the hotel's current state. The 1920s-style staff-operated elevator gave our bikes a

62 Excerpt from the February 8, 2012 issue of *Territorial News*.

high-class ride, and the guest quarters still charmed, but a tiny stream of cold water dripped out of the marble-tiled shower. The place was almost empty. Hotel staff moved the one working TV into our room.[63]

At the turn of the twentieth century when the Gadsden was at its zenith, it was a favorite of oil tycoons and copper bosses. Copper was king here. Phelps Dodge Copper created Douglas and the Mexican town of Agua Prieta to service their mines and smelters on both sides of the border. There were no fences, barbed wire, or checkpoints then. The company would leave piles of industrial waste lying across the borderline.

The Mexican Revolution was, in part, a revolt against this blatant US corporate imperialism. The hotel claims that Pancho Villa rode his horse into the Gadsden lobby and up its marble staircase, denting the seventh step. Maybe. We do know that Mexican anarchist Ricardo Flores Magón delivered his revolutionary manifesto in Douglas in 1906, demanding an end to foreign control of Mexican subsoil resources. In 1920, Mexican revolutionaries met on the other side of the border to sign the Plan de Agua Prieta, ousting President Carranza for failing to protect Mexico's resources from US companies.

Phelps Dodge maintained its border copper conglomerate until 1975, when they closed the Bisbee mine. Today Douglas and Agua Prieta depend on cross-border commerce to keep afloat. Douglas is a Border Patrol town, and Agua Prieta is home to border factories and a power plant.

We crossed into Agua Prieta on foot. A few steps into Sonora, Mexico, was a small hut where deportees—people dumped by US Border Patrol buses—lined up to receive water, food, and advice. Returning to the US, we stood in line behind Douglas restaurant workers armed with giant bags of tortillas and oranges. Douglas appeared quieter, richer, and more spacious after an afternoon in Agua Prieta. We walked back to the hotel through downtown,

63 The Gadsden has new owners and has since been restored.

passing the general store, Mejor Precio, sporting Valentine-themed displays of plastic flowers, meant to attract Mexican customers. It was empty.

The new Walmart, where we stopped to use the bathroom on our way out of town, was busy with customers from both sides of the border. I laid my helmet on the bathroom sink, and an elderly white woman asked where I was going. "I grew up in Douglas," she said. "We left after the smelter closed. Just here to shop. The Mexicans have taken over. They saved this town."

TWENTY-THREE VERTICAL MILES FROM Douglas is the former center of the Phelps Dodge conglomerate: Bisbee, Arizona. Our climb to Bisbee was steep, winding, and lacked a shoulder most of the way. Purple-red copper cliffs rose in steps to the sky on either side of the road. As we entered town, the central mine glowed orange, gold, and gray in front of us.

It was clear as we entered that Bisbee was capitalizing on the charm of verticality and curves, attracting tourists with its natural and human-made beauty. Small shops sold Apache, Navajo, and Mexican artistry for immense markups to retired hippies and snowbirds who filled overpriced hotels. Judging from the prevailing smell of pot, this was a drug-enforcement-free zone. Prescribed marijuana was legal in Arizona, but use here appeared to be more than medicinal. We were ten miles from Mexico, yet we saw no Border Patrol vans marring the hip feel. Bumper stickers took sides on the border war. None of them read *How many must die so you can get high?*

Seeing the road rising at the town's egress as we walked the steep block to our motel, we decided to stay two nights, immobilized by the climb we faced leaving town. We spent the day off at the Bisbee Smithsonian Museum, learning about the copper workers' uprising and deportation of 1917. Showing more than typical interest, we got an audience with the curator of the exhibit, Annie Larkin, an impressive young PhD.

"When Phelps Dodge heard the Industrial Workers of the World were planning a strike," Larkin explained, "they organized a local militia to deport two thousand US miners to a desert military outpost in Columbus, New Mexico."[64]

Larkin's goal was to understand what moved neighbors to arrest and deport neighbors. "It was six months after the Zimmerman Telegram. We had just entered World War I. The company told their vigilante recruits the Wobblies were an imminent terrorist threat, part of a German-Mexican cabal intent on giving the Southwest back to Mexico."

"My dad was not happy with my conclusions," Annie added. "He grew up hearing that the Wobblies posed a danger to Bisbee and America and that it was the duty of patriotic citizens to remove them. My adviser, on the other hand, accused me of writing the 'Phelps Dodge perspective.' But the Wobblies are quite happy with my exhibit."

"Your exhibit is essential," I said. "It shows that deportations, then and now, are about labor control, not security."

Larkin wasn't the only local grappling with the 1917 legacy. Townspeople had discussed erecting a monument but were divided over who to memorialize. Two men died: Orson McRae, a deputy sheriff, and Jim Brew, a Wobbly organizer. Brew killed McRae when he and other vigilantes were forcing their way into his home. In retaliation, the vigilantes killed Brew. McRae had a large stone in the Evergreen Cemetery in Bisbee. Brew had a simple grave marker until 2006, when someone quietly erected a memorial stone that read, "James H. Brew refused to work under conditions of 'involuntary servitude' as defined in the 13th Amendment to the Constitution. Brew's death and the 'deportation' are symbolic of our continuing struggle for freedom and equality."[65]

In 1917, President Wilson's Federal Labor Commission ruled it was unconstitutional to deport US workers into the desert because you didn't like

64 Now Pancho Villa State Park.

65 Excerpted. Read the full dedication from a labor perspective at weneverforget.org-we-never-forget-fw-james-h-brew

their politics. But then the case went to the Supreme Court, who ruled that since the federal government hadn't contained dangerous radicals, locals had no choice but to take the law into their own hands. I saw an anti-immigrant bumper sticker in Bisbee that mimicked the century-old Supreme Court decision to mock the Constitution:

Arizona: Doing the job the feds won't do.

BISBEE SEEMED SETTLED INTO its tourist identity, but Freeport-McMoRan—which merged with Phelps Dodge in 2007—was allegedly considering reopening the mine. First, they had to deal with arsenic, copper, lead, and manganese polluting gardens and school playgrounds. "The copper company's giving us new soil and building us designer patios," a woman staffing the museum bookstore told us. She felt the company was overdoing it.

"Are Douglas residents being compensated?" I asked. High lead levels in Douglas and Agua Prieta had spiked learning disabilities. Both towns demanded an investigation in the 1980s, to no avail.

"No." The bookstore worker seemed discomfited. "They haven't asked for it. They didn't have the mine there, just the smelter."

37

TRAILING JUDY BLUME IN TUCSON

Arizona

Censorship grows out of fear . . .
—Judy Blume[66]

We climbed and dropped two thousand feet before reaching downtown Tucson, at rush hour. The annual Gem Show was on. Thousands of distracted rock lovers swerved through Tucson's intersections. As we made our way up the north side of the valley, we felt lucky to be alive. Our destination was a gated community covering a small mountain. At the end of a long day, it felt as though it curved upward forever. Stopping to catch my breath, I admired a saguaro cactus, rooted horizontally in a secluded yard, hiding an understated mansion.

We stayed with a young family. They were welcoming to us and loving to each other, but we picked up on an inexplicable sadness. David tried, unsuccessfully, to connect with their middle-schooler. We had better luck with their third-grader, Joey, who showed us his Gem Show treasures.

After dinner, their mother, Nancy, handed me a coin-sized clay disk. "I want you to carry this with you," she said. "My friend started making these tokens for personal healing when she lost her two-year-old son, Ben. When

66 Judy Blume talks about censorship. https://judyblume.com/judy-blume-on-censorship/

a gunman shot Congresswoman Giffords, killing six constituents, including a young girl, Ben's Bells became a way for Tucson to show our hearts were broken. It became important to me personally after we lost our fourteen-year-old son, Noah."

"What was Noah like?" I asked, grasping for something helpful to say.

"He read books voraciously," Nancy replied. "Shortly before he died, he joined an online group, BookCrossing. You register your books, then release them to the world. I am slowly continuing what he started—releasing his books."

"What was Noah's favorite?"

Nancy did not hesitate. "*Double Fudge* by Judy Blume."

I smiled. "My twenty-one-year-old prefers *Fudge-a-Mania*."

At Nancy's urging, we visited the Beyond Bread café next to the Safeway, where Congresswoman Giffords was shot. A man finishing a cinnamon roll moved his coffee cup to a closer seat. "They just removed the teddy bears and the six wooden crosses," he told us. He pointed at a political lawn sign at the edge of the parking lot. "That's the Republican running for Giffords's seat. He stuck it right on the spot where she used to put her Congress on Your Corner sign, inviting constituents to gather."

I HAD BEEN TO Tucson once before. In May 2010, Arizona Governor Brewer signed House Bill 2281, outlawing ethnic studies in public schools. The ban targeted one Tucson high school Mexican American studies program transforming young lives and increasing graduation and college enrollment. That was the same week I was laid off. Sitting in my pajamas, I contacted a handful of professors asking what they thought of a national ethnic studies week campaign with the tagline "Ethnic Studies: You Ban It, We Expand It."

Eventually, two hundred educators signed on. As the volunteer organizer of the November 2010 Ethnic Studies Week campaign, I came to Tucson that July to meet educators and students involved in the banned program.

In 2012, the struggle continued. At the Tucson Revolutionary Grounds bookstore, where we spent an hour eating zucchini bread, they had a shelf latticed with CAUTION tape, filled with books banned from the Tucson high school Mexican American studies classroom. They included volumes by Isabel Allende, Gloria Anzaldúa, James Baldwin, Sandra Cisneros, bell hooks, Jonathan Kozol, Elizabeth Martínez, Paulo Freire, Cesar Chavez, and William Shakespeare.

LEAVING TUCSON, WE STAYED the night in the Catalina Foothills with Syrell Leahy, the mystery writer. I asked her how she got her first novel, *A Book of Ruth*, published.

"I shared a book agent with Judy Blume," she began.

38

BEYOND HOPE

Arizona

People from Owatonna, Minnesota, bring their Midwestern grass. Before you know it, there's mosquitoes in the desert.
—Debra from Sierra Vista

A saguaro can weigh sixteen thousand pounds, grow sixty-five feet tall, and live two hundred years. For forty-two miles, on Highway 79 beginning in Oracle Junction, it was us and the giants.

AFTER DINNER IN FLORENCE, Arizona, David turned pale and threw up. We spent Valentine's Day at the Blue Mist Motel, across from a brown field enclosed in barbed wire. It seemed wholly unromantic, until I realized Blue Mist was a house of devotion—a motel for visitors of incarcerated loved ones.

By the next afternoon, David had enough energy for a slow walk. We found ourselves at the Pinal County Historical Museum, where prisons were the tourist draw.

"How many prisons are there in Florence?" I asked the docent.

She counted on her fingers. "Federal, state, county, private, drunk driving, juvenile, and immigration. All the male prisoners from Hawaii are here."

"I guess family visits are not a priority."

She moved on to greet another visitor.

There were 130 inmates currently on death row in Florence. We were encouraged to go online and read graphic descriptions of their crimes. Death row accoutrements—nooses, electric chairs, straps, and a double chair used to execute two brothers at once—were on display. Mug shots and "last supper" requests filled one wall. There were lots of eggs. "Executions must take place in the morning," David said. One fellow requested a Rolaids.

AT THE FLORENCE FUDGE Shop & Café, we listened to a man lament to the counter staff about his day. He was a prison contractor who "had some tools stolen—a few, not a big deal. The guards caught the guy, tied him to a tree, and left him there. He died. Now I have to take time off work to testify."

AFTER A DAY OF rest, David managed ten miles to Coolidge, Arizona, home of the Casa Grande Ruins, where the Hohokam—descendants of O'odham people currently living in the region—had farmed until 1450, building canals to water their fields and growing drought-resistant corn and beans.

In the morning, we reviewed directions to Ahwatukee, a southern suburb of Phoenix. My phone suggested we leave truck-filled Route 87 for a side road, a mile shorter. We figured we needed something mellow, as David was still recovering.

After four miles, the pavement disappeared. David, declaring himself all better, lurched ahead. "It's been a long time since we've had an adventure road!" he yelled.

I rechecked my phone. We'd connect with Highway 87 in ten miles. David beckoned, shouting, "It's hard packed!"

The desert wonderland was seductive. We stopped often to take photos. Two miles in, it narrowed and softened, forcing us off the bikes.

Four miles and another hour later, walking rocky undulations and powdery sand, we saw a white jeep in the distance. At the top of each twenty-foot undulation, we glimpsed it, getting closer. Border Patrol? The border was two hundred miles away.

As we approached, a uniformed man was standing by the jeep, waiting for us.

"Told my wife, 'You're not going to believe this. Two people, walking bicycles across the desert!'"

Ranger Dixon informed us that we were trespassing on the Gila River Indian Community, home of the Akimel O'odham (Pima) and Pee-Posh (Maricopa) peoples.

"Since you are on this great adventure, I'll let you go."

Dixon's job usually consisted of accosting rustlers who borrowed other people's free-ranging cows and horses. We exchanged cards. He grinned and said:

"I'll drive through later, see if the vultures have picked your bones yet."

The reservation land was parched. In the 1870s, European immigrants siphoned the Gila River upstream to irrigate their farms, sapping water from Indigenous fields of corn, beans, and squash. Initially, the Coolidge Dam, built in 1934, replenished water for the Gila River Indian Community, until farmers and cities used it to divert the water again. Deprived of subsistence farms, the Indigenous people depended on government-processed food, leading to a diabetes epidemic. The community sued; in 2004, they won the largest water settlement in US history, a plan to divert the Colorado River through underground aqueducts back to the reservation.

(In 2012 we could see no results, but returning to the Gila River Community in January 2015, we saw newly planted olive and orange orchards; fields of cotton and alfalfa; a new casino, hotel, and industrial park; and a community building filled with workout machines, art, and meeting spaces. Amazing what a little water can do.)

Throats dry as the desert, we quenched our thirst at the McDonald's on the corner of Highway 87 and East Riggs Road, just outside of the reservation.

Turning west from there, we entered a Phoenix suburb: housing units were decorated with human-made waterfalls, canals and ponds, and lawns of fluorescent green grass.

VY—FAMILY OF FAMILY—WAS NINETY-THREE. Every morning before dawn, she climbed a small rocky mountain outside her Ahwatukee, Arizona, apartment. She'd check the newspaper to see when the sun was rising, leaving ten minutes beforehand. Pausing halfway to watch birds do a swooping dance, she'd wonder, *Who decides the pattern they make?*

Vy led us on her daily meditation. As she walked, she kept her eyes on the ground, picking shards of glass and paper and putting them in a plastic bag. We reached the top just as the sun peeked over the horizon. Heading down the backside, another group of birds lined up on the telephone wire, waiting for Vy to pass by.

"When I go for a long drive, I look for a hill to climb," Vy told us. "My legs need it. I also need the sky."

IN AGUILA, ARIZONA, I had my version of David's stomach ailment. Had I been well, we would have spent one night at the Burro Jim Motel, eaten at the gun-toting Coyote Café, and figured Aguila was an Anglo cowboy town. But we spent two days, walking dirt roads in the back of the motel, followed by skinny dogs, past storefront churches and tiny domicile cafés, discovering that Aguila was also a Latino town. The major employer in Aguila was

Martori Farms, an agribusiness notorious for exploiting prison and child labor. Martori supplied Walmart with most of its cantaloupes.[67]

At a dusty street corner, a boy of twelve held out two cartoon drawings. "Which do you like best?" he asked David. One looked like a tracing, the other original. David chose the latter. The boy beamed. "I'm going to be an artist!" Toward evening, the boy found us again, standing by a house dressed in colored lights, emitting music and laughter. We began our ride to Hope, Arizona, early the next morning as women set out clothing, toys, and food stalls for the weekly Aguila Swap.

The RV Park in Hope had a Marlboro billboard where others might put a welcome sign. Instead of a cigarette, the cowboy held a revolver. The caption read, *Gun control means holding the gun with both hands.* The Park wasn't pleasant, but the tenants were friendly and the location pretty.

As David heated oats in the park microwave, we regretted not purchasing food at the Aguila Swap, but retirees playing cards offered us Rice Krispie Treats, adding another cereal to our grain diet. The early spring air, and the desert, beginning to flower, were enticing. We still had energy after our thirty-mile ride. Thinking of Vy, we found a hill to climb. In the distance, framed by the burning blossoms of an ocotillo shrub, we could see Route 60, our road to California. From our perch, it was a tiny seam slicing a distant hill, decorated with happy toy vehicles.

Riding that road was not child's play. It took us over a mountain on an interstate filled with fumes, trash, and recreational vehicles not expecting to encounter anything going slower than them. Like us, all the RVs stopped at the Mountain Quail Café in Quartzsite, which resembled a Minnesota Lutheran church basement. I considered moving in, washing dishes, and living on omelets. The last thing I wanted to do was rejoin my RV-hauling diner-mates on the road, buzzed as they were on steak and eggs and lemon meringue pie.

67 Human Rights Watch, *Fingers to the Bone: United States Failure to Protect Child Farmworkers* (New York: Human Rights Watch, 2000).

Our day ended with a sand embankment. We pushed loaded bikes up the steep incline, onto the pedestrian bridge, across the Colorado River, into California.

39

LOVE WITHOUT BORDERS

California

In Blythe, California, we waited at a nearby café for the one-room Black History Museum with stunning outdoor murals to open. At 10:00 a.m., we saw a white man unlock the door. We walked in. The room was empty, the man on his knees, fixing electrical wires.

"Just bought the place," he said. "It's gonna be my office."

THE GOLDEN ALGODONES DUNES were a new and breathtaking sight, but a rutted road and a stream of white buses filled with day workers tempered our enthusiasm. As it got dark, the white buses multiplied and drove more erratically. We walked the last three miles into Calexico, California, when we could no longer see the ruts.

Calexico's cultural arts center was showing a free play performed by a transnational Mexican and US troupe: *What Is Love* was a comedy with a transformative moral—love is real; the borders we erect, artificial. Outside the arts center, a live drama played out on the streets of Calexico. Drug dealers and buyers exchanged goods from cars as they did in South Minneapolis. Only here, law enforcement sat in plain sight, ignoring illicit commerce, focused on cross-border labor control.

Border control in Calexico/Mexicali was a one-way enterprise. At 4:30 p.m. college students and retirees with license plates from California, Nevada, and Arizona lined up on Imperial Avenue. David asked the hotel clerk what was going on.

"It's Friday night. They're waiting to hit the bars in Mexicali."

Leaving Calexico, we passed farmworkers picking broccoli in withering heat. Some farms had shade canopies. Others did not.

This was the Colorado Desert. It felt more desolate, more uninhabitable than the 1,500 miles of Chihuahua and Sonora Deserts we'd already crossed. A sign seemed to agree with me.

No Cross-Country Travel: Limited Use Area.

I got off my bike and sat in the sand. "Limited use does not include me."

"It's three miles," David coaxed. "Like a ride around Lake Nokomis in Minneapolis. We can *always* do three miles."

"You can't fool me with that shit today!"

David helped me to my feet, but I wouldn't get back on the bike. We inched on foot through merciless sun, endless dust, devil wind.

LIFE LOOKED DIFFERENT SITTING in the air-conditioned café in Ocotillo, eating icy blueberry smoothies with real frozen fruit, followed by double scoops of frozen chocolate ice cream. The next day, we'd climb a mountain—4,500 feet, half of it on the interstate—but I wasn't worried. It would be Sunday—less traffic. We could take a whole day to descend. We'd be in San Diego by Monday night.

The brain is a funny muscle.

IT WAS HOT ON the mountain. RVs careened. When we turned a corner, we could see a dozen switchbacks snaking, Escher-like. Well-meaning people had warned us about scorpions, mountain lions, and lack of water. We swerved around a lion, eyes open, laying on the shoulder, innards out. There was plenty of water, a barrel every half mile to rescue overheated vehicles in distress. Stenciled on each barrel: *Not for Drinking*.

At the top of the mountain, dark clouds moved in. We were seven miles from the Mexican border, and snow was in the forecast. They closed the road. The blizzard took twenty-four hours to come, forcing us to stay in Boulevard—population 400—for an unwelcome three nights. The town's RV park owner had died, so they were "taking no tenters." We stayed at the overpriced Lux Inn next to a Border Patrol station. The debris of failed Boulevard businesses filled the motel yard. The TV didn't work, and neither did the Wi-Fi, but border patrol vans put on a show, riding past our window at all hours.

The bright spot of our stay in Boulevard was the snow, and watching informal mutual aid in action. At the Manzanita Diner, a jobless man and an elderly woman worked it out: "I'll fix your toilet, you make me a pie."

HIGHWAY 94, OUT OF Boulevard, skirted the US/Mexico border. It looked friendlier on the map than the freeway route recommended by Adventure Cycling. It wasn't. With narrow switchbacks, blind curves, and truck traffic, 94 was no place for a bicycle. At the Barrett Junction Café halfway down the mountain, we ordered a second salad, more cornbread, a piece of apple pie, trying to make friends, looking for a ride. Everyone was friendly. Everyone had a pickup. Everyone was, "Sorry, not going your way."

The road out of Barrett Junction ascended and descended at angles defying gravity. Spectacular mountain and valley views made it hard to resist a peek. Sightseeing on a tightrope.

AT A SUBURBAN SHOPPING strip outside of San Diego, my high school friend Tari picked us up. She looked taller than I remembered. We hadn't seen each other for thirty-five years. As I hugged her, a memory surfaced: Tari on the floor of our high school library, leading a feminist consciousness-raising group, using words like *clitoris* and *masturbation* without laughter. Now, Tari was part of a six-person nuclear family. Daughters Maia and Priya—adopted by Tari and her partner—also had a parent relationship with two men who were a couple. The girls saw their dads on Saturdays and vacations. Wednesdays, the entire family ate together.

It was Wednesday. A kitchen counter laden with fresh greens, salmon, mangos, wines carefully paired, fresh flowers, everything bathed in yellow light—that's how I remember the home of dads Gregg and Ishmael. Priya did homework with Ishmael. Maia flitted from person to person until Tari got her to practice her piano.

Listening and praising the young musician, I took in this new world. We had crossed a border. No wall or barbed wire, watchtowers, or machine guns—this border divided desert and sea, hinterland and coast, rural and urban. I did not want to forget desert friends, apparitions with messages, the singular beauty of burr, rock, and sand. But I was done with isolation, shadeless days, bone-chilling nights, low-intensity border warfare, and cactus-killing drought. Now, in this new land of floral opulence, a family made of love gathered us in their arms. I relaxed.

Later, sitting at Tari's dining room table, below a framed California

Domestic Partner license and a mash of child milestone pics, I asked my friend how she landed in San Diego.

"I came to escape a Wisconsin winter," she said. "Stayed two years. No seasons here, you know? It's hard to keep track of time." She laughed. "When I became a nurse practitioner and HIV researcher, I came back here to practice. That was twelve years ago."

Tari's partner, Sarah, interjected proudly, "She just got a million-dollar NIH grant to take her AIDS work to Peru."

Perhaps the AIDS conversation got too easy in the US, I thought. Tari was still that bold young feminist, holding forth on the schoolroom floor, making people talk about what made them uncomfortable, telling them what they needed to know.

Exhaustion hit as I melted onto Tari's pullout couch. Lost in this haven of gold, red, green, and blue, knots released. Maybe it was the Buddhas eyeing me from all corners. Or something more earthly: feeling the human love.

OREGON
CALIFORNIA
California
(40-43)
○-41-○ Chapters
☆ Cities
San Francisco
43
42
41
Los Angeles
40
San Diego
Colorado River

40

TSUNAMI

California

In Case of Tsunami, Head Away from the Coast.
—California highway sign.

Our southern California bike map took us through the Camp Pendleton Marine Corps Base. It was peaceful compared to the beach towns on State Road 1—like a lovely state park if you ignored road signs—*Caution: Troop Movement* and *Tank Crossing*. I stopped for water in front of a billboard with three stony-faced Marines and the words, *D-stress. Fight the Inner Battle.*

Back on the Pacific Coast Highway, cute shops sold endless summer. Mothers with strollers jogged the street, followed by a pert coach shouting, "Good job, ladies! Pick up the pace." I grew anxious, agitated. Stopping at an outdoor café, I wrote to make sense of an inexplicable wave of desolation.

When did I start to identify with the trauma of veterans? I think it was listening to Jerry Rau, in Dinkytown, sing folk music for the dimes of passersby. There was an intensity to his performance that I recognized; a man twice my age, playing to stay alive. I didn't find out until five years later when I heard him speak against US intervention in El Salvador that Jerry was a veteran. It was the 1980s, and Vietnam vets were dying in public, homeless, drinking, killing themselves slowly or quickly. Jerry was in the struggle. I recognized the vigilance. My affinity with him seemed ridiculous. I shared it with no one.

I was diagnosed with PTSD at age forty. I resisted the label. I did not reenter the traumatizing event often. Instead, I would feel the emotions associated with it, unattached to conscious memory. Eventually, I agreed to try EMDR therapy, a method effective with some veterans, but the historian in me thwarted the process. The way I understood it, the idea was to retell the trauma, changing my interpretation of the outcome. Though I called myself a rape *survivor,* I rejected a revision that gave me more power than I had. I had survived. I could have died. Some people do die.[68]

Early March, when melting ice forms deep puddles on sidewalks in Minneapolis, was the worst time of year for these seemingly irrational emotional outbursts. It was early March now, but here in southern California, intoxicating flowers in outrageous colors provided no temporal signs it was early spring. "No seasons in San Diego," Tari had said. Was the subconscious keeping track?

I had hoped the bicycle trip would lead to a cure for everything dysfunctional about me. Now, it seemed dubious that I would find an answer to my mental conditions on the side of the road like David found hats or Santa stockings. Daily exhaustion wouldn't lead to permanent "D-stress." No mountain, no desert would be tough enough to overcome "the inner battle." No number of miles would be enough to cure me.

That night we shared a Bike & Hike site with a man who appeared homeless. He invited us to join him with a silent nod and point. After the tent was up, as we walked the beach, I cried in a manner incompatible with this semitropical paradise by the sea.

The world looked different in the morning. On the top of a ridge, a toy village glistened in the sun. Above it, jagged green mountains dimmed with distance. Beyond the mountains were white sands and blue sea. Yesterday, I had not seen the beauty. I took long, slow gulps of air.

---

68 In 2021, reading B. A. Van der Kolk's *The Body Keeps the Score: Brain, Mind, and Body in the Healing of Trauma* (Viking, 2014), I realized my EMDR practitioner did not correctly administer the therapy, and I made it a goal to try it again.

41

DUELING MISSIONS

California

"A California schoolchild's first interaction with history begins with the missions . . . how Father Serra and the priests brought civilization to the groveling, lizard and acorn-eating Indians . . ."
—Douglas Monroy[69]

We fluctuated between blissful bikeways and terrible traffic. When the Laguna Beach Festival turned the road into a parking lot, we took refuge at an oceanside park where several people held peace signs. A petite woman in a military jacket with a POW-MIA patch extended her hand to me, her words a salute.

"Lee, Vietnam vet."

"She is also Iroquois," boasted a man in a Marine Corps jacket.

"My husband," Lee explained. "We've been coming here Saturdays for nine years. This year, we call ourselves Occupy Laguna."

I asked Lee how a soldier became a peace activist.

"I enlisted in 1960. Thought China was a grave threat. If the men had to go, I should too." She smiled ruefully. "And sure, I wanted to leave my small town and see the world. I got stationed at an air force base in Japan where my job

69 Douglas Monroy, *Thrown Among Strangers: The Making of Mexican Culture in Frontier California* (Berkeley, California: University of California Press, 1993), pxiii.

was to ship people home in pine boxes. Home on leave, I was horrified that nobody knew what was going on, how many soldiers had died, and for what?"

"How did you cope after the war?" I asked.

"I became a psychiatric nurse."

"Healing others to heal yourself."

She nodded, eyeing me sharply. She gestured toward her husband. "Now we're retired. Full-time activists. We have two causes: end war and get money out of politics."

"Let's count votes, not dollars," her husband chimed in.

OUR DESTINATION WAS THE home of my college friend Patti. We'd met in Mulford Sibley's political philosophy course at the University of Minnesota in 1982. She was nearly six feet, statuesque, with black hair and an exotic air. When Patti and I walked across campus, we looked like a feminine Mutt and Jeff. After class, we'd head to The Valley, a restaurant where I once waitressed that had an all-you-can-eat salad bar and all-you-can-drink coffee. We'd stay long enough to make two meals out of it, bouncing ideas off each other, glad to find someone else whose brain refused to stay in one place. In the years since, Patti had moved to Irvine, California, married Argyris, had two daughters, become a linguistics professor, and joined the Greek Orthodox Church.

Patti took us to the Mission San Juan Capistrano. We joined visitors strolling between perfectly restored buildings, recreated workshops, and a garden in full bloom. A young man meditated in an alcove. A bride smiled at the camera. A model posed.

David and Patti wandered while I sat on a bench against an eighteenth-century wall facing the sun, waiting for a phone call. *How sanguine this historic site is!* I thought. In California, fourth graders learn their first lessons in historical research here. Some teachers were joining Indigenous leaders to change the depiction taught to children. The missions were not akin to technical colleges and Christian retreats. Instead, they were more like concentration camps and plantations, stealing Indigenous labor to build an overseas empire.

I wondered if California's embrace of the Spanish missions made it easier to gain public acceptance for other oppressive institutions, like reservations, Indian boarding schools, Japanese internment camps, migrant-exploitative factory farms, and military bases. Camp Pendleton Marine Corps Base had been a mission. Before that, it was the territory of Indigenous people. *Give the land back. That's how you break the cycle of exploitation . . .*

Jose Lara called. The Los Angeles educator and I were going to meet, but he was too busy protesting proposed preschool education cuts. I asked him why early childhood programs were so important to him.

"I can tell which of my teenage students learned their colors, their numbers, how to socialize and play fair when they were four," he answered. "Besides, the Black Power and Chicano movements in LA demanded these preschool programs. Closing them throws away our civil rights legacy."

Jose was hopeful. "There's a resurgence of the historic movements of the seventies. Many participants in our campaign are undocumented parents. We chant in Spanish and English. The Occupy movement has given us a new language. We fight the one percent's influence over public education."

LEAVING THE MISSION, PATTI treated us to java prepared by baristas in lab coats—nothing like the rotgut at The Valley that sparked our youthful jam sessions. Still, we played off each other's brains, as we had in college. "California thinks of itself as trendy," I ranted, pausing to take a sip of the exquisite brew. "But dismantling preschool? And sanitizing the missions? That just perpetuates historical trauma." I licked the last foam from my latte.

FROM IRVINE, WE HAD a short, sweet ride on a canyon bike path through a salt marsh to the sea, to sleep in a waterbed on Captain Jack's houseboat in Long Beach. Jack served delicate salmon, new asparagus, and stories of scientific magic. He sold machine tools to build artificial body parts. A client had given him a piece of coral. The tools Jack sold shaped the rock into a ball that fit into an eye socket. The body, in its infinite wisdom, sensed the eyeball and grew a white film in which a pupil could be placed—a marriage of natural healing and high-tech engineering.

I asked Jack why he lived on a boat.

"I used to have a wife. We divorced. I got the boat."

Jack's home was small, but he had the biggest front yard in the world.

HOW DECEIVING THE CALIFORNIA coastal bike path was! All those sunbathers, and the majesty of the ocean—none of the visual marks of struggle accompanying a Texas headwind, yet resistance was as fierce as we headed north. We inched past Marine World to the Los Angeles River path, across the western edge of the city, and back to the coast, through Playa del Rey, Santa Monica, Pacific Palisades, Malibu. We passed people living on the beach, some in five-million-dollar bungalows, others with sleeping bags and shopping carts.

As we put up the tent at Leo Carrillo State Park, I shivered. A cold shower did not help. I awoke with a scratchy throat, runny nose. At home, I would have called in sick. But dawn came, and we pedaled, eleven miles before the wind rose.

In Oxnard, we squashed grapefruit-size strawberries—too big for pint containers—littering the road. Farmworkers, finishing their shift, headed to their cars. A day later they would begin a work stoppage protesting unclean bathrooms, "drinking water that tastes like the ocean," and harassment.

NINA INVITED US TO stay in Goleta. I hesitated, not wanting to get her sick, but she insisted. A provider of curative touch to people battling cancer, she sensed I needed care. Her husband, Charlie, was also a caretaker—director of the nations' first hospice. He had also been a colonel in the US Army, Korea through Vietnam. I asked his opinion of current military conflicts. He was succinct.

"We do not need any more wars."

The couple had met in the demilitarized zone in Korea. "You've seen *M*A*S*H?*" Nina asked. "That was us. My job was 'recreational health.' I performed skits for the troops."

"I was lucky," Charlie interrupted. "Out of twelve thousand soldiers, she picked me."

A night with these two healers revived my spirits. The forty-six miles from Goleta to Lompoc were the first in California I enjoyed. Perhaps I was figuring out Zen and the art of Pacific coast headwinds?[70] Or maybe it was leaving the touristy coast. We had been on the road too long to enjoy being treated as vacationers. When always moving, you desire to feel at home, wherever you are.

We took a tunnel under the mountain and turned on to State Road 1 for a three-mile climb, followed by eighteen miles of gentle descent against a headwind. Marveling at the phenomenon of pedaling downhill and not going over ten miles per hour, David mused: "Given a three percent downgrade with a

70 Apologies to Robert M. Pirsig, author of *Zen and the Art of Motorcycle Maintenance.*

forty-mile-per-hour headwind, what's the correct gear ratio?" We never figured it out.

By the time we reached Lompoc, however, we both felt ill. We walked to Herb Home Thai, hoping their chili, lime, and ginger concoctions would cure us. Outside the restaurant, an inebriated man with a fresh face wanted to know our story. "Thought you were homeless," he slurred. "Lots of 'em with bikes here."

We'd noticed.

He was in town for prison guard training. "Lompoc has the best dive bars in the country," he said. "You should check 'em out."

We stuck with soup.

Walking slowly across town to our motel, we admired murals that told the town's past. One depicted the Chumash people fishing. Another imagined the utopian vision of Lompoc's first Europeans: an alcohol-free oasis in the Wild West. In a third, a soldier stood in the foreground. Behind him, fields covered with flags illustrated the town's transformation from farm to military economy. Vandenberg Air Force Base and a federal prison were the town's primary employers.[71]

In the middle of the night, we awoke to the sound of sirens. In the breakfast room, the local broadcaster revealed the night's tragedy: Across the street, at the Embassy Suites, two young men, high as kites, in town for the prison guard training, played with a loaded gun in their hotel room. One friend accidentally killed the other.

WE LEFT LOMPOC EARLY, grateful for a peaceful climb out of the valley. We took the lane, relishing a road to ourselves, until seven speeding police cars forced us back to the edge. When the law enforcement parade ended, it was calm again. It wasn't long before I had to pee and began wishing for less peace

71 Vandenberg Air Force Base changed its name to *Space* Force Base in May of 2021.

and more commerce. I had just let go of my gas station bathroom fantasy and settled for a stand of trees when we alighted the hill. On the edge of a farmer's field sat an outhouse. I wasted no time questioning my unlikely good fortune. It was new and clean inside.

When I emerged, David pointed at a spirited group marching toward us holding signs:

No Nukes! No Drones! Vets for Peace. How's the War Economy Treating You?

Behind them were seven police cars.

At the stone gate of the Vandenberg Air Force Base, a woman in her sixties holding a *Stop ICBMs* sign cornered me, rattling off protest bullet points. "Intercontinental ballistic missiles are tested here," she said. "They land four thousand miles away, leave depleted uranium in the Marshall Islands, and pollute our coast with rocket fuel exhaust. Two weeks ago, Daniel Ellsberg—you know, *Pentagon Papers*—got arrested with us. They constantly change the rules on us. Today they put up an outhouse to keep us from requesting a bathroom."

While we talked, a military policeman approached David. "Bicycles are not permitted at the main gate," he warned. We rode off as a handful of protestors sat on the asphalt, blocking the Vandenberg entrance.

TWICE WE HAD POSTPONED our stay with Candy and Bill, in Santa Maria. Now we tried not to sneeze on these generous strangers.

Candy taught first grade in a Lompoc school that was 90 percent Mexican American. "I teach in English, scold and praise in Spanish," she explained. "I do a bang-up job. By this time of year, my students are all reading." The school district had just issued nine teacher furlough days to balance budgets. "They're hurting everyone equally," Bill noted wryly.

From Santa Maria, we rode fields of light green, sweeps of yellow and magenta ringed by mountains, into Guadalupe, a Mexican American town five miles from the beach, filled with enticing, independent, permanently closed restaurants. On the north side there was a small house with an intriguing sign: *Guadalupe Cultural Arts & Education Center.* The door was open. Seeing no one, we stole into a side room and squinted at a photo labeled "Mexican workers on strike, 1933."

A door squeaked. Two square-shaped men in their sixties stood in the doorway. One wore a Native Vietnam Veteran cap. We exchanged reasons for our presence.

"Never want to miss a historical exhibit," I explained.

"A community meeting to discuss how we can revive Guadalupe," they said.

I nodded sympathetically, mentioning our search for lunch.

"When we were young," the one with the hat said, "Guadalupe's strip was hopping: movie theater, cafés. Now, it's closed by 8:00 p.m."

"We used to have the best restaurants in the county," the other one chimed in. "Now, people go to Santa Maria to shop, eat at McDonald's. We lost two grocery stores. The population has grown, yet we can no longer support local businesses."

"What do people do for a living in Guadalupe?" I asked.

"Farm work. Five hundred trucks ride through our town every day, hauling broccoli, cabbage, bok choy, celery, lettuce, tomatoes, strawberries—and this year, blueberries."

Like Louisiana, I thought. The fruits of Guadalupe's labor pass through town in semis, leaving foreclosed shops and diesel exhaust.

Outside the city limits, broccoli and cabbage split a verdant field. Then strawberries, with human figures, bent in half.

42

HOME, SICK

California

When you are sick, a tent doesn't do it. A hotel can make you sicker and eat your funds. In other people's homes, you feel like a pariah, sniffling on those sheltering you. You don't want to hug people or shake their hand. You feel untouchable. You need a home.

We weren't homeless. We had a home waiting for us in Minnesota and people taking care of us. But some thought we were. In San Luis Obispo, people with stuff like our stuff claimed a corner of each block.

We weren't homeless, but we were sick. I called our host.

"Should we get a hotel? We don't want to make you ill."

"Kids at the preschool expose me to everything," she replied. "Come. Stay a couple nights."

WHILE CONVALESCING IN SAN Luis Obispo, an eddy of factors whirled us in a new direction. Our colds were getting worse. A dangerous storm was brewing north of us. David's parents needed help moving into an assisted living center. My mom was in the hospital again. A friend in San Francisco had a place for us to stay until we got well. California headwinds.

Bill in Santa Maria had given us his copy of *Bicycling the Pacific Coast*. The preface described a young man's disastrous ride north against headwinds. We weren't young. We needed a break.

We decided to take a bus to San Francisco, get well, fly to visit parents, come back to the Bay Area, take a train to Seattle, bicycle back to San Francisco, and drive a friend's car back to Seattle. If you, dear reader, are confused, I know how you feel. We were too. We were loath to interrupt our circle, but reversing course seemed to solve several problems at once. We were trying to take care of ourselves and our parents while heeding the advice of *Bicycling the Pacific Coast*:

Ride with the wind.

43

OAKLAND SPEAKS

California

HOWARD WAS IN THE process of moving from San Francisco to Seattle and had offered us his nearly empty apartment with views of Golden Gate Park. Suddenly recipients of luxury, we took in how sick we were: riding on a fever, pedaling pneumonia. Able to spend days in bed, our bodies told us it was impossible to do otherwise.

After a week, we were well enough to venture out. We wandered on foot, bus, and boat, blending in, attracting no attention. I was overwhelmed by the beauty of San Francisco's public spaces and appalled by its current social engineering. So many people who couldn't afford housing lived in parks, left to urinate on streets, sick, hungry, cold. I tried not to stare at a man sleeping at the base of the Gandhi statue, wondering how we would have fared, spending our ill days on the streets.

IN THE LOBBY OF the de Young Museum in Golden Gate Park, we saw a painting of a white woman eating gumbo, oblivious to images of slavery and poverty surrounding her; a "parody," the placard for the painting said, "of those who sample exotic cultures, avoiding their complex origins." Afterward, we had dinner at a dim sum restaurant on 47th and Balboa, where no one spoke English and forks weren't an option. A slippery slice of bean curd fell into my lap. We ate the spring-green stalks of Chinese broccoli, stuffed eggplant, and shrimp in paper-thin rolls. Without our loaded bikes to attract conversation, we shared not even a pleasantry. Just two people experiencing the exotic.

WE TOOK TWO SEPARATE planes to see our parents. Coming back to San Francisco felt like coming home—not to our serene, borrowed space, but to our bikes and each other. We were not happy about reversing course. We felt like Bike to Alaska, the man in Marfa, Texas, who had put a sail on his bike and ridden backward.

Our train was leaving Oakland at 10:00 p.m. In the early morning, we walked our bicycles past hippies and head shops, down Haight Street, to take the ferry from San Francisco to Oakland. Our friend Ingrid had invited us to visit her third-grade classroom. She met us in the school vegetable garden. As we watered the cucumbers, she told us how school inequities played out in Oakland.

"Rich schools in the hills, poor schools in the flatlands. Franklin Elementary is a flatland school: eight hundred kids, twenty-seven languages. My students relish teaching each other about their differences. Mexican and Vietnamese parents share food and plant knowledge in this garden. But to sustain those intercultural relationships, we need support. We have no art or gym. Our playground's torn up. I have third graders with PTSD, kids separated from parents who came from refugee camps to my classroom. I work one-on-one with the traumatized kids. We make progress on the trauma, but not on reading."

"I vote Ingrid education queen," I said as she opened the school door, beckoning us to follow. "What will you do first?"

"Repeal Prop 13, which froze property taxes in 1978, a big source of school funding. Before it, California was an education beacon, preschool to grad school. Community college used to be nearly free."

In the colorful classroom, I squatted on the tiny chair Ingrid offered, watching parents and kids flock around her. No question: she was already queen to them.

WE SPENT THE REST of the afternoon at Oakland's African American Museum on 14th Street. An exhibit interviewed locals of diverse ages and perspectives. I was struck by an agreement: while racism in Oakland was the constant, decent union jobs made earlier decades the "good old days." The city's Black community flowered during World War I, when people migrated west to work at shipyards and canning factories. The Brotherhood of Sleeping Car Porters had a strong Oakland chapter, and the Black Panthers originated here. When the jobs went, foundations of a healthy society—neighborhood organizations, cultural opportunities—frayed. The Panthers stepped in, offered free breakfasts, health care, security, and pride, while the dominant society criminalized unemployment and hunger.

We needed a bike store close to the Oakland Amtrak that would box our bikes. Bikes 4 Life, a community-based program for adjudicated youth, was two miles from the train in a neighborhood of empty lots, fences, fast food, and Black-owned co-ops. We drank tea at the Revolution Café while kids disassembled our bikes under a wall-size rendition of Oscar Grant, a young Black man killed by police at a transit station in 2009. The Bikes 4 Life staff helped us locate a taxi big enough to transport eight bags, two bike boxes, and two people to the Amtrak station for an overnight train to Seattle.

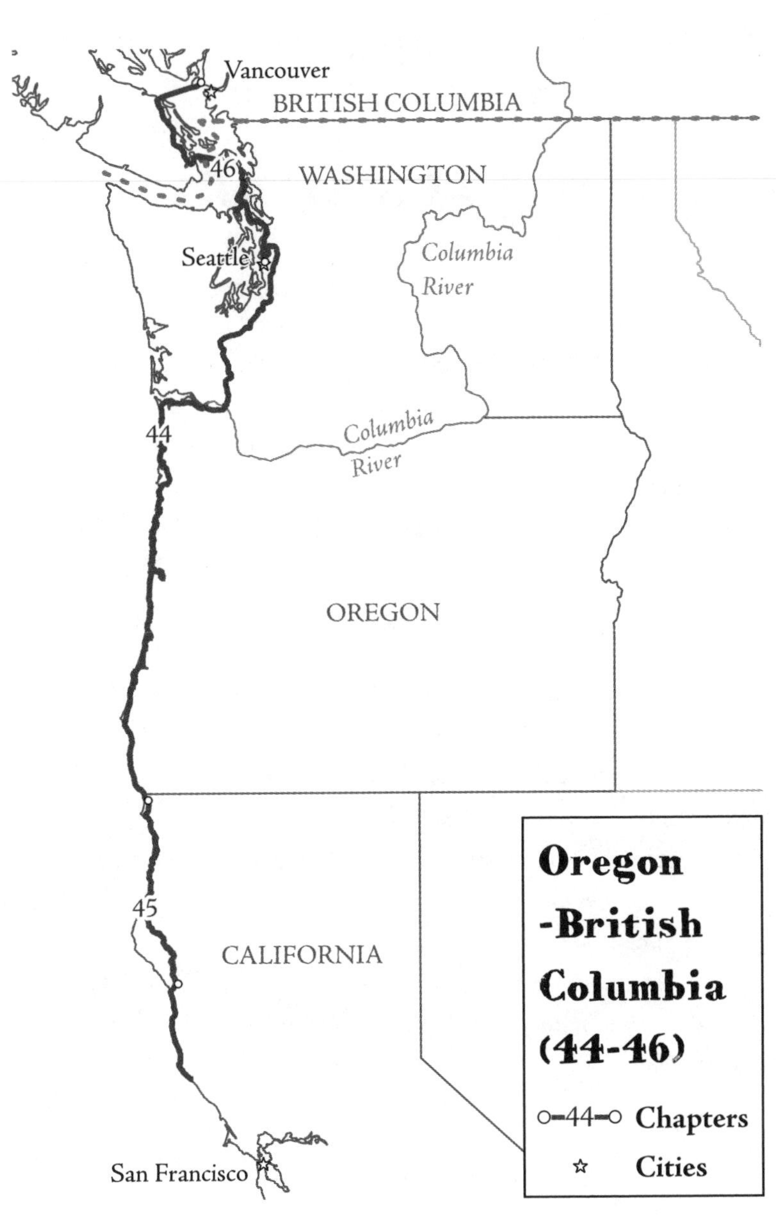
Vancouver
BRITISH COLUMBIA
46
WASHINGTON
Seattle
Columbia River
Columbia River
44
OREGON
45
CALIFORNIA
San Francisco
Oregon -British Columbia (44-46)
44 Chapters
Cities

44

WINTER WINDS

Washington State and Oregon

It's 6,534 miles from Oregon to my home in
Guangzhou. You could have gone to China!
—Waiter, Chinese Restaurant, Waldport, Oregon

Safeway is a store.
—Diane, North Bend, Oregon

It was thirty-nine degrees and blustery as we began our trek back to California on April 1. Seattle's Lake Washington Bike Loop and the Interurban Trail were flat, but a persistent headwind gave us a workout. We laughed at the contradiction. We were going south now.

The day ended with a steep climb to Puyallup. We felt like the tough aunt and uncle, until we watched our young relatives chase two-year-old twins. Nephew Stephen made a veggie pasta with almond sauce. Toddlers made a mess. The dog and the cyclists had a feast. Niece Heather mapped our route to Centralia, Washington, so all we had to do was gasp at the changing faces of Mount Rainier—a day so good, we almost didn't notice the headwinds.

LUSH LANDSCAPES COVERED THE walls of Jean's bedroom in Centralia, Washington. A high school art teacher, she had taken a circuitous route to her career. When her first husband, a Vietnam vet, died of Agent Orange poisoning, art therapy helped her express what she couldn't voice. As her kids got older, she did art projects in their schools. "I got my teaching certificate at fifty," she said, laughing. "I'll be paying student loans into my eighties."

"Centralia is a working-class town," Jean told us. "Parents work lumber, coal, farms, or the outlet mall. With unemployment up and salaries down, I have more homeless kids in my classrooms. I bring food and don't give homework. Too many don't have a place to work. I dumpster-dive for art supplies. We do lots of 'found object' sculptures."

IN CENTRALIA'S CENTRAL SQUARE, competing public art told contradictory accounts of a historic labor battle, similar to the 1917 conflict in Bisbee. Two years after the Arizona deportation, returning veterans in Centralia—primed by timber bosses to see the Industrial Workers of the World as a domestic enemy—made it a campaign to attack labor activists. On Armistice Day 1919, a street battle ensued, and four Legionnaires were killed.

The *Sentinel* monument in the center of the square, erected by the American Legion in 1924, honored the four veterans. A bright mural on the top half of a side building, dated 1999, celebrated the IWW's struggle for labor justice. Fifteen feet behind the Legion monument, sitting low on the ground and hidden by a coffin-shaped war memorial, a small black marble plaque embossed with a hammer and noose was etched with these words:

"Because unions were willing to die for equality . . . the eight-hour day, social security, workers' compensation, occupational health, safety, and job security are now a reality in the lives of their children."[72]

Cynder Villas was fourteen in 1989, when she completed her National History Day project, and eighteen when she realized her wish to have her findings carved in stone in the Centralia square. The American Legion fought the installation of her marker. When she won, they erected the coffin-shaped war memorial to dwarf it.

AT A TEXACO GAS station in Cowlitz County, we parked our bikes next to a truck with *Don't Tread on Me* bumper stickers. To get to the bathroom, I walked a gauntlet of racist anti-Obama decals, submachine guns racked to the ceiling, and a life-size effigy of a bloody Osama Bin Laden. Leaving, I noticed a flyer on the door: *Cowlitz Friends of the NRA Fundraiser: All Dinner Packages Include Chance to Win a Firearm.*

As we approached Longview, the political messages changed. Nearly every lawn and small business window sported *We Support ILWU* placards. The community was expressing its solidarity with the International Longshore and Warehouse Union's recent militant action. A developer had received tax exemptions to build a grain terminal with a proviso to create union jobs. He broke his promise. The union picketed, stopped trains, and stormed grain elevators. Cops arrested labor activists. The union sued the county for police brutality and denying their right to a trial. A sign over the parmesan shakers at Papa Pete's Pizza in Longview expressed the sentiment of the community: *ILWU: fighting for a decent standard of living.*

72 Excerpted from the plaque.

LEAVING THE TINY TOWN of Westport, Oregon, we had a push-downhill headwind. We complained about it to our host in Seaside. "Fishers know this well," he responded. "From Washington to northern California, the winter winds run south to north until May, sometimes June."

We had planned a ride to Bay City, forty-two miles away. After three miles, I had an internal flat. The wind left my sails. I deflated. Insert your own damn wind metaphor. One thought did a hamster wheel: *Our reverse course ensured we'd catch every headwind the Pacific coast had to offer.*

I cycled on empty four more miles, to Cannon Beach, and insisted on a room with a door to a garden patio. We left it open, letting sea breezes blow any which way they wanted, and took an afternoon nap. Afterward we walked the beach and admired Haystack Rock, a favorite breeding spot for migrating puffins. Children were having a Welcome Home rally, with banners and orange-tufted puppets, though the feathered guests of honor had yet to arrive.

THE OREGON COAST CHALLENGES the biker any time of year: steep hills, winding roads, disappearing shoulders, frightening bridges, tunnels. In April, cold rains and fog made pavements slick and visibility low. And those headwinds! We removed and put on clothes, sweated, and froze. In our favor, traffic was low. Inclement weather kept RVs and smart cyclists away.

The natural beauty was a salve. Our route from Cannon Beach to a farm outside Tillamook took us from beach to coastal mountaintop. At each turn, we glimpsed ocean, rock, and fir from a different angle, a different light. The afternoon sun threw a spotlight on a mountain crest and a field of free-roaming goats. A roadside placard informed us some of this beauty was preserved by public policy a century ago. Governor Oswald West had declared the seashore—the land between high and low tide—a public way. No one owns the shore, so we all do.

Rain sent us into the 2nd Street Coffee House in Tillamook, with its large peace sign and small military recruitment poster in the window. Photos of a young child and a woman in uniform were taped to the wall next to the bathroom. The owner had a gray ponytail and a turtle necklace. He didn't sell food, and we were hungry. Noticing a loaf of whole-grain bread on his desk, I asked if he'd sell slices.

"Toast with butter, no charge."

He kept giving us food to try—an egg roll, bean cakes—and advice: "If you have a cold sore, bite into a kiwi and rub on the juice."

We ate our bread and bean cakes. A young woman walked in, cell phone to ear. "I'm almost there," she said. "I love you." Hanging up, she addressed the room, anxiety written on her face. "Haven't seen my little daughter in a long time."

She didn't have money for coffee. The owner handed her a cup. "Pay me next time," he said.

MY BROTHER, WHO HAD lived in Seattle, reserved us a night at his favorite retreat in Newport. The Sylvia Beach Hotel was literary themed. Each room celebrated an author. We had J. K. Rowling. David donned Harry Potter glasses and played with Hogwarts paraphernalia. At dinner, staff led guests in a game of Two Truths and a Lie. It was fun. If I'd learned nothing else from my ten months on the road, I knew this: People love to talk about themselves, and everyone loves a good story.

AT A COFFEE SHOP in Florence where we waited for David's sister Susan to pick us up, I stared at an inspirational wall poster: *How often do you take a chance and do something you've never done before?*

"Every minute," I answered.

Susan and her husband, Jeff, shared living quarters with their ProCycle motorcycle parts company in Eugene. We slept above the shop. Our bikes went to bed with the big boys. Susan is a nurse practitioner, but it wasn't her profession that led me to approach her with my most pressing health issue. Susan could make or fix anything. If anyone could build a portable penis, it would be her. I tried her models on for size. My urinary issues remained unsolved, but our laughter was therapeutic.

It was raining hard when we wished Susan farewell and got back on the bikes. Outside of Charleston, my wheel wedged into a seam, obscured by the slippery white lane line between us and the cars. I fell. I wasn't hurt, but all my fears came to the surface. "Don't ride in the seam!" I yelled at David. A few minutes later, David rode the seam. I lashed out at him.

Fear and anger. One seemed to follow the other in quick succession with me.

At the Sylvia Beach Hotel, our dinner-mates had asked how the trip had changed us. The assumption—which I shared—was it would be transformative. But it seemed that all the riding did was lay my issues bare. If anything, I expressed more anger. On the bike, ferocity had no container. The depths of my fury scared me. Distance and wind meant David did not hear every word, but enough.

And then it dawned on me. The road had unleashed a well of emotions, and so far, I had not died. I had allowed myself to feel and no disaster had befallen me. My rage turned to giggles, imagining explaining this change to our Sylvia Beach friends, who wanted to hear I'd learned to live each moment, enjoy God's beauty, love my fellow human.

I calmed down as we entered Shelter Creek in Bandon, Oregon. After her divorce fifteen years ago, Mary created this haven, surrounded by cranberry bogs and sheep farms, to help friends recover or transition through life's challenges. Her wood house was small and oblong, filled with windows, stained glass, and colored tiles. A long porch faced a fantasy of flowering paths, reminiscent of Frances Hodgson Burnett's *Secret Garden*. She had a greenhouse, a bit of old-growth Oregon woods, and a hot tub where the three of us soaked and drank wine—Mary naked, me and David in suits.

After forty years of nursing, Mary got laid off when she was a few years too young for Medicare. "Chronic conditions make me uninsurable," she said. "I bought the tub while working in hospice. Life is delicate. If you want something, go for it." Mary grew up in northeast Kansas. "The pretty part of the state." Her guest cottage had a Wizard of Oz theme. She missed her homeland. "No thunderstorms here. Rain, fog, wind, yes, but no lightning."

"There's no place like home," David said.

ENTERING CALIFORNIA FOR THE second time, I was stunned. At both crossings—Arizona and Oregon—the landscape on the border transformed into industrial farms. On a small, elevated road off 101, we paused to take in bright green fields. We had lunch in Smith River, the Easter lily capital of the world.

45

EARTH TO EARTH

California

Wildly came the wind all through the half lighted night,
clouds black and cold hanging about the summits.
—John Muir[73]

The Klamath nation lost the bulk of their territory after European contact, but they rebounded and built one of the most sustainable, self-sufficient economies in Indian country until the 1950s, when the Eisenhower administration targeted them for termination, stealing prime hunting, fishing, and logging territory. In the 1980s, some land was returned, but by then, forests and fisheries had been decimated from overharvesting.

The town of Klamath, California, sat in a wide valley surrounded by mountains and redwoods. It had a couple of bars and independent fast-food joints and an intriguing community building. We slept at a white-owned motel and had breakfast at a Klamath-owned gas station.

Outside Klamath, on the Newton B. Drury Parkway in Redwood State Park, moss crept onto the road. The majestic trees brought out my inner child. We met Mark—a twenty-two-year-old cyclist from England—and he played with us among the giants. Mark had biked Europe.

73 Linnie Marsh Wolfe, ed., *John of the Mountains: The Unpublished Journals of John Muir* (Madison, Wisconsin: University of Wisconsin Press, 1938), 159. Muir, founder of the Sierra Club, was a racist who knew more about wind than people.

"The US Pacific coast is harder," he asserted.

Mark started the descent out of the park with us until he became impatient with my braking. Reuniting at a diner in Orick, we lent him our phone to check his email and send his mother a photo. Mark was traveling without technology. He read us an excerpt from his journal, about a white guy who shared fresh-caught salmon with him and then complained about the Klamath restricting his fishing. I told Mark about the Indigenous fight to retain spearfishing rights in northern Minnesota. "Minnesota is the land of ten thousand lakes, but there are still whites who claim there's a lack of fishing spots for them."

"In England, the *Daily Mail* scapegoats single mothers on welfare," Mark said. "Indian treaty fights are new to me."

DANIEL LIVED IN A one-room structure in Eureka, California, made of reclaimed wood and bamboo. An attached greenhouse was filled with pot plants, medical license displayed on the glass. His toilet and shower had no door. He was half-naked when we arrived—and high. A giant brass instrument, big as a tuba, lay on the couch, so we sat on the floor around a low table. He fed us chili that was delicious and satisfying. As we ate, he mended leather pants that appeared to be his only pair. His underclothes—a loincloth of sorts—barely covered him.

"Tell me about Eureka," I said, searching for another focus.

"Three thousand years ago, they fished salmon, used shells for currency, and traded in salt," Daniel said. "Smallpox, destruction of habitat, and stolen land decimated the Indigenous population."

As he explained how redwood logging and salmon fishing became the mainstay of the European-American economy, my initial discomfort melted away, replaced with a growing affection for this serious, eccentric, tiny man who shared my passion for getting to the root of things. Clearing the dishes, I moved aside a food-stained pink paper lying on the table. Daniel rushed to retrieve it and beckoned me to follow him outside.

The small yard was encased in a forest of bamboo, shutting out the mid-afternoon sun. On one side was a fishpond. Daniel held up the pink paper. "This is a recipe for ferrocement," he said. "I built my pond using it: chicken wire, sand, water, and cement. It's waterproof."

I matched Daniel's enthusiasm for renewable building materials, telling him about tabby walls made of sand, straw, water, and oyster shells that we had seen in Darien, Georgia, and cob houses made of dirt, sand, hay, and water in Oregon that withstood the rainy climates. He nodded vigorously, a bit of color appearing on his wan face. "It's all better than timber, especially redwood that takes centuries to grow back."

Daniel's fifty-seven-year-old emaciated frame spoke of grave illness but did not say its name. I hoped the pot leaves he ate with goat milk provided relief and gave him the munchies. Over the sink was a photo of a heartier Daniel, posing with a brass band. Seeing me looking at it, he pointed at the instrument lounging on his couch. "My 1904 French horn," he said. "Don't have the lungs for it now."

"It's like a lazy roommate," I ventured, relieved to see him grin.

An alto recorder sat on his table. "Do you play?" I asked. He shook his head.

"May I?"

He nodded. I fingered "Wayfaring Stranger."

"A friend gave it to me," Daniel said. "I told him I wasn't going to play it. He told me to give it to someone."

Daniel saw us out the next morning, making sure I packed the alto recorder. He was heading somewhere on his own bicycle, wearing a homemade helmet with brown horns.

SCOTIA, IN THE HEART of Humboldt County, north of the Avenue of the Giants, looked like any company town: small, identical homes facing the redwood lumber yard. At Taco Loco, four retired lumbermen were surprised to find us in their regular spot. Another foursome—a town doctor, a church lady, an aging Catholic priest, and his young Polish replacement—filled the third table. Their conversation dominated the room.

"Priests and parishes have abandoned doctrine," the church lady said. "They are the church's worst enemies on issues that define what it is to be Catholic: women's ordination, abortion, gay marriage."

"Catholic Lite," the doctor quipped. "Like you said, Father, if you agree with more than a tenth of your parishioners, you're not doing your job." He continued, "All of Europe will be Muslim in a decade because so-called Christians are using birth control. God is playing a joke on liberals who support Muslims' right to worship. After all, they hate abortion and gays as much as we do."

"What happened to the God of Love?" David interrupted.

They brushed him off with glances that said, *Exactly what we were talking about.*

David apologized for his outburst. "Tell the owner you're sorry," I said, but the proprietor was smiling at him warmly.

DURING MY LAST SEMESTER at Saint Cloud State, after a publicized incident in which Somali high school students were bullied, my students created a video on Islam to precipitate a dialogue. A young woman—tall, blond, who wore short skirts that accentuated long legs—took leadership of the project. At one point, she asked a Somali classmate about Muslim attitudes toward gays. He told her most do not support gay rights. The two students worked together on the project. At the end of the semester, the young woman compared her experience of coming out as a lesbian to that of Muslims in Saint Cloud. When she finished, her Somali classmate clapped hard.

AFTER THE PRIEST AND his entourage left, the regulars whose table we had stolen spoke up.

"He's about to retire," one said.

"Good riddance," said his friend.

A duet of amens from our corner of the room.

MOST ESTABLISHMENTS ON ROUTE 101 through Humboldt County were closed, catering to a still-dormant tourist trade. We looked forward to a good meal, some quality groceries, and company in Garberville. We weren't disappointed. Chautauqua Natural Foods had a deli with taco salads and a staff eager to trade adventures. Afterward, we walked the main drag. A three-foot pot plant stood outside the flower store. A dozen people were sitting or lying on the sidewalk in front of the Marijuana Connection Dispensary. An unmistakable sweet smell permeated the air. Outside a saloon, a toking German student told us,

"I'm on a bike tour too. Six weeks, Seattle to San Diego." He pointed at the cloudless sky, mumbling, "But the weather's been so bad."

He stumbled back into the bar.

THE FORTY-FOUR-MILE RIDE FROM the peak at Leggett, California, to the coast included a mountain, hairpin curves, no shoulder, drop-offs, and

rough pavement. I cursed whoever had decided this was a suitable bike route and longed for the open roads of West Texas. Still, I had to admit that our landing spot in Elk, California, was spectacular. We spent a day staring at a rock shaped like a water buffalo taking a long drink.

ON THE FIRST OF May, President Obama took a surprise trip to Afghanistan to celebrate the first anniversary of the killing of Osama Bin Laden. People held May Day rallies in cities across the nation, supporting public sector workers, health care for all, an end to home foreclosures, immigrant rights, and justice for the murder of Trayvon Martin. David changed a tire. I sat on a pannier, staring at a farm that could have belonged in the Midwest. A jet drew puffy lines on a solid blue canvas.

By the time we reached Gualala, California, the blue canvas turned black, and we were soaked. We waited three nights for the torrent to stop. On the fourth day, we passed Howard's deadline to pick up his car in San Francisco. A couple of retired Jehovah's Witnesses driving south found space for David.

When he returned in Howard's car, David said, "There's no way we could've biked from Gualala to San Francisco." However, as we drove north the next day, marveling at switchbacks, steep grades, and precipices, we asked over and over, "How did we do this?"

46

OLD GROWTH

Washington State and British Columbia, Canada

Loggers are sensitive to the wind. A sudden change and a tree could crush them.[74]

When David turned twenty-four, I gave him two books: *Little Bear,* illustrated by Maurice Sendak, and a lesser-known work about a boy named David and his red bike, Speedy. Although David denies it, he was disappointed. A serious fellow, he would have preferred the complete works of Gabriel García Márquez. At thirty-four, he was reading *Little Bear* to our toddler. At forty-four, he got a bike for his birthday. He named it Speedy. We went on our first bike tour as a family, from Hinckley to Duluth, Minnesota.

On the eve of his fifty-fourth birthday, we arrived back in Seattle and returned Howard's car. I said, "We should celebrate! How about we bike from Seattle to Port Townsend and see your sister Barb?"

Barb made David a flourless chocolate cake and took us to Better Living Through Coffee, a café with a splendid view. As we sipped lattes and admired the gorgeous bay, Barb pointed at a picturesque tugboat. "It looks harmless from here, but it's armed and escorting a nuclear submarine from the Navy munitions depot on Indian Island."

Barb was working with the local Occupy chapter. She told us about a

74 Informational Video on the Timber Industry, Chemainus History Museum, Vancouver Island

Border Patrol station outside of town. "ICE agents recently roadblocked the Hood Canal Bridge, the only way off the island. They questioned people at Catholic churches and on buses, offered themselves as Spanish interpreters, then deported people without papers. We're three thousand miles from Mexico and ten miles from Canada, but they didn't pull over Canadians."

Later, Barb took us to visit the County Museum, where a 130-year-old photo showed a constable standing guard in front of a Port Townsend brothel. Not far from the museum, we saw a cop with an uncanny likeness to the nineteenth-century constable, standing guard in front of Bank of America.

"Our foreclosure rate increased tenfold in the last five years," Barb explained. "The bank hired the cop after we held an Occupy demonstration here, demanding they open bank-owned homes to those in need."

WE HAD TWO WEEKS to zigzag the Pacific Northwest before road crews cleared the snow over the Cascades. So, from Port Townsend, we took the ferry to Whidbey Island. The southern portion of Whidbey was green and lush, dotted with bungalows tucked into heavily wooded reclusive lots—the first or second homes of Seattle commuters. The northern side was filled with apartment complexes, fast food, and naval stations.

On the southern side, we met a vigil. A woman wearing a button that read *War Is Terror* greeted us. "We've been here every Saturday since 9/11, standing for peace." She introduced us to David Anderson—mid-sixties, trim, and mustached—who invited us to follow him home on his bicycle.

Anderson had just read *The Man Who Cycled the World*, and he laid out a feast fit for cyclists who ride two hundred miles a day. We sat on his deck overlooking the Admiralty Inlet, sampling avocado and tomato aspic, chickpea soup, tuna sandwiches, tangerines, and rhubarb pie. To the left was Seattle's

Space Needle; to the right, the snowcapped mountains of the Olympic Peninsula. We sat mesmerized, watching cormorants, herons, sea lions, massive container ships, Victoria ferries, and small fishing boats.

Our new friend had been many things, including veterinarian, golf course owner, and Washington state senator. Of all the hats he'd worn, the fisherman's cap represented his soul. "My father was a fisherman," he said. "It's in the blood." He pointed to a logging ship headed to China. "Sustainable fishing depends on protecting habitat, which makes for interesting politics among loggers, farmers, and fishers."

Hours passed. As we tore ourselves away from the gorgeous view in the late afternoon, Anderson tempted us. "You should see the sunsets."

IN COUPEVILLE, THE DIVIDING line between southern and northern Whidbey, we bought ice cream cones and strolled the pier, admiring snow-peaked mountains, exchanging stories with an African American couple on a short vacation. They were both nurses. The Supreme Court was debating the Affordable Care Act. I asked Pearl and Michael what they thought of Obamacare.

"My patients at the VA have public health care," Michael began. Pearl, who worked at a military base, finished his sentence: "That population's sure to grow, so our jobs are secure. With ACA, we get more access, but we all need what the veterans and politicians have."

WE TOOK A FERRY to Vancouver Island in Canada. A woman who taught gardening and ballroom dance waited with us for the Brentwood Bay ferry. She pointed out giant starfish and spouting porpoises. Jutting her face skyward, she said, "We all get happier when the sun comes out."

Riding out of Mill Bay, past crystal waters and evergreen forests ringed with soft green peaks, David repeated a mantra: "Doesn't get prettier."

"Or hillier," I would add.

David's blissful state wore off as hunger set in. The one-word signs, barely noticeable, stuck in trees every two hundred feet, teased Wall Drug style:

Coffee. Latte. Mocha.

Anticipation mounted.

"Been closed for a year," a man said when he saw us trying to force the café door open. It was twenty miles to the next town. David whined like a child. The role reversal was welcome.

The town of Chemainus, where we finally found sustenance, had forty-three murals that celebrated workers. The town museum overlooking the log-filled Stuart Channel showed a video of loggers felling a giant tree in real time. "Loggers like old growths best," the video narrator said.

A FERRY THE SIZE of a shopping mall took us from Vancouver Island to Horseshoe Bay on the Canadian mainland. We stood in front of semitrucks and watched dots become snowcapped mountains. As we disembarked, David sighed.

"This is the most beautiful spot in the world."

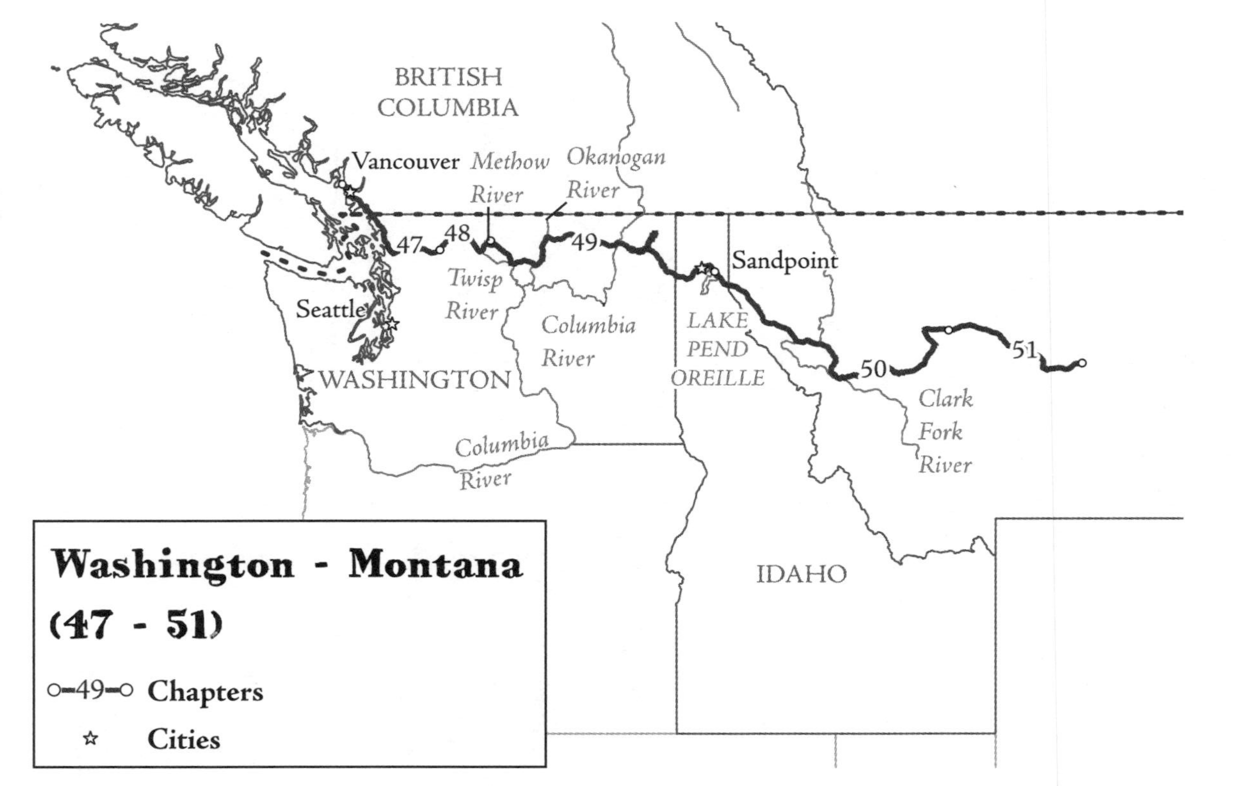

BRITISH COLUMBIA
Vancouver
Methow River
Okanogan River
47
48
49
Sandpoint
Twisp River
Seattle
Columbia River
LAKE PEND OREILLE
50
51
WASHINGTON
Clark Fork River
Columbia River
IDAHO
Washington - Montana
(47 - 51)
49 Chapters
Cities

47

RESERVATIONS

British Columbia, Canada, and Washington State

Carnivores are measurements of the health of our
eco-system: if they survive, we all do.
—Grizzly Bear Outreach Project

In front of Darryl's Coffee & Native Art in downtown Vancouver was a carved figure with a sign on its hat: *General Custer, It's Payback Time.* Darryl was a large man with an inviting demeanor. We sat at one of his two tables, surrounded by jewelry, pottery, paintings, masks, and ground coffee beans packed in glass jars labeled *Stolen Land for Sale*. An eagle feather hung from the ceiling. I told him the room was beautiful.

"The store's my retirement," he said. "A chance to celebrate the artwork of my friends and relations." He directed us to a wall map of British Columbia. "I come from three tribal chief families, on both sides of the border. My mother's Alaskan Tlingit."

I asked him about the eagle feather.

"The Squamish people gave it to me. When I was ready to open, I asked them for permission to use their land. We had a ceremony, walked around the block carrying Custer before placing him in front of the door."

"Mr. Payback Custer?"

He nodded. "I told the carver to make him short so we could look down on him—a log of shame. Payback for all those cigar stores that display Indian heads like trophies. I've had one negative reaction. A man from Texas called me 'boy' and demanded I remove the statue. I had him removed instead."

We told Darryl we were headed across the Cascades. He arched his eyebrows. "Are you ready for bears?"

I was worried about our Cascades climb: temperature changes, lack of services, access to water, doubts about my ability. Bears had not entered my consciousness. Panic must have registered on my face.

"Don't worry," he said. "Make as much noise as possible. Bang a tin cup. You don't need a weapon." He paused. "I hate guns. When I was twelve, my father took me hunting. We came upon a big buck. My father gave me the gun and told me to shoot. I shot in the air. He took me home and told my mother, 'He's never coming hunting with me again,' which made me happy. For punishment, he gave me a hunk of fat from the deer to eat."

A friend walked in, recently diagnosed with diabetes. Darryl wouldn't let him buy a baked good. He handed him an apple and advice: "I've been off bread for two weeks. The weight's dropping quickly."

When I went to pay, I noticed a button on the register that read *The Bullying Stops Here*, and a rainbow-colored sign: *Safe Harbor*. For us—travel-weary—the colorful room with its engaging proprietor was an oasis. I suggested an addition to his sidewalk sign: "No reservations needed—just give the land back."

RIDING SOUTH AGAIN, WE approached Bellingham, Washington, our gateway to the home stretch. The town was preparing for Ski to Sea, a relay race with swimming, road biking, mountain biking, running, kayaking, canoeing, and skiing. The competitors used to go it solo until someone died. The youth had their own Ski to Sea. The thirteen-year-old twin daughters of our hosts, Jeremy and Peg, competed on the Team of the Mismatched Socks.

Jeremy was my brother Daniel's childhood friend. It was no surprise he settled in this community of outdoor adventurers. When he and Daniel were small, they were always scheming to make a sled or boat faster. Jeremy remembered me too. "A serious person, head in a book. Of all the members of your family, you're the last I'd imagine on such a tour."

Jeremy showed us two routes to Sedro-Woolley. We chose the six-mile ascent on Samish Way instead of the breathtaking views, sheer cliffs, hairpin turns, and predicted weekend traffic on coastal Chuckanut Drive. After two months on the coast, I was happy to head inland, where cows and green pastures replaced craggy coast.

A CROWD DRESSED IN white shirts, ties, and long dresses revived the gospel in Sedro-Woolley's Hammer Heritage Square. The minister bellowed about "heathens in Bellingham." One believer approached, pointing to his brethren. "We are Apostolic Pentecostals."

He paused, waiting for my reply.

"We are headed east," I said.

I was still thinking about the Apostolic revival when we ducked into a motel in Concrete, Washington, to get out of the rain. In the motel lobby, I picked up a "Carnivore Heritage" brochure put out by the Grizzly Bear Outreach Project.

Lying on the motel bed, I saw *Carnivore Heritage Square. Grandpa Grizzly was testifying about glory days of meat-eating ancestors. The den mother fetched more chairs, exclaiming, "The outreach worked!"*

"What's so funny?" David asked.

According to the GBOP brochure, the grizzly population in the Lower 48 has gone from 100,000 to 1,000 in the last century due to human encroachment. The organization offered a helpful hint if you are lucky enough to encounter one of the survivors: Learn bear language. But be aware of double meanings. Standing on hind legs could mean "I want to get a better look at you" or "I want to eat you."

In Concrete, lying on a flat mattress on a creaky bed, rain pelting the window, the GBOP brochure provided high comedy. In Marblemount, where we hunkered at a hostel for three days, waiting for the precipitation to stop (rain down here meant snow on the mountain), I lost my sense of humor. Four young women—gorgeous, athletic—joined us. I envied their independence, fearlessness, and beauty. Jealousy is an ugly emotion.

ON MAY 23, DARK clouds filled the sky, but it wasn't raining. As we rode to Colonial Creek Campground at the mountain's foot, we passed the sign: *No services, 74 miles.*

48

ALTITUDE AND ATTITUDE

Washington State

Nothing is etched in stone.
—Carved into rock, Sandpoint, Idaho

I had come to believe in the power of expectations and attitude. Seventy miles or twenty—whatever I expected was my capacity for the day. I reined in my fear with math: I knew I could climb a mountain. I had done the Berkshires, West Texas, and eastern California climbs. Our first mountain in the Cascades was four thousand feet up in thirty-two miles, down in eighteen. Climate change from sunny bottom to snowy top provided another challenge. We'd leave at dawn to take advantage of all available daylight, bring extra water and food. One pedal at a time. This was possible.

Attitude. David had his. At Diablo Lake, he bubbled, "It's like glass! A perfect reflection of clouds moving over the mountain." He pointed at a snowy crest. "That's where we're going!"

Borrowing from David's playbook, I sang, "What the world needs now is love, sweet love."[75]

Overlooks and turnouts were still closed, filled with snow roadblocks. We rested on the slope, leaning against a guardrail, facing a cascade of weeping

75 The lyrics come from "What the World Needs Now Is Love," written by Hal David and Burt Bacharach. Copyright 1965.

rock. David was ecstatic. "Look at how it shimmers, capturing the light. Can a photo ever do justice?" *Click, click.*

I sang, "No, not just for some, but for everyone."

Fifteen miles on, I didn't dare sit down. I feared I wouldn't get up. David clicked away, hardly containing his enthusiasm. "Wow!" he said. "The trees are rivers, undulating and flowing, dancing with each other!" Snow accumulated on the side of the road.

I sang. One line became a mantra: "Lord, we don't need another mountain."

David didn't seem to notice. He was happy riding, happy resting. "It gets more gorgeous with each mile," he said.

Twenty-five miles. We had cold toes, even as we wiped sweat out of our eyes. I drained our last drop of drinking water. The snow was three feet deep. "This is the hardest thing I have ever done," David admitted, "and the most exhilarating."

I stopped singing.

Mile twenty-eight, Rainy Pass. A thirty-foot wall of snow lined the road. I did the math: 600 feet to the peak, 4 more miles. Calculate the elevation, calibrate my expectations. But at mile 28.2, we descended sharply, 350 feet. I'd have to climb each foot again. This was a violation of my expectation calculus. "Fuck this!" I told the mountain. "Fuck you," I yelled at David. A couple of bike racers went by. "Fuck you!" I yelled at them, and every car, every truck.

Fucking adrenaline pumped me up the unrelenting rise.

A couple, about our age, doing the reasonable thing—driving—cheered as we edged to the top. They didn't know I was the fuck-you monster. "You made it!" they said. "How long did it take you? Seven-and-a-half hours? You made good time! Can't believe you've come so far." A fearless mountain jay stared at me from atop its snowy perch, two feet from my face. Walls of creamy white snow filled the closed overlook road. Purple mountain majesty.

Love, sweet love.

Bliss was short-lived. It started to snow. Shivering, wet to the bone with sweat, we pulled on sweatshirts, winter jackets, rain pants, and thick gloves for gripping brakes for eighteen miles of switchbacks. Hands brittle, shoulders hunched. Down three thousand feet. Too scared to sing or swear.

In Mazama, it was early summer. At a sporty resort, I declared, "Tonight, cost does not exist."

49

WATERSHED MOMENTS

Washington State and Idaho

"Are we back in Arizona?!"

David shook his head in wonder. We had just turned the corner onto the eastern side of Loup Loup summit. Green forests ended abruptly, and we entered a desert, carved into mountain cliffs.

Howard in Seattle had told us about the moment fifteen thousand years ago that explained this geographic whiplash. A glacial dam had broken on the Clark Fork River, unleashing the ancient Great Lake Missoula from its shores with a force that split mountains. In two days, lake had reached ocean, leaving massive holes in its wake, including the Grand Coulee Canyon, Dry Falls, and this desert bowl before us. Howard worried Lake Missoula's voyage foretold impending environmental disaster.

"Many tiny changes over eons, and one day the dam broke," he had said. "What will happen when a glacier in the Arctic reaches that point?"

We rode toward the town of Okanogan, Washington, dodging tumbleweeds rolling across the road.

IN OMAK, WASHINGTON, WE followed the sound of a mariachi band to the top of a steep ridge. Between us and the lilting tunes was the Okanogan

River. Rills bounced over rocks, dancing to the music. The river was the lynchpin of Omak's economic life, irrigating the valley's lush orchards. It also provided a death-inviting obstacle course for Omak's Suicide Race.

"Horse and rider drop off the cliff into the ravine, cross the river, and end at the Stampede stadium," the volunteer at the Omak Visitor Information Center told us. "Every few years, horse and rider die. Boys in Omak don't want to be Michael Jordan," she added. "They want to be last year's Suicide winner."

The volunteer seemed to think we had something in common with the suicide boys. We chatted about the chances people take, until a man wearing a VFW cap and Korean War Vet badge interrupted us. "Gonna be a Memorial Day parade in Omak?"

"No, sorry!" the volunteer answered. "Perhaps in the next town?"

As the man let the door slam, he shouted, "I heard the Valley's anti-veteran." He was the second man we'd seen dressed to be honored, looking in vain for a parade. I wish he had stayed so we could have heard his story.

AS WE CLIMBED PAST Mount Anne and Little Bonaparte Mountain, traffic was low, the weather pleasant. The sheep, horses, cows, and red crossbills were fun to watch. Being a good union family, we took an hour-long lunch break at the Wauconda Café. Just as we passed the sign, *Entering Republic: Peddlers Permits Required,* David's front tire split open. A woman came out of her car repair shop and walked toward us as if we'd entered her store and she wasn't sure if we'd buy or steal something.

"Can I help you with anything?"

"A new tire!" David said.

She considered us for a moment. "If they don't have it at the hardware store, you can order it. A courier comes in once a day from Seattle."

The hardware store clerk sent us into the basement to look for ourselves. Behind a stack of yard signs that read *I have a constitutional right to shoot you if you trespass without a warrant,* we found one lone serviceable bike tire.

Republic defied left and right political categories. The Civilian Conservation Corps had saved the town from oblivion in the 1930s, reforesting the mountains and protecting the land for generations. Murals and posters celebrated early miners, loggers, ranchers, and farmers with the slogan "Without you, there would be no us."

Assertions of local control and individual freedom were everywhere. Stores and cafés displayed pro-gun and pro-hunting signs. The organic food co-op featured items grown, sewn, and built by local back-to-the-landers and do-it-yourselfers. We talked to a co-op customer who had an off-the-grid sheep farm and homeschooled her kids.

In Ferry County, they grow it, teach it, fish it, shoot it, govern it themselves. Or it comes by courier, once a day, from Seattle.

THE DESCENT OUT OF Republic was easier—or I was getting used to it. I lifted my head, smelled cedar, heard effervescent streams, enjoyed encounters with other human beings. We met five young white men cycling cross-country to raise diversity scholarships for their private Christian college. As we pulled damp layers over frozen sweat, they climbed into a warm support van stocked with snacks and sweatshirts. I heard one exclaim as they raced by us on the descent, "I hit forty miles an hour!"

On the other side of the age spectrum was a seventy-two-year-old couple riding tandem, heaven-bent for Bar Harbor, raising money for the Shriners Hospital where the man had spent his childhood. "I spent my first decades in a wheelchair," he declared. "I'm determined not to spend my retirement that way."

At a former CCC camp not far from Kettle Falls, we met Shannon and Louise, living in their van, hitting every national park in the West. "Our new life began when Louise got pink-slipped and the dog died," Shannon explained. "I quit my job. We sold the second car and our house in Seattle and hit the road."

Another couple at the wayside were from England, a retired teacher and a social worker doing a Pacific Northwest circle in a rental car. The social worker and David talked shop. She warned, "In Britain, a private company is replacing public services, turning our profession into low-wage work. They took over our prisons. I hear they are coming to the US to profit from your large prison population."

WE CLAIMED A BENCH at the Colville, Washington, town square, next to an iron statue depicting hunter, angler, miner, logger, below an eagle's nest. A retired high school principal stopped on his way to the bank. He looked quizzically at David.

"School Social Worker? We don't have those here. Education funds don't reach this part of the state. Our illiteracy rate is 25 percent."

The principal took care of business and returned, holding two chocolate chip cookies. "They're free in the bank." He walked away from us, turned back, handed us the cookies, and got into his car.

IN EASTERN WASHINGTON, NO one confused Minnesota with Michigan or Minneapolis with Indianapolis. It seemed like everyone here had a relative in our home state. "My dad drove the train for Burlington Northern," one person told us.

"My son works for a car dealer in Bloomington," said another.

"My grandparents had a hardware store in Brainerd back in the day," said a third person.

One woman couldn't contain her disdain for Minnesota, but her roots were hard to deny. "I spent four years in Two Harbors, north of Duluth. Winter wonderland eleven months of the year. You know the Paul Bunyan statue in Bemidji? That was my grandpa Cyril Dickenson's project. My great-uncle added the blue ox."

WE SPENT THE NIGHT in a free bicycle hostel outside of Colville. It was raining at 6:00 a.m., and I thought, *what a cozy place to spend the day*. But it cleared by nine. Cascade mountain five was smaller and the last climb until the Rockies. We glimpsed an eagle, a wild turkey, and Texas longhorn cattle. All was right with the world until clouds unleashed frozen rain. Fingers stiff and toes numb, we reached the Beaver Lodge Resort & Campground. The owner brought a space heater to our table, lit a fire, invited us to put our wet shoes by it. Before they were dry, the rain stopped.

In the parking lot, a man who got soaked on his ATV put his face to the sun. We joined him. He had been a housepainter in Spokane before the Great Recession. "The company I worked for had twenty-six employees five years ago. Now they have three." He made an assumption. "Are you going to vote for Obama again?"

I shrugged, said I heard the big banks were supporting both candidates.

The man squeezed water from his headscarf. "We steal something, we go to jail. Banks stole millions, and they get a handout."

ON AN EMPTY TREE-LINED road, we reached the 10,000-mile mark and wished we had someone to tell. Before mile 10,001, European cyclists Alison and Matt appeared. They were four hundred kilometers into their trip from British Columbia to Mexico City, with visas requiring them to exit the US in ninety days. They had brightly painted plastic bakery buckets—free, accessible, waterproof panniers. Waterproofing was important. As we took off in opposite directions, it thundered.

In Ione, Washington, the sky was cloudless again. It looked like a perfect night for camping, but we knew that could change instantly. We booked a room at Ione's Riverview Motel, where the other guests were all men, living in the motel while building a bridge funded by Obama's American Recovery and Investment Act.

After hearing about the 10,000 miles, the motel's owner, Dan, offered to take us on his pontoon on the Pend Oreille River "to see some bears." As we sailed, he provided political commentary on government intervention, historical and contemporary. "The government granted the land along the river to railroad and timber companies 150 years ago," Dan said. "Today, all government does is create hurdles for a small business like mine. I nearly went under in '08."

Nearing the shore, we passed the firepit where his other guests, working construction on the government's dime, sat enjoying barbecue and beer.

"No bears this evening," Dan said as we anchored. "Guess you'll have to come in." He ushered us through the door of his small home. In the living room, a bear snarled at me from the couch. A cub lay on its back, glass table atop its paws. Deer, elk, and antelope heads and two stuffed squirrels decorated the living room. A red fox stood sentry between the kitchen and the dining room. Dan took us into his bedroom, where a bearskin with head, eyes, and teeth covered a queen-size bed. Straining to make a hunting connection, I ventured, "We were surprised to find no regulations against baiting in the South. Gas stations sold bags of deer corn."

Dan scowled. "I don't support Washington's baiting regulations. If you bait, you can watch the animal for half an hour, make sure it's big enough to kill. People think every bear they see is big. Most estimate their weight to be three times what it is. They kill anything, even cubs and sows." As we left, a stuffed cub whimpered at me from atop the refrigerator.

IN THE 1860S, THE US stole Kalispel Indian territory and distributed it to railroads and immigrants. Some settlers abandoned their 160-acre homestead plots. A few of those plots were turned into tiny national parks. At one such park, in the Colville National Forest, we had lunch. An informational display near our picnic table asserted that the Kalispel were never forcibly removed from their lands. It's true they weren't force-marched hundreds of miles like the Miami in Ohio, or the Dakota in Minnesota, but the US expropriated their land with such destructive force that by 1900, their population was in the tens.

We rode through the Kalispel Reservation, awed by its dense forest and lush meadows stretching for ten miles along the glassy Pend Oreille River. A herd of buffalo ran in a field next to a modern tribal office and wellness center.

Peace ended for us at the reservation border. The road to Priest River, Idaho, was barely two lanes, with a steady stream of logging trucks moving fast.

The Priest River Museum and Timber Education Center was a

disappointment, a pile of logging implements awaiting context. The rest of the museum was a typical jumble of local memorabilia: dresses, guns, farm tools. We were about to head out when I eyed a stapled sheaf stuck in the middle of a shelf: *Memories of Vietnam,* essays collected in 2001 when the Mobile Vietnam Memorial Wall came to Sandpoint. I slid to the floor and read about a soldier's time in a mental ward:

What makes a man go over the edge, or a woman for that matter? . . . The constant shelling or cold-blooded murder on his battlefield? . . . Maybe it's filling corpses with heroin to be sent home. . . . Into this [mental] facility they herd by the hundreds, dreams shattered by the price of war and duty to country. Whites, Blacks, Hispanics, Indians. The poor who fought the war are united again.

I left Vietnam and returned to Priest River, Idaho.

At AJ's Café, two men talked timber. "Been driving logging trucks for thirty-two years," said one of them. "Rolled only once."

"If I had a dollar for every truck I unloaded, seventy to a hundred a day for thirty-seven years . . ."

The man sitting closest to us left the sentence unfinished. I introduced myself. He had retired and was now the town fire chief. Thinking of western Florida, I asked him if the timber industry was still operating at full capacity in Idaho.

"A couple mills have closed. We have this industrial park now, computer businesses and the like," he said, continuing his thought. "Washington has a higher minimum wage, so they come here to pay seven dollars an hour. They would pay five if they could get away with it. Loggers get twenty dollars. We need jobs, but these cut-rate companies? We're better off without them."

When we got up to leave, he warned us, "Get to Sandpoint and stay there. Big storm's coming. Could be a tornado."

WE MADE IT TO the natural food market in Sandpoint before the storm. As we munched on black bean quinoa salad and some fantastic cookie-thing, the sky turned green. A woman approached and invited us to stay the night. We rode to her home, wind whipping through us.

Suzy was a bluegrass musician and community radio host. We woke up to guitar and her mellifluous voice. The storm had subsided, but it was still raining. She invited us to stay another day, but rain was forecasted for all week, Sandpoint to Missoula. No point in prolonging the wet ride.

The lake, mountains, forests, and marshes on Highway 200 out of Sandpoint looked pristine. Even in the rain, the beauty did not escape us. At a scenic pullout in Idaho, we stopped to admire glassy Lake Pend Oreille. These pristine waters were what remained of the ancient Lake Missoula.

BETWEEN OUR SPOT AND the water were railroad tracks. A train passed, filled with black gold, making the scene even more picturesque—until we remembered something Suzy told us: "Warren Buffett wants to transport coal to China, on trains along Lake Pend Oreille, throwing coal dust—thirty tons per trip—into crystal river waters, into our water table. The Sandpoint Waterkeepers are fighting him, but the billionaire is a formidable foe."

50

CONTINENTAL DIVIDES

Idaho and Montana

This is windy, eagle country, where Montana's Rocky Mountains spill down to the Great Plains.
—A roadside marker in Montana

Beware the woman with 10,000 miles *and* hips under her belt.
—Me

Her hair flowed below her slim waist. She met a boy. They took a trip to the Mexican border, across Texas, into the Deep South. Sometimes people were nice to them. Other times, they didn't like hippies, and the lovers felt lucky to get out of town alive. On the way back to LA, they stopped in San Francisco. For all she knows, the boy never left Haight-Ashbury. She left him, took another road trip, stopped at a wayside in Hope, Idaho. An osprey hovered above her, its wings cocked backward. It dove and caught a trout with its talons. She stopped traveling and opened up a resort where Lake Pend Oreille meets the Clark Fork River.

In June 2012, the woman—silver hair below her ample waist—was agitated. It had been sleeting for a week. She gave up on chores and drove to town, picked up the *Julie & Julia* DVD. Making herself a chef's salad with anchovies and a nearly raw egg, she slipped the movie out of its jacket, careful not to touch the machine with her yoke-covered pinky finger. Someone knocked, startling her. Yellow goo dripped, jamming the DVD player.

At the door, two soaked and muddy bicyclists shivered. They claimed to have ridden 10,000 miles but let slip that their day started in Clark Fork, four miles away. They wanted a room. They had no PayPal account. A vague memory surfaced from the woman's sojourn with the boy. Was it Morganza, Louisiana, or Chattahoochee, Florida? A motel clerk, or a gas station attendant? Someone "didn't like their kind," turned them away in a rainstorm. She heard herself agree to take three twenties for a room worth triple. She reminded them that checkout was 10:00 a.m. and regardless of the weather, there was no vacancy tomorrow.

AFTER AN EMBARRASSING FOUR-MILE day outside of Clark Fork, we crept, doing twenty-five-mile days, hoping the weather and the road would get better. We'd picked a spectacular route to Missoula: a glacial bowl between mountain ranges, meandering the Clark Fork and Flathead Rivers through the Flathead Reservation. But the twisting, two-lane highway was also a major truck route—death for cyclists, even without the freezing rain. In Plains, Montana, halfway to Missoula, we hunkered under covers at the Dew Duck Inn, watching a PBS World War II special. The next morning, I was ready to go AWOL, but momentum had already kicked in. I pedaled. The wheels turned.

IN MISSOULA, I NEEDED a new jacket. The bike shop didn't have women's sizes. "Try the men's large," the young man said when the men's size medium didn't fit over my hips. His innocent suggestion set me off, unleashing frustration accumulated from a year of encounters with a bike industry geared toward men, who viewed biking as competition, paraphernalia as status, and touring as male bonding.

Men took to the road, fulfilling a lifetime dream. They lost their paunch, exchanged stats: miles, speed, equipment, how much they could eat. They'd boast of surviving in the wilderness, seedy hotels, days without showers, stealth camping, beautiful women on the road. The bike shops, manufacturers, and organizations catered to them.

I didn't go fast or care a stitch about equipment. I hadn't lost a pound, couldn't eat whatever I wanted, didn't feel safe most anywhere, couldn't go without a shower or I'd get a rash. Biking alone added another level of fear. Biking with even the best guy added a level of dependency, a constant source of tension.

I'd met so many women who said they would bike cross-country if their partner would go slower, if they felt safe. I'd been on the road long enough to say touring is for people like us—not just men or wiry athletes, but femmes of a certain age who want to get out of themselves and into the world. I was having my cycling adventure. Was it too much to ask for a jacket wide enough for my women's hips to go with it?

FORTY MILES OUT OF Missoula, where Highways 83 and 200 intersect, I found the *Missoulian* on a wayside picnic table. The headline read, "Montana Guard Unit Prepares for Afghan Heat, Language Barrier." In the accompanying photo, nineteen-year-old Montanans stood in full gear in 110-degree heat at Fort Bliss, Texas, preparing to teach community policing to Afghan villagers.

I thought of Shiro, Texas with its *All Citizens Are Armed* sign. What if they deployed young Montanan recruits to teach *Texans* how to secure their communities? How long before Fort Bliss ran them out of town, guns blazing? What does it do to the mind of a young person when you tell them they can teach another culture, half a world away, how to police themselves?

FOR THE NEXT TWO days, we intersected with a mountain bike race following the Continental Divide to the Mexican border. Our first contact with the racers was in the high valley town of Ovando—population ninety—where we spent the night. Contestants arrived in dribbles and droves, eating massive amounts of food at Trixi's Antler Saloon. Most were between the ages of thirty and fifty. Eleven of the 110 were women. They had survived snow, mud, bears, sheer cliffs, wet socks, and little sleep. One guy was med-evac'd with hypothermia. Another dozen had quit. They seemed like creatures from another planet, but we conversed with a massage therapist from Tucson who appeared thoroughly human.

At the Stray Bullet, we and the racers ate breakfast and watched a storm come, go, and come again. Four more bikers arrived, covered in mud. Stories got more fantastic with each cup of coffee. One rider was on his way home. The others had convinced themselves Montana was the hardest part. "It has to get warmer as we go south."

Leaving Ovando, we biked twenty-seven miles in a thunderstorm. The racers charged the slope in marble-sized hail. We all ended up at Scapegoat Pizza in Lincoln. "You cheated," they said.

"We are playing a different game," we responded.

Their game had some pretty convoluted rules: It was OK to ask us, but not their competitors, for a tire pump. They could hitch a ride back, but not forward, to get a part for their bikes. They were microchipped. The whole world could watch them go to the laundry, the grocery store, the bar, and, I suppose, the toilet. They all spent the night in Lincoln because, like us, they had a long stretch coming without towns.

One racer in his mid-forties who had ridden fourteen hours without sleep or food, stared down a black bear, and slept near a cougar's den, sought me out at the laundromat. "How do these machines work?" he asked. "Never done laundry in my life."

Another racer, a square-jawed man from Denver, sat next to us at lunch. He looked at me wistfully. "If my wife would ride cross-country with me, I wouldn't have to do this."

"Would you be willing to go slower?" I asked.

My question went unanswered.

The next day, the racers went south toward Helena. We headed north toward Great Falls.

THE ROGERS PASS CLIMB to the Continental Divide was gradual—nothing like the Washington Cascades. I felt a thrill as we emerged from the mountains onto the high rolling plains. Sky brought a sense of peace to this claustrophobe. It wasn't flat, however. Hills appeared to lead to the end of the earth.

The wind was with us until we turned north toward Augusta, Montana, where construction workers servicing the North Dakota mines had doubled the population of 234 and toppled the gender balance. At the campground, one hundred men slept in their trucks. I was the only female, until a dappled mare in the adjacent field came by to say hello. When I got out Daniel's recorder, she leaned in to listen.

At 2:00 a.m., we awoke to the sound of a low grunt outside our tent. My horse friend? A flash of lights, a truck motor—the grunting stopped, and I fell back asleep. The next morning, patrons at Mel's Diner compared sightings of the grizzly sow and two cubs who had taken a midnight jaunt through town. David looked at me.

"I *knew* it was a bear."

Maybe, I thought. But we'd both been ignorant enough to think no woods meant no bears. We had used bear boxes in the mountains. Here, on the prairie, we brought our food into the tent. I picked up a souvenir sticker for my bike at the drugstore. Around the name of the town of Augusta was the silhouette of a grizzly bear.

ENTERING A RESTAURANT IN Simms, Montana, we greeted a dour-looking couple at a nearby table. They did not respond. Back from the bathroom, I gave them a big smile. Still the cold shoulder. Halfway through our meal, the man blurted, "How far ya come?"

David recited the whole song and dance. The man responded curtly, "In Great Falls, you must see the C.M. Russell Museum."

The perky waitress made up for the quiet couple. She showed us a photo of her sitting next to a tranquilized grizzly. "Mother and cubs have been hanging around my family's home for a year," she explained. "The Montana DNR refused to remove them until the mother killed livestock. They transported the grizzlies to the Bob."[76]

The couple stopped at our table on their way out to wish us a safe trip. When David went to take care of our bill, the waitress shook her head. "You don't owe anything," she said. "That couple paid for your dinner."

76 Bob Marshall Wilderness Complex

51

DISCOVERY AND CONQUEST

Montana

Some people in Montana quote the diaries of Lewis and Clark like others quote the Bible, reciting chapter and verse concerning creek, trail, or mountain. The diaries describe a Montana landscape, in many ways, still the same.

I understood why Lewis and Clark felt like discoverers. We experienced that feeling—especially when territory was new to us. Our sense of ownership increased if getting there was a struggle, and Lewis and Clark certainly met adversity on their sojourn. But they were not just explorers. They were robbers casing the joint to empty its coffers. Clark's role in Native dislocation and genocide was direct. He became Superintendent of Indian Affairs for St. Louis, under President Andrew "Trail of Tears" Jackson.

At the C.M. Russell Museum in Great Falls, I talked back to a man in a wall-length photo, posing next to a mountain of buffalo bones. "Discovery is not the problem," I said. "It's the conquest."

THE RAILROAD TYCOONS WHO founded Great Falls were from the Twin Cities, and it showed: wide roads and easy grid, like Minneapolis, and one-and-a-half-story homes with porches and stoops, reminiscent of working-class Saint Paul. Unlike the Twin Cities, however, Great Falls ended abruptly. No suburb or exurb, not even a strip mall. Just open road and sky.

Our destination was Fort Benton, fifty miles northeast, where Lewis and Clark spent ten days debating which of two rivers was the Missouri. At the intersection of Highway 87 and Highwood Road, where we were supposed to veer north toward the fort, we saw a sign: *Belt, 20 Miles*. We spent ten seconds debating which of two roads to take.

A mile from the Belt exit, a fierce crosswind forced us to walk. At the fork/spoon/gas pump sign, we turned. Wind at our backs, we soared. Belt was deep in a valley, so low and gusty it had to be the one where you "hang your head over and hear the wind blow."[77] The hill bottomed onto Main Street, at the Belt Creek Café. Outside the café was a small park suitable for a tent. Tomorrow, we'd battle hill and headwind.

The town was jumping, an impending rodeo and a high school ball game the attractions. The café was full, as were two saloons. Even the history museum was rocking with visitors. A museum photo showed the green hill above Belt's Main Street filled with clapboard houses. The coal mine had closed in 1969. Now many of the seven hundred people in Belt worked at Great Falls Clinic or Malmstrom Air Force Base.

One of Belt's founders, an African American woman enslaved at birth, had owned a popular hotel in the center of town. She—reportedly—had donated the land to the city, and they had turned it into the park where we planned to camp, but we got into a conversation with Meg, the docent at the museum, and she invited us to tent in her yard.

"Come by after you see the rodeo," she directed. Meg's son was the rodeo chairman. She sat in the front row and waved up at us. The calf-roping seemed cruel—a race to tie the legs of a young calf while riding a horse. Bull and man seemed more equally matched, and the women's barrel racing was impressive.

77 The folk song "Down in the Valley" refers to Birmingham, Alabama, but it sure could have referred to Belt, Montana.

Contestants came from all over the country. A local girl won, so everyone was in a good mood.

Meg's ranch was down a long gravel driveway, set off at an angle from the road. She and a friend sat in a yard lined with roses and vegetables. She invited us in for dinner. We combined our avocado and pear with her lettuce and cheese and had a feast. After we ate, she invited us to sleep inside and use her washing machine.

Meg had been an elementary school teacher in Belt. She still substituted. She was also the town's special education assistant, librarian, museum docent, music teacher, and piano player. "I used to be the church organist," she said. "Now, I just do funerals, weddings, veterans' events, and school musicals. Retirement means doing what you love, refusing to do what you don't."

She had decorated her living room with Tanzanian art collected during four years of teaching in Dar es Salaam. We spent the evening singing. Meg sat at the piano, I played Daniel's recorder. David took over Meg's drum with the zebra-skin top. Meg's favorite was ABBA's "I Have a Dream." I loved that song too. The verse about destinations and pushing through another mile resonated differently this time.

In the middle of the night, two calves were born. While we slept, Meg and her son branded and aided the newborns, one of which slipped under the fence where it couldn't reach its mother.

FROM BELT, THE FIRST relief from intense sun was a café forty miles away in Stanford, Montana. For us, shade and water were the most heavenly items on the menu. For the couple at the next table, the café was a destination worth the hundred-mile ride to and from Lewistown, Montana. Charlotte—bubbly, covered in striking turquoise jewelry—and her dapper companion,

Gene, were interested in our venture. When I told them about our night with Meg, Charlotte invited us to stay with her in Lewistown the next day.

But first, we had to complete a seventy-mile day. With a strong tailwind, it was doable. At mile fifty, however, a detour added seven extra miles and a side wind. While we rested at the Utica bar, the wind reversed, and we emerged to dark clouds racing west. The last twenty miles took as long as the first fifty-seven.

As it began to hail, we could see the contours of Eddie's Corner, a café and motel featured prominently on the Montana state map. We took their last room. Throughout the night, I opened the door to watch trucks grow and shrink. Storm clouds raced. The hail stopped, and a billion stars lit the black. Faded into purple. Orange. Yellow. Morning.

During breakfast at Eddie's, the next table stuffed forty dollars into slots and came up short on the bill. The waitress shrugged. She had taken a day off for her thirtieth wedding anniversary and was making up for it working a string of shifts: eight hours on, eight hours off, none for what she willed. We doubled our tip.

OUR LEWISTOWN HOSTS HAD recently lost their spouses. They met in a grief group. Charlotte lifted an eyebrow. "You can imagine dating in a small town like this." Charlotte and her husband had been teachers in Bozeman, Montana. Gene had been a rancher, politician, and jewelry store owner. Gene sold Charlotte the locally-mined yogo sapphire she had been wearing when we met them in Stanford.

Gene served two terms in the state legislature in the 1980s. "I want you to know," he said, "I got the endorsement of the teachers' union."

"Isn't this a pretty conservative place?" David asked. "How did you get elected?"

"Human contact," Gene explained. "I visited every farm and ranch, traveling the twenty miles between each one. I knew every family in central Montana. Politics was less sectarian and more sensible back then." He gave an example: "A state senator proposed closing a small school district to save money. I asked him to meet me at four-thirty a.m. to ride the daily distance with the superintendent, who was also the principal and the school bus driver for the district. The senator declined the invitation and withdrew his bill. Now, common sense does not win out. People are too busy posturing to do what is right."

It rained the next morning. Charlotte insisted we stay another day. She brought me to her workroom to show me a charcoal landscape she had drawn. "I was so happy when I realized how easy it is to depict a cow." She picked up a piece of charcoal to illustrate. "Draw a rectangle, smudge it a little bit . . ."

Not all budding landscape artists need to draw a cow, I thought. But in Montana, where cattle outnumber people, it's a necessity, like perfecting Spanish moss in South Carolina or saguaros in Arizona. "I love the way people love the landscapes they inhabit," I told the reporter at the *Lewistown News-Argus* when Charlotte took us to meet her later.

The *News-Argus*'s current feature story was about the Hutterites, a local religious sect prohibiting school attendance beyond the eighth grade. "Subcultures thrive in Montana," Gene said. "The Freemen, a government-hating Christian organization in Jordan, was busted by the FBI in the 1990s. An agent questioned me because I went to grade school with one of the leaders. He asked me what people were talking about. I said, 'The weather.' He thought I was evading, I told him, out here, no subject is more important than the weather."

Charlotte and Gene took us to Lewistown's watercress-filled spring in a lovely Civilian Conservation Corps park. Charlotte was worried. "With North Dakota's Bakken oil fields, how long will we have the purest water in the world coming out of our kitchen taps?"

On the morning of our third day in Lewistown, the sky menaced. Charlotte invited us to stay another night. I tried to imagine what would have happened had we met Gene and Charlotte early in the trip. We were grateful but no longer surprised to receive such supreme hospitality. As we left, the sun glinted through clouds. Charlotte saw us off, dressed to work out. She was training for the National Senior Olympics in Cleveland.

Montana - Minnesota (52 - 54)
53 Chapters
Cities
MONTANA
NORTH
DAKOTA
MINNESOTA
Jordan
52
53
54
Minneapolis
Mississippi
River
LAKE
SUPERIOR
Mississippi
River

52

EASTERLY WIND

Montana

There is no longer a prevailing wind, an effect of climate change.
—Joyce, Bismark, North Dakota

Easterly wind usually means trouble.
—Man in café, Jordan, Montana

We had survived Florida, Texas, and California. Among the giants, Montana is fourth in size but first in emptiness. The stretch from Great Falls to Lewistown was an urban core compared to the yawn from Jordan to Circle. "If I have to go to eastern Montana, I bring a good book for the drive," a woman at the Lewistown gas station said.

Bicyclists warned us about isolation, sun, wind, and elevation going west, but we were going east. We looked forward to floating gently, quickly, down the Montana plains. The fierce headwind out of Lewistown was a cruel joke, a violation of the law of expectations.

BATTERED BY FIFTY MILES of gales and sun, we joined three men and a woman in their thirties at the picnic table under the awning of Winnett's Kozy Korner Bar & Café. A man wearing an 1889 Montana ball cap grinned at us. "We are planning the new Freemen," he said. "Legal this time. Want to join?" David—sure they were joking—laughed. I—positive they were serious—stepped away from the protective awning, back into punishing sun.

Winnett—population 182 and the central hub of Petroleum County, Montana—had seen better days. We circled two permanently closed motels before settling at a tiny park. A twenty-two-year-old cyclist from Brooklyn, New York, showed up a few minutes later to share our makeshift campground. He gloated. "Nothing but easterlies in the foreseeable forecast. I'll make it to Portland before the wind changes."

The next morning, a young woman at the Kozy Korner Bar & Café sat next to us at breakfast. "I'm tired!" she sighed. "Spent fifteen hours yesterday. *Aaad* a whole herd."

"Aaad?"

"Artificial insemination."

"Woah! Sounds like a lot of work."

"I'm saving money for college in Billings."

"What do you want to study?"

"Welding. I want to work on an oil rig."

THE EASTERLY WIND GATHERED strength out of Winnett. Our Brooklyn friend must have had a ball. At a palatial rest area, we made a note of accommodations: water, bathroom, air conditioning. Montana waysides were a camping option. We would have stayed, but we had reservations at the Hill Ranch Oasis B&B, where fifty-five dollars bought us supper, breakfast, and a window into the lives of a ranching family. Supper was simple: tomato soup, grilled cheese on white bread, milk, packaged cookies, canned fruit. We passed around a gallon of bottled water. We were one hundred miles from

Lewistown's freshwater spring, and the tap water was undrinkable. Dolores, the rancher, shrugged. "It tastes like the sea," she said. "Has for several years."

The ranch was downsizing. Dolores was wistful. "We used to have 1,200 head of cattle and as many sheep. Had to work 'round the clock during lambing season, separating mothers and babies from the others. A baby was born every hour or two. We took eight-hour shifts."

"Dolores loved the night hours," her husband, Phil, interjected.

Dolores smiled. "Now, we have 120 sheep and as many cows. We check the sheep a couple times a day for babies. Our dog protects them from the coyotes. The cattle are still a heap of work. Tomorrow's branding day."

"Gonna be a long one," Phil added.

"Next week, we become a boarding house for oil workers. They want breakfast at six." Dolores rolled her eyes. "The oil is a mixed blessing. For the communities, it's a strain. A town of three hundred is now six hundred. Housing prices are through the roof. And there's more crime. They killed a teacher in one town."

Phil leaned in, lowering his voice. "Our nephew was in an accident on an oil rig in Louisiana. He watched coworkers burn. Before he came to stay with us, I didn't believe PTSD was real. The nephew and his wife are living in our mobile home while he gets therapy, goes through the lawsuit ordeal."

The next morning, Phil spared us the rough driveway and dropped us off on the highway. We told him his gray soil was unlike anything we'd ever seen. He grinned proudly. "Take a step when it rains, and you grow six inches."

THE EAST WIND WAS relentless, and there was no indoor respite. We ate lunch on a gravel road near a tiny school sitting alone on the horizon—one room, one flag, one swing. Ranches were five, ten, and twenty miles apart. A hundred hills rose to meet the sky. Our anticipation for Jordan grew with each peak. We knew the town would be small, but it was twice the size of Winnett.

Two miles from town, I got off the bike. We were so close, but I needed a rest. A guy in a pickup saw me sitting on the side of the road and insisted on giving us a ride. In our minutes together, we heard about his son's wedding, the ex-wife, the stag party. He dropped us off in front of an abandoned service station, whose gas pump and tires were buried in weeds.

Walking toward downtown, we passed a faded dinosaur mural. There were two bars on Main Street. The bigger one was for sale. The grocery store was open. The cashier who took our money looked to be twelve. The bag boy, who was younger, took a running jump onto the back of a stack of grocery carts and flew down the aisle.

Two women stood in line behind us, buying water, talking lambing. "We'll come over to your place tomorrow," one said. "We can do ours on Saturday." She looked at me, dressed in neon, holding my helmet. "There's a hail storm and tornado brewing east of here. You don't want to be riding tomorrow."

There were two motels and an RV park in town—all filled with oil workers. "You're lucky," the motel owner said. "I've got one room." We booked two nights and walked to the Hilltop Café, where twenty dinosaur diggers were ordering pie. The rest of the tables were full of small groups eating the dinner special. Noting the real estate sign, I asked the elderly owner, "Looks like business is booming. Why are you selling?"

"Because I'm tired. My ten-year-old grandson and I work tables and kitchen, morning to night. We have no workforce to draw from. Everyone is working oil."

AT NIGHT, LYING ON the motel bed, I watched poplars bend and thought about the Freemen, the militant anti-government group Gene told us about, that the young people in Winnett wanted to resurrect. The eighty-day standoff between them and the FBI in 1996 had brought unwanted attention to

Jordan. It was easy to see why people felt taxed and not represented here. The Freemen faced farm foreclosure—too many agricultural loans, not enough flowing back. The government should have helped. Instead, the law prohibited them from killing a coyote eating their lambs. And now, the government couldn't provide the most basic life force. The water was undrinkable.

WE DEBATED A THIRD night in Jordan. Forecasters said the wind would change in twenty-four hours, allowing us to do sixty-eight miles to Circle, Montana. Or we could huff thirty-four miles through another easterly to a Montana wayside. Either way, we'd get to Circle at the same time. Both days, the temperature would be over one hundred degrees. We went for the two-day plan.

As we left town and reentered the emptiness, David mused, "They're talking about farming on the moon. Why not come to Montana instead?"

A placard at Jordan's eastern exit told us the moon had come to Montana sixty-five million years ago in the form of an asteroid. In 1969, Apollo 11 astronauts brought back armalcolite—"the same mineral found in the igneous rocks at Smoky Butte." Montana's mussel shell region felt otherworldly: red, green, and gray soil, and rock formations shaped like the dinosaurs whose remains they stood over. Over eons, dinosaur bodies had become deep veins of oil—a treasure now fracked using tons of trucked-in sand and water.

In Garfield and Petroleum Counties, some changes took millennia. Some were meteoric.

OUTSIDE OF JORDON, WE met two men cycling west, enjoying an unexpected week of tailwinds. They wanted to know, "Does touring get easy after a while? Old hat?"

"Nope," we told them. "Each day has its drama."[78]

As if to prove our words, by late morning the east wind rose, and the temperature soared to 105. A stream of oil trucks spat at us, leaving a layer of crud on our skin. The wayside we'd planned to camp at had no air-conditioned building and no water, just a pit toilet and a sign: *No Camping.*

EIGHT MILES PAST THE rest stop, I noticed David was sweating profusely. My skin was dry. With eleven more miles to the nearest indoors, we poured half our water on me, hoping to avoid heat stroke.

At the Brockway Bar, red, filthy skin covered in a layer of soot, we sipped water and iced tea. The manager took a six-shooter out of his hip holster and gave it to a patron to look at, an interaction that would have had me heading for the door any other time. Now, I didn't care if they had a shoot-out. Nothing was moving me from water, seat, and cool.

Mary, the bartender, lived in Circle. She offered us her yard for the night. Revived by this generous offer, we got ready to ride the last thirteen miles. As we mounted, the sky darkened. "Thunderstorms coming," said the bar owner, a skinny woman of middle age. "You're not going anywhere." She pointed at an old camper twenty feet from the bar door. "It's filled with junk, no water or electricity, but there's a bed in there. You can shower in my mobile home.

"I'm doing this for my uncle," she said. "He biked across the country to celebrate his eightieth birthday. He was crazy. You are too."

The storm ended as quickly as it came, and the evening was gorgeous. Clean, cool, we sat on a truck bumper and watched the sunset, holding hands, laughing at this twist in the day's drama. The camper was next to an old school bus, filled with what had once furnished a house. It blocked sight of the bar

78 Theoretically, one could bike from Jordan to Circle drama-free. If you had a tailwind, no oil trucks, a seventy-degree day, and a wayside building—like the one Montana built in 2015—you would still have hill after hill, but you could enjoy those spectacular claw-shaped buttes, dancing sage grouse, and bluebirds backdropped in shale.

door, giving us a sense of privacy. We opened the windows. I slept, cool breezes blowing on clean skin.

WE HAD BEEN WITHOUT internet or phone connection for a week. The Lunch Box in Circle had Wi-Fi. We plugged in and discovered David's sister Susan had filed a missing person's report with the Lewistown police department. The officer had told her, "There's nothing between here and Circle. You'll hear from them when they get there."

IN THE EVENING, A five-minute hailstorm brought a rainbow,
and a cool
westerly
wind.

53

OIL AND WATER

Montana and North Dakota

In Glendive, Montana, piping for the Keystone Pipeline was piled a block wide and four stories high. The national debate over the project raged. Environmentalists objected to tar sand exploration; a spill would contaminate water tables. The company claimed it would provide "twenty thousand jobs for ten years." At Mexico Lindo in Glendive, a group of men sitting behind us calculated what a decade of work would do for family finances.

As we neared North Dakota, oil replaced the weather as the central topic. The local refrain on fracking: "a mixed blessing" and "inevitable." People who had lived through the 1980s boom knew a bust would come—facilitated, they believed, by Obama, environmentalists, or falling oil prices. The manager at Beaver Creek Inn in Wibaux, Montana, was ecstatic about oil exploration. "If you're making money, you love it," she said. "I don't care about those who are not."

Obviously. Eager for a shower to remove the crud from oil trucks, we called ahead to reserve a nonsmoking room. Our sheets stank, and our eyes swelled in the morning. The manager was unconcerned. She knew who buttered her bread—not a couple of bicyclists.

Remove Frack Sand Before Washing read the sign in the Belfield, North Dakota, laundromat. The owner, Barbara, told me, "In 1982, when the Bakken oil exploration halted, this town filed for bankruptcy. We struggled to keep the laundry open. Now you should see this place on Saturdays."

But even with the spike in business, she didn't feel the change was all good. "Truckers hauling water and natural gas are barely trained. They have so many accidents they don't report them anymore. And we have an extreme worker shortage. The Dairy Queen in Williston pays sixteen dollars an hour and still can't keep staff. Walmart sells off pallets, and restaurants are drive-up. Even construction companies can't find people. They're talking about bringing in labor from Monrovia, fast-tracking people from underrepresented immigrant groups."

FROM BEACH, NORTH DAKOTA, we savored pot-holed, abandoned Highway 10. There were too many gorgeous buttes and tinted hills to contemplate going fast. Houses, barns, and sheds were painted to accentuate natural beauty. We stopped to admire color. Sentinel Butte made a face: a row of blue teeth, red-rock mouth, sun-gold canola scarf. Below it, an orange road between verdant fields looked like a zipper cinching a green jacket. Our commune with the buttes was interrupted by the frenzy of Medora, a western-themed tourist mecca, but the magic resumed once we left town. We passed Theodore Roosevelt National Park, a source of North Dakota pride. Now, some were debating if it would be right to place oil rigs there.

AN OIL WELL ON a grass strip in front of a cul-de-sac let us know we had arrived in Dickinson, North Dakota. At every corner, construction teams were building hotels. By some miracle, we found a room. Guests left their doors open, revealing stashes of junk food, beer, and work clothes. They took over the halls, like a men's college dorm.

We were about to search for a quiet coffee shop when fire trucks surrounded the hotel across the street. Two of the women who poured out of the building came over "to ask about the bike." One was from Beijing, the other Taiwan. They had been recruited to come to Dickinson to clean rooms at the burning hotel, with the promise that they would learn English. They'd met three months earlier in the Minneapolis airport. "We are not learning much English," the woman from Taiwan said.

"Problem is," the young woman from Beijing said, laughing and pointing at her friend, "I met her."

WE FOUND THE BREW Coffee House, a serene spot in an old chapel. I had just gotten settled with my computer when a man came in, looking for apartment leads. The barista shook his head. "Great time for landlords, bad for renters." The home-seeker was from Virginia. He had a degree in environmental science and had been hired by an "environmental agency connected to the Dakota oil companies." I told him about the undrinkable water in eastern Montana. Was that the result of fracking in North Dakota? He looked alarmed but did not answer directly.

"Some people say water is more important than oil. The oil in North Dakota is two miles down. We are breaking barriers between sediment layers, putting water at risk of contamination. We frack natural gas. It could affect the water table. That will hurt us all. We can't uncontaminate that water in our lifetimes."

AT A TRUCK STOP outside of Dickinson, a teamster driver talked labor with David. His son had a non-union trucking job with the fracking industry. "He's making retail," he told David. "Nothing you can live on. He got no training. Union drivers need one hundred hours before they can haul sand or water."

Another trucker, driving from New York to Oregon with a load of Snickers bars, asked me about the weirdest place we'd been. I said, "North Dakota! It has businesses folding and people without housing like everywhere else, but for opposite reasons. And here, the falling price of gasoline is *bad* news. If it falls any farther, the boom is over."

While fracking wasn't saving North Dakota towns, the state had accumulated a $2 billion budget surplus. Some called for a dividend. Others pointed out needs created by the new population: schools, housing, health care, infrastructure. Time was of the essence. As surely as two cyclists would run out of borrowed resources to burn on cheap motels and café meals, the subsoil resources would disappear. The question was, what would they have to show for it?

AFTER DICKINSON, THERE WERE few places to stop. We took a detour and found a gas station with two tables. At the other table, a farmer complained about his son. "He said he opposed the war in Iraq, said it was a war for oil. I told him, 'You're right, but are you going to support fracking?' He said no. I hate it when people refuse to see the big picture."

When they left, a seventy-three-year-old retiree took their place. He wanted to hear our story. "Making lemonade of lemons," he said, sighing. "My dream was to sail the Missouri River to New Orleans. But I do love North Dakota. People don't realize our geological diversity: the Black Hills to the west, plains to the east. In the middle, our potholes—glacial puddles. More ducks are born in our wetlands than anywhere else in the continental US."

The watery potholes were welcome. Ducks and pelicans glistened in flat pools against green fields. But North Dakota's plains came soon enough: endless fields, endless exposure. We rode the freeway. Traffic—though low—went eighty miles per hour, spewing hot exhaust. We stopped under each freeway underpass and willed ourselves to reenter the sun. The air was noisy with silence. The sound of a semi or a goldfinch reverberated for minutes and miles. Sometimes I was in awe. Most of the time, I wished for the indoors.

We shared a public campground with cyclists young enough not to mind the lack of shower facilities. I had a three-week hot-weather rash, the kind David's body didn't get. His enthusiasm about this free night with new friends and a scary solo trip to the dark-pit toilet—a vulnerability I didn't want to have and didn't want to have to *remind* him I had—enraged me. He returned from his chat with the neighbors and met me at the toilet door, startling me. I screamed.

When I calmed down, I tried to joke, "Over eleven thousand miles, and patriarchy has yet to fall." I was trying to lighten the mood, to quip that I was sorry I still carried terror and poured it on him in unfair ways, expecting him to correct for his gender.

David did not laugh.

SIXTY MILES FROM FARGO, we descended, a one-day float to a welcoming home on the Minnesota border. Our Fargo hosts, Dan and Sharon, were displaced farmers. When they were a young couple, they had purchased a medium-sized plot and planted oats, barley, wheat, and flax. But like so many other independent growers in the eighties, they couldn't survive the farm crisis. Agribusiness bought them out and abandoned their diverse yield for corn and soybeans. Now, Sharon was a financial officer at a Fargo clinic. Dan worked at the post office, but his heart was still in farming. I told him about a Rhode Island farmer we'd met who also went belly-up in the eighties. In 2011, laid off from his high-tech job, he had returned to growing food, engaging in community-supported agriculture and a farm-to-school program.[79]

As I spoke, Dan grew pensive. "The city of Fargo is built on flat and fertile land," he mused. "It's a real waste. Why not have a city in areas where nothing will grow?"

79 Jeff Booker, Elisha Farmstand, Greenville, Rhode Island.

54

STRANGERS WITHIN RANGE

Minnesota

We gave them five Super Bowl rings—five years of
record profits. They traded their best players.
—Becki Jacobson, American Crystal Sugar worker, Moorhead, Minnesota

From Fargo, North Dakota, it was a four-day ride to Minneapolis. Instead of heading home, we zigzagged around Minnesota. Friends and family were incredulous. For David, a Minnesota circuit was fine, but he would have been happy at home too. He repeated my righteous assertion to his mother: "Anne says she has no right to say anything about other states if she doesn't interrogate her own."

True, but also a cover. I hoped that circling below the clouds might soften my descent. If I decreased miles, spiraled ever slower, my vision would have time to focus on the new me emerging. The bicycle was my chrysalis, metamorphosis still in process.

ENTERING MOORHEAD ON A footbridge, there was no *Welcome to Minnesota* sign, but the *American Crystal Sugar* let me know we had crossed the state border. *Fitting,* I thought. The sugar company had deep roots in

Minnesota. In the early twentieth century, migrant workers from Texas and Mexico harvested the beets, building a foundation of agricultural wealth for the state. Mostly mechanized now, Crystal still squeezed labor to increase its bottom line. A few weeks after we'd left, they had locked out workers to punish the union for rejecting a give-back contract. Thirteen months later, workers were still locked out.[80]

Cresting the hill into Barnesville, we saw a banner draped over a church wall: *Marriage = One Woman and One Man,* proclaiming the church's support for an anti-gay amendment on Minnesota's November 2012 ballot. It marred the beauty of the steepled chapel and dampened our enthusiasm for our home state.[81] We sat, deflated, at a gas station café in Glyndon, until a bouncy baby with four teeth, born as we rode across Virginia, grinned and waved at us from her mother's knee.

A BLACK MAN WALKED into a white café. At least that's how it appeared to me.

He was young, with a bicycle helmet in hand. David beckoned him to join us in our booth at the Rothsay Truck Stop, situated blocks from the town's giant prairie chicken statue. John was a college student studying "physics and human consciousness," spending his summer cycling from Maine to Washington State without GPS or iPhone, living on peanut butter and the aid of strangers. "Everyone has been so good to me," he asserted. We gave him our northwest bicycle maps. He shared his scientific mysticism: "There are no single entities,

80 Interview with Becki Jacobson, April 2014. On May 28, 2013, Minnesota Governor Dayton signed a bill stipulating workers locked out by management in contract disputes would get a year in unemployment benefits, twenty-six weeks longer than previously.

81 The anti-gay amendment was defeated. Gay marriage became legal in Minnesota in 2013.

like a person or a cup. No boundaries mean no limits. That's what makes it possible for me to do major athletic feats like triathlons. Next trip, I'm going to run across the United States."

John gave me much to think about. He knew no boundaries; I saw countless roadblocks. Only a day of exhausting myself on a bicycle allowed them to dissipate, trading fears for discomforts. This extreme method of overcoming hurdles, real and imaginary, would be useless when I returned to civilian life.

John left. Sitting two booths ahead of us was a trucker from Boston. A couple with a boy about eight slid into the booth between us. The boy and the Boston trucker got into a conversation I wished John could have heard. The boy was a fellow believer. No boundaries, no limits. He asked the trucker:

"Did any of your children go to college?"

"One went to community college," the Boston trucker answered. "He's going to be a chef."

"I'm going to be a German shepherd," the boy responded.

RIDING INTO WALKER, MINNESOTA, we passed massive stumps and pilings—nature's public art installation, entitled *Global Warning*. Two weeks earlier, much of the northern Minnesota forest had succumbed to ninety-mile-per-hour winds and torrential rains. Minnesota's north wood majesties are key to the tourism and timber industries that keep this region afloat. In the summer, people from the Twin Cities migrate north for glassy lakes and cool forests. Today, however, it was so steamy we spent the afternoon in the cool of Walker's Cass County Museum.

"Hot day," I said to the docent.

"If this heat continues, what doesn't burn will blow away," she replied. "Another dust bowl is on its way."

Walker is on the edge of the Leech Lake Reservation. During the 1880s, the Anishinaabe had sold wood to immigrants at a rate that kept the forest healthy. In the 1890s, timber barons destroyed this equilibrium, felling old-growth forest as fast as their brethren slaughtered the buffalo. They denuded the land and divided it into homestead plots to attract more European immigrants. Railroads came, knitting together burgeoning white towns. The destruction of woods devastated the Indigenous economy. The 1898 Battle of Sugar Point, referred to in the museum as the "Last US-Indian war," was, in large part, about this economic crisis.

The Civilian Conservation Corps replanted the Northwoods in the 1930s, but another late-twentieth-century frenzy thinned the forest again. Now, this "storm of the century" decimated much of what remained. For us, the storm meant campgrounds were closed for cleanup. We checked in at a B&B near the Bemidji State University campus.

We sat with the innkeeper on his porch overlooking the lawn, where a downed oak smothered a flower garden. He shook his head. "I've never seen winds like this. When I was a kid, the average snowfall was one hundred inches. Now, it's thirty. I'm feeding Baltimore orioles earlier every year. The growing season is extending. Yet some people who've lived here all their lives deny climate change."

Also staying at the B&B was a Serbian American couple, refugees of a NATO bombing campaign in the 1990s. They joined us on the porch. Andjela was the director of the Diabetes Center at the University of Nebraska. She talked about the US health-care system: "The belief is, more is better—tests and procedures with no correlation to health outcomes."

I thought she could have been talking about Minnesota's clear-cutting timber barons, or North Dakota frackers, or bicyclists who don't know when to quit. Andjela's husband, a father of two, summed up our discussion of unsustainable appetites: "If you give a moose a muffin . . ."[82]

THE INNKEEPER HAD TRAVELED to Latin America. He was alarmed that we planned to ride through the Leech Lake Reservation fifteen miles from his home. "Get out before dark!" he instructed.

Horseflies attacked our ankles as we entered the RV park on Lake Winnibigoshish in Bena. The office doubled as a bar. The bartender/resort manager served beers with one hand, took registrations with the other. The atmosphere was frantic, the crowd a yard deep. Little kids played in the outdoor pool. Teenagers hung out in a room next door. Most of the adults were inebriated. At this white-owned establishment, all the campers were white, on the reservation to fish. The couple next to us had a thirty-foot trailer, a boat, a truck, and a car. At 4:00 a.m., they revved three engines and headed out.

We pushed our sleepless bodies onto the road early, planning to finish our miles before the heat of the day. At the intersection to the town of Ball Club, we stopped at the liquor store, hoping to pee. It had three *No Public Bathroom* signs. About to move on, we heard a loudspeaker. We followed the sound down a side road. In a large clearing ringed with US flags, people of all ages and physical abilities danced. Others sat on bleachers and ate.

Ball Club was hosting their fiftieth annual powwow. A man whose business card read "Tribal Comptroller for Northern Lights Casino" pointed us to breakfast: six dollars for oatmeal with bacon grease, two eggs, potatoes, and meat. We got one plate and had second breakfast. I ate the eggs and oats, David the country fries and ham. Drinking wasn't allowed. Serious dance competitions were on the schedule. "We provide the prize money," the comptroller told us. Dancers honored veterans, one dance for each war, one US flag for each veteran. Children moved from family group to peer group, reveling in

82 He was quoting from Laura Numeroff's *If You Give a Moose a Muffin* (New York: HarperCollins, 1991), a children's book about a moose who always wants more.

the reunion. A woman saw our gear and showed us where to put up our tent. We thought of our sleepless night in the RV park and kicked ourselves for not making it this far the night before. Now, we had a motel reserved in Hibbing and hosts scheduled in Duluth.

Not wanting to leave, we spent the cool hours in Ball Club, hitting the road in the heat of the day when we should have been seeking shade. Bean soup in an air-conditioned café in Deer River went down well, but we had an infantile argument about iced tea. On the surface, it was a rift between two cyclists who needed sleep and relief from the sun. Below swam worries of cost and expectations seeping into our collective consciousness. Out of money, racking up debt, we were haunted by questions of the trip's worth. The argument spilled onto the sidewalk, where unrelenting sun and heat incensed the nonsense.

At a shaded picnic table, we rested our foul moods. A thin white man, about sixty years old, with veteran's cap, Vikings tee, and missing teeth, approached us with the usual questions. He addressed David: "Well, you have a wonderful woman that she would come with you." Reconsidering, he pointed to both of us with two hands. "You must love each other very much."

IN HIBBING, MINNESOTA, WE sampled potica—the walnut-rolled sweetbread Slovenians gave to the Iron Range—at the Sunrise Bakery, then ate dinner at Zimmy's, a shrine to local star, Bob Dylan. Italian Americans had reserved the main room. A quartet sang haunting folk tunes from the old country. In between songs, Minnesota rangers haltingly spoke the language of their ancestors.

European ethnics spoke thirty languages in this northeast Minnesota mining region through the late twentieth century. Rudy Perpich, Iron Range native and Minnesota Governor in the 1990s, spoke Croatian until grade school.

Finnish immigrants brought radical economics and political organizing to the Range. Strong unions and cooperatives demanded more return to the community than other US mining regions. Fruits of this historic collective power were still visible in regal school buildings, but the Iron Range had not rebounded from the Great Recession. In one range town, we rode the wide streets—built big enough for ore-hauling trucks—passing clapboard houses once owned by the iron company, looking in vain for an open business. Cafés and bars were permanently closed. We found an open door and a bathroom in a union hall, where a *Solidarity with Wisconsin* poster was taped to the door.

We toured Hibbing High School, admiring priceless chandeliers, the state-of-the-art theater, Olympic-size pools, the professional pipe organ, and a library mural depicting miners of different ethnicities—multiculturalism circa 1910. Our guide, a high school sophomore, gushed, "We go to school in a museum. Vandalism is unheard of. When we have a performance, we fill all eighteen hundred seats."

"Hibbing began as a lumber town," our young guide explained, "until they found iron ore under the city streets. To persuade townspeople to move, the mining company built this school, five miles out of town."

The Hibbing mine closed in 2009. In 2012, it was running, but with a fraction of the workers. I wondered how the downsizing affected our guide's young life. She sidestepped the economic question. "They only blast once a week now," she said. "It shakes the school. We don't notice it. Foreign students think we're having an earthquake."

IN FLOODWOOD, MINNESOTA, THE "Catfish Capital of the World," a swarm of boys on banana bikes peppered us with questions while we put up our tent. The recent storm dominated the conversation at the Floodwood Bridgeman's Ice Cream Parlor.

"You heard he found a giant catfish swimming in his basement?"

"Yeah. I told him he should put the photo on YouTube and crowdsource financial relief. Instead, he put his hand in a tip jar and landed in jail."

OUR VISIT TO DULUTH began as a one-day stop with a couple we'd never met and stretched into three days. They suggested we take their car to the Fond du Lac Reservation to see Jim and Pat Northrup—a generous offer that made an afternoon visit possible. Four years earlier, I'd asked Jim to speak to my class at Saint Cloud State. I had assigned his book, *The Rez Road Follies*. The students were thrilled to meet an author from Greater Minnesota. As a "cidiot"—Northrup's term—I had a credibility problem with my students that he did not have. Yet Jim was a neighbor they did not know. I had no students from "the Rez." Many lived close to reservations but had never had a conversation with an Indigenous person.

I'd told Jim that we would visit by bicycle at the end of an epic adventure. Instead, we drove up in a red car, in civilian clothes, cleaned and rested—which seemed like a violation of the invitation. We sat at their kitchen table. Jim carved holes in a piece of birch bark. Pat watched the Summer Olympics. Jim occasionally interrupted the conversation to explain what he was doing:

"We only make baskets in the summer."

"The oil in the bark makes it curl."

"Pat sews. I carve and make the holes."

"Making baskets, you can't be angry or in a hurry."

"We found that's true for bike touring as well," David said.

I told Jim about our experience at the white-owned resort on Leech Lake.

"White ownership goes back to the Dawes Act of 1887," he said. "The government turned reservation land into eighty-acre allotments. What was not claimed by Indians was open to anyone. Allotment was an extreme form of divide and conquer."

Pat, who is Dakota, added, "On my reservation, we are supposed to own ten miles on either side of the Minnesota River. They created that war in 1862 so they could have that land. Look at how valuable it is today: rich topsoil and access to the river all the way to the Twin Cities."

We bought a copy of Jim's *Anishinaabe Syndicated*. His 2012 book, *Rez Salute*, was about to come out. "I write in the morning and a couple days past deadline," he explained. "I write about what pisses me off. Now I'm pissed about the news coverage of the mass shooting in Aurora, Colorado. Reporter Brian Williams said it was the worst incident of gun violence in American history. What about Sand Creek? One hundred and sixty people shot with cannons and guns—unarmed people. I guess it doesn't count because they were Cheyenne."[83]

Jim's works were acerbic, witty confrontations with the trauma of colonialism that never ends and the trauma of war that keeps on giving. A Vietnam vet, veterans' issues were central in his writing. I asked him how he would design a memorial that honored soldiers *and* ended war.

"The Vietnam memorial has fifty-five thousand names," he said. "I would depict fifty-five thousand families crying."

WE SPENT ONE MORE day up north, walking eight miles across Duluth, viewing the flood damage. The gash in the Whole Foods Co-op parking lot looked like the work of an earthquake. The city on a hill suddenly seemed vulnerable; another natural disaster, and it might slide into Lake Superior. At the Willard Munger Inn we heard about the donkeys, goats, and sheep in the

83 Jim was referring to the 1864 Sand Creek massacre in Colorado.

zoo next door who perished, and the polar bear and seal who escaped onto roads transformed into streams.

On the Willard Munger State Trail, we walked muddy detours where the flood had taken out giant chunks of asphalt. We stopped in Moose Lake, Minnesota, to visit the Fires of 1918 Museum. The town is ten miles from the Fond du Lac Reservation. Their glassed-in display of arrowheads and a jingle dress made by the Moose Lake Camp Fire Girls, revealed less cultural competency than the Native American exhibit at the Penelope Barker House in Edenton, North Carolina.

Like Columbus, New Mexico, Moose Lake had one event they deemed most worthy of historical documentation. In years to come, perhaps there will be an exhibit on the 2012 flood to join the 1918 fire.

"The flood destroyed the first floor of our school," the docent told us.

Strangely, the 2012 flood and the 1918 fire covered the same geographical region. Both disasters included the Fond du Lac Reservation and the surrounding white communities. During the 1918 fire, white survivors caught passenger trains, but rails did not go through the reservation. Anishinaabe survivors went into the lakes. Many European homesteaders on the reservation did not make it. Courts found railroad and timber companies responsible for the fires. White farmers eventually received compensation, but Native Americans received nothing because, the argument went, the US government held reservation resources in trust for the tribe.

THE LAST TWELVE MILES of the 12,087-mile journey retraced the first twelve.[84] From downtown Saint Paul, we ascended the ridge overlooking the

84 These miles include riding and walking bikes. We traveled another 2,000 miles by ferry, bus, train, and car, not counting two trips up the West Coast by train and car, another 1,600 miles.

Mississippi River. At the Ford Parkway Bridge, we paused in the middle to take photos. Stopping at the giant bronze rabbit on the corner of Portland Avenue and Minnehaha Creek, we watched a preschooler climb its slippery body. I looked down at my handlebars. The horn with a smiley face from the woman in Cleveland and the white plastic flower from the child in New Orleans were still there.

At my insistence, we slowed time, walking the last six blocks to our doorstep.

We arrived home on a Sunday. Monday morning, David put on his Minneapolis Public Schools ID, got on his bike, and rode to middle school. I put my computer in my backpack, walked to Turtle Bread, ordered a decaf coffee, and started to write.

EPILOGUE

A RIVER NEEDS NO FLAG

I dragged my diaper in this sand. So did my mother and her grandfather. There are probably other places with better wild rice, but this one is mine.
—Jim Northrup, Fond du Lac Reservation, July 2012[85]

Love the crust of the earth on which you dwell more
than the sweet crust of any bread or cake.
—Henry David Thoreau, 1858[86]

When we practice this kind of radical hospitality . . . we make room for the possibility that fear does not have to compel our every response.
—Christine Valters Painter, 2012[87]

In an age of empire, hospitality is, in many ways,
politically subversive—challenging dominant and prolific racist
rhetoric, anti-immigrant fervor, increasing nationalism, and more.
—Tess Varner, 2021[88]

85 Comment to author, July 31, 2012.

86 Henry David Thoreau, Journal Entry, January 25, 1858.

87 Christine Valters Painter, "Radical Hospitality and Holy Disruption." *Progressive Christian*, September 30, 2012.

88 Tess Varner, "Transformative Hospitality: A Pragmatist-Feminist Perspective of Radical Welcome as Resistance." *The Pluralist* 16 (1):41 (2021).

The daily practice of seeking comfort in strange places taught me how to be at home inside my skin. Often, the road did a magic trick. Liabilities became assets, transforming the definition of a successful life. I learned I could do the impossible if I calibrated my expectations—but things often didn't work out how I expected. I expected I could outride my ghosts. I could not. But the road toppled my hierarchy of fears, and that led me to question everything that caused me trepidation.

Fear is endemic in this nation. And like me, most people—in real danger or not—rely on imaginary thinking to protect themselves. At worst these coping mechanisms add to a spiral of violence and rob us of the resources we need to build healthy communities. What makes us safe? Not more guns in our closet. Not more cops on our streets. Not a bigger border wall, or a larger gate around our community. Not another bomb, or another war. Full security is illusive in a world of climate crises and pandemics. But we will be safer when we embrace radical hospitality, build sustainable economies, and address historical trauma.

Embrace Radical Hospitality

LISTENING TO MY DAD'S stories about Nazi Germany, I came to understand how Hitler manipulated love of the fatherland into fear of the other to build his fascist movement. In graduate school, I studied the nationalist movements of oppressed people, concluding that unless those movements embrace global solidarity and economic justice and reject patriarchy, they too can devolve into racist, sexist, classist ideologies divorced from liberating social change.

National allegiance is manufactured, but attachment to *place* is real. I learned that on my bike trip. Jim Northrup and Henry David Thoreau both understood this. The problem comes when our love is poisoned by notions of colonization, of conquering, of racial superiority—when we revere our footprint on the land and not the environment itself. Conquest leads to security states that require slogans and flags to convince us we need gates, armies, and border patrols. A river needs no flag.

On the bike tour, people shared their love for the places they called home, and they opened those places up to us. As perpetual strangers, we were the recipients of a generosity that went beyond elemental kindness. To welcome in and share food, shelter, and stories with someone you are not likely to ever see again is profound.

We were safer where there were other humans. We were also safer in communities that invested in their own welfare. We lived in parks and campgrounds, used public bathrooms, and visited libraries and museums. We noticed when roads were in disrepair, celebrated bike paths and safe bridges. We saw that when communities combine resources for the public good, magic happens.

To sustain the local places we love, we need a robust public sector. But commons without equity become resources for the resource-rich, paid for by the resource-poor. In 2014, twelve-year-old Tamir Rice was gunned down by police in one of those Cleveland public parks I so admired. Our shared resources need to tip the scales toward those without, otherwise they can become places to police poverty and deepen inequality.

Both public and private entities can limit or enhance access and equity. The left/right argument over public versus private social supports—big or small government—is overdrawn. If we focus on community sharing and justice-building instead, we may find new bridges across manufactured blue/red divides.

The concept of "radical hospitality" has been taken up by religious groups, anti-racist organizations, feminists, immigrant rights activists, and arts and social service entities. These entities are embracing both personal generosity and public policy transformations. Their efforts are underground streams, forming a river that can overrun the hate rhetoric, the shibboleth about a divided and irreconcilable nation, and the nativist calls for a militarized border.

Radical hospitality is the opposite of conquest, the opposite of nationalism, the opposite of extractive capitalism.

Build Sustainable Equitable Local Economies

EXTRACTIVE CAPITALISM LED US to build communities based on one-product economies. Trees were felled, ore removed, water polluted, profits extracted, and then the jobs disappeared. When all the eggs are in one basket, the boss gets the omelet, and workers get the shells. Today, when corporations leave, meth labs, military recruiters, and prisons fill the void. The social cost of relying on these life-destroying enterprises is devastating to the US body politic.

Even diverse economies are unhealthy if workers are super exploited. People need meaningful work and dignified compensation. Too many places are like Louisiana and Guadalupe, California, where trucks and ships haul out profits while subsistence wages deplete local economies.

Perhaps you are thinking that extractive capitalism is here to stay because people want it. But in 2010, two researchers discovered that 92 percent of Americans—from blue states and red states, urban and rural—wanted a society profoundly more egalitarian than our status quo.[89]

So how do corporations get away with robbing communities of their resources and labor and then abandoning them? We got a hint of how that works in Cross City, Florida, where the timber mill closed, and the unemployed town was exhorted by their local paper to rise up, not against the timber corporation, but in support of a Ten Commandments tablet.

In 2021, those who divide to conquer attack immigrants, trans youth, Black Lives Matter activists, and teachers who talk about race. Many of these campaigns pit urban against rural people. But actual differences between urban and rural life are narrowing. As manufacturing is dying in urban centers, rural

89 Michael Norton and Dan Ariely, "Building a Better America, One Wealth Quintile at a Time." *Perspectives on Psychological Science*, 2011, 6:9.

areas are industrializing and becoming more racially diverse. Suburbs, created as oases for white people fleeing urban centers, are no longer racially homogenous. Most reservations are rural. Immigrants, LGBTQ people, and people of color live everywhere.

In the context of the devastation caused by boom-bust economies, the North Dakota fracking frenzy was madness. However, embedded in the absurdity of moving tons of water and sand across the nation to frack a nonrenewable resource, I saw a kernel of hope. Humans can move mountains.

The Indigenous people and others who occupied the construction site at the Standing Rock Indian Reservation in 2016 to hold the line against the Dakota Access Pipeline recognized this. In 2017, water protectors in Minnesota took up the mantle, fighting the construction of a new Pipe Line 3 through the Leech Lake and Fond du Lac Reservations. The water protectors have done more to break down racial and urban/rural borders than perhaps anyone else. Their argument that waters connect us all is hard to refute.

Rural people, like inner-city dwellers, are victims of environmental injustice. An urban/rural coalition of those experiencing the brunt of climate change and pollution could be unstoppable. The policy proposals are out there. Environmental activists are demanding alternatives to non-renewable industries. Labor movements are demanding both living wages and livable communities. They are talking together about green, just economies. We can be for the miners and not for the mine.

To make it happen, we need to connect the issues corporations rely on to keep us apart. And we need to repair the transgressions of the past.

Heal Historical Trauma

RECONCILIATION IS POSSIBLE. ADDRESSING historical trauma allows us to repair the potholes so we don't fall into them again. Only then can we focus on making the places we love hospitable for ourselves, our children, and the strangers who enter.

Public history can begin the healing process. Every trail where US troops force-marched Native people is a chance to tell the history of a government intent on making Indigenous America disappear; a chance to tell stories of resistance and resilience; a place to advance reparations. The sites of Indian boarding schools, California Missions, and slave plantations are places to center victims so, as they do at concentration camps, visitors pledge, *Never Again*. It will be up to us to make current connections—to show, for example, how histories of conquest expose the obscenity of the current border war.

The new monument, which opened in 2020, honoring Native American soldiers in Washington, DC, is a long time coming, but like most other war memorials, it celebrates battles and does not depict the pain of survivors, as Jim Northrup imagined. We need to allow veterans and those who lost loved ones to tell their truths—not just on slips of paper hidden on a shelf in a timber town in Idaho, but in marble and brass, giving their stories the power to end war.

In June 2015, Bree Newsome pulled down the Confederate flag from the South Carolina statehouse, igniting a movement to remove the monuments and official symbols venerating slaveholders. The reaction from those still embracing those old symbols made the Confederacy a central issue in the 2020 election.

The campaign against critical race theory, absurd on its face, is a reaction and an indication of a decade of progress to overcome the foreclosure of Black history. The Smithsonian National Museum of African American History and Culture took its place on the National Mall in Washington, DC, in 2016. The Legacy Museum: From Enslavement to Mass Incarceration, which opened in Montgomery, Alabama, in 2018, refuted the prevailing narrative of an inevitable march of progress. The New York Time's 1619 Project transformed our sense of time, leading policy makers and protesters to cry "Four hundred years is enough." The Minnesota African American Heritage Museum and Gallery in North Minneapolis opened in 2018 after decades of such attempts. During the Minneapolis Uprising of 2020, it had the flexibility and power to respond to and support the movement in the streets.[90]

What We Do Matters

POLITICAL AND CORPORATE ELITES have an interest in disaggregating and erasing people's history. It is up to us to celebrate the trajectory of grassroots transformational social movements, learn their lessons, and build on their momentum. The Occupy movement mirrored the nineteenth century "Gilded Age" revolts against the wealth divide. Yet Occupy Wall Street was small compared to the uprisings of 2020.

The Grangers and railroad workers of the nineteenth century would have applauded the diversity of the Wisconsin Uprising and the geographic and sectoral breadth of Occupy. They would also have warned us to prepare for reaction. Their movements devolved from demands for radical economic restructuring to white supremacy. Post-Occupy, we saw a similar resurgence of white supremacist movements.

We also saw a proliferation of anti-racist movements.

Three women initiated Black Lives Matter after the murder of Trayvon Martin.

Young people in Ferguson, Missouri, commandeered the streets after the killing of Michael Brown. Since then, the call for Black liberation has deepened and broadened.

Four Canadian women formed Idle No More, advocating Indigenous sovereignty and uniting Native nations across colonized North American borders.

In the Trump era, Muslims, Jews, and immigrants from all parts of the world built alliances to oppose the Muslim ban, the border wall, and detention camps.

90 America's Black Holocaust Museum in Milwaukee reopened as a virtual exhibit in 2012. As of this writing, it was still planning an onsite reopening.

Other social movements addressed gun violence, LGBTQ rights, climate change, raising the minimum wage, and rape culture. Labor activists followed the lead of the historic IWW and shifted focus to those at the economic bottom: fast-food workers, janitors, and undocumented people. They expanded their scope beyond the workplace to incorporate concerns fundamental to workers' lives, like housing, environmental justice, and the well-being of people who use what they produce.[91] The #MeToo movement exposed the pandemic of sexual assault and harassment. Survivors told their stories and took down high-profile perpetrators. Trans and nonbinary people said *We are here*, and many were front and center in other liberation movements. People too young to vote built campaigns of unprecedented size and global reach against gun violence and for climate justice.

When police killed George Floyd ten blocks from my home, police brutality in Minneapolis and the US was not new. Neither was the movement against it. But we reached a tipping point. The murder was filmed and viewed across the globe, and a levee broke. Immovable ideas and institutions began to shake. The seismic eruption that began in my neighborhood spread across the world, bursting open myths about public safety and what makes us secure. Twenty-six million people stood up. Solidarity obliterated local, state, and national borders. In Minneapolis and cities across the nation, the role of police in public safety was under scrutiny. Calls for abolition grew.

In the aftermath of global protests, institutions considered their responses. Amid the COVID-19 pandemic, the question of racial justice took center stage in organization Zoom sessions. Emblematic of changes, real and rhetorical, was the Cleveland baseball team, which, invoking the name of George Floyd, changed its moniker.[92]

91 The strategies of the Chicago Teachers' Union, the Minnesota Nurses Association, the Coalition of Immokalee Workers in Florida, and CTUL in Minneapolis are a few examples.

92 https://www.theguardian.com/sport/2021/jul/23/cleveland-major-league-baseball-indians-guardians

As people fought for a just future, they scrutinized the past. Monuments were torn from their pedestals—including statues of Junípero Serra, mastermind of the California missions. In Jamestown, Virginia, the Settlement Museum revised its purpose from "history as fun" to history as meaningful and intersectional, telling stories that center Indigenous and Black experiences.[93] Cities drafted slavery reparation plans.[94] Calls—not just for truth—but also for financial reparations for Native Americans built on this momentum, after the mass graves of children at Indian boarding school sites in Canada were uncovered in 2021.[95]

Backlash was swift. One day we swam a tidal wave; the next we battled a riptide. Change requires persistence. Often it feels like we are fighting a headwind in a West Texas desert. The temptation to turn around, set sail, and ride a breeze that promises movement—even if it is backward—is huge.

The future is unwritten, and progress not assured. But the uprisings of 2020 showed us that what we do matters, and, once in a great while, our efforts can become a mighty force. Like the ancient Lake Missoula, a drop of water, united with a billion other drops, can break a dam, split a mountain, find a path to the sea.

---

93 Complete interview with the museum director on National Public Radio: https://www.npr.org/2021/03/20/979491451/some-museums-have-found-a-new-audience-online.

94 Durham and Asheville, North Carolina; Providence, Rhode Island; Evanston, Illinois; Kansas City, Missouri; Amherst, Massachusetts; and Washington, DC, to date.

95 Pastor Jim Bear Jacobs argued reparations should be a line item in annual church budgets. https://www.mprnews.org/episode/2021/07/29/atonement-and-reparations-for-native-american-boarding-schools

QUESTIONS FOR BOOK CLUBS AND CLASSROOMS

To request book club discounts or a virtual or live visit by the author, email awmpedalstory@gmail.com.

For more resources on all of these issues: see annewinklermorey.com

Do you have a local place you love? What makes it special? Is it public or private? How do you enjoy it, care for it, share it with others?

Consider the public assets (i.e., the commons) in your community. Which do you use? Who has access to them? How could your community increase its commons and equitable access to its public wealth?

In chapter 16, labor organizer Blair talked about the economic changes in his community, when they lost a dominant product and the political will to share its fruits. Consider the economic engine(s) of your community. How have they changed? Have the profits been used to develop the commons?

Consider the public history sites in your community. What stories are told? Which are left out? What sites need transforming? What new ones are needed? Design one.

Twice, the author uses the phrase "the brain is a funny muscle." Have you had experiences where your brain dictated what you could and couldn't do physically?

In the epilogue, the author talks about the rise of social movements since 2011. What social movements have developed where you are? How have they built on each other?

Do you have fears that lead you to irrational coping mechanisms that make you less safe? Have you seen this in your community? Your nation? Globally?

Define the words *public* and *safety*. Design a public safety system. What would a safer society look like where you live?

The author asserts that gates, borders, guns, armies, detention camps, and police forces actually make us less safe. Do you agree? What would you do instead?

What skills do you use to empathize with the trauma experienced by others?

"A river needs no flag," the author asserts. What does she mean? What early stories shaped your ideas about nationalism and/or patriotism? What identities are most central to you?

Do you ever want to escape? Where would you go? How would you travel?

Have you been to, or do you live in, any of the places described in this book? What did the author get right? What did she get wrong? What are the problems and possibilities with first impressions and "telling a slice of the truth as you see it"?

Exchange stories with one person in your group. Listen carefully. Take no notes. Write down what you remember.

Discuss the urban/rural, racial, ethnic, class, and political divides where you live. How can you bridge them to build a more equitable community?

ACKNOWLEDGMENTS

Though I am responsible for the words on the page, thousands of people directly influenced my thoughts, and supported this effort, making both the bike trip and the book possible.

Trail angels

One hundred and forty-three households put us up during the bike trip. Hundreds more people offered food, water, rides, directions, advice, and stories. There would be no book without the trail angels. I hope that some will consider this book partial payment forward.

Teachers

Writing educators at the Loft Literary Center in Minneapolis, Minnesota, provided invaluable lessons in the writing process. Memoirists, Cheri Register, Laura Flynn, and Nicole Helget, were especially helpful. The students in my Loft classes provided comradery and feedback that also influenced the outcome of this work. Alex Kuo's writing workshop in Winthrop, Washington, revived me at a moment when I had nearly given up.

The voices of my students at Metro State University, St. Cloud State University, and the University of Minnesota, were always in my head as I wrote. I thank them for the education.

My graduate school adviser Dionicio (Dennis) Valdes, and dissertation committee members August Nimtz and David Roediger are still teaching me.

The one hundred people who participated in the Minneapolis Interview

Project profoundly influenced my thinking about life stories and the importance of place.

Supporters

I am grateful to siblings David Winkler, Daniel Winkler, Michael Winkler, John Morey, Susan Homolka, Jean Morey, Nancy Bauer, and Barbara Morey, and their spouses and children, who were there for us during the trip, during the writing process, and in life.

I thank friends, for support and inspiration: Adriana Cerrillo, Alan Dale, Roya Damsaz, Valérie Déus, Sara Dick, Anna Dick Gambucci, Kristin Dooley, Emily Donovan, Drew Edwards, Liz Faue, Shari Geistfeld, Polly Kellogg, Sally Kundert, April Knutson, Polly Mann, Howard Metzenberg, L Papalamaitcalli Meza, Eric Mueller, Roxxanne O'Brien, Ingrid Perry-Houts, Patricia Schneider-Zioga, Marjaan Sirdar, Betty Tisel, Gilberto Vazquez Valle, Ruth Voights, Donna Vukelich, and Bianca Zick.

Teachers and friends from high school came through for me in ways that still confound me: Avis Elson, Michael Brockmeyer, Suzy Grinrod, Ed Feeny, Bill Feeny, Howard Metzenberg, Tari Gilbert, Enrique Valdivia, Todd Weiss, Cata Morgana, Donna Vukelich, Beth Miller, Leslie Davenport, and Larry Iles.

Betty Morey has been supportive every step of the way, for a decade. She always asked: will it have a happy ending? I hope that she thinks it does. My child Emily Winkler-Morey and their partner Lluvia Alcázar, inspire me with their very beings. They have been a constant source of support throughout this project. David Winkler-Morey, my number one cheerleader, believed in this project and in me, when I did not. His consistent, unrelenting support made everything possible.

Collaborators

Emily Donovan's painting is on the cover. Tori Hong drew the bicycles.

Heather Spates created the maps. Eric Mueller shot the author photo, and Patrick Maloney put it all together. Together they made the book lovely to behold. The staff at Wise Ink provided advice, support, cajoling, patience, and wisdom.

Inspiration for the book's title

The title went through many iterations. It was not until I read Robin Wall Kimmerer's *Braiding Sweetgrass* in 2021 that the current title emerged. I thank her for her inspiring book, for her thinking on nationalism and ecology, and for her concept of waters and winds as plural, ever moving and ever changing, and yet at home, wherever they are.

In memory

To those who have passed on since the bike trip: Marjorie Winkler, Arvid Morey, Maja Gorland, Bob Eddy, Gerry Eddy, Vy Homolka, Sam Hughes, Dick Isaac, Tom McCart, Stan Metzenberg, Jim Northrup, Micheal Trueheart, and Gilberto Vazquez Valle; my memories of you are a blessing.

I have not stopped arguing with, and running ideas by Stefan Siegfried Winkler, though he died in 2000. In many ways, this book is making those discussions public.

Readers and listeners

People who read early versions of the book: Lluvia Alcázar, Liz Bartholomew, Kristin Dooley, Drew Edwards, Patricia Weaver Francisco, Ann Hohenshell, April Knutson, Alex Kuo, Jeanne Landkamer, Sherry Quan Lee, David Lyons, Loan Mai, L Papalamaitcalli Meza, Kim Sabow and her book group, Lucy Saliger, Lizabeth Fiedorow Sjaastad, Amy Noelle Smith, Emily Winkler-Morey, and Bianca Zick, thank you for your essential feedback.

David Winkler-Morey read all iterations, and put up with this constant refrain for a decade: "Can I read you this paragraph?"

My mother, Marjorie Winkler, and my 101-year-old friend, Polly Mann, invited me to read segments of the book to them, every time I saw them. I watched their faces for emotion, grateful to see tears and laughter. Their rapt attention gave me hope I was on the right track. Marjorie loved the stories of natural places. Polly focused on stories of people. Reading to them helped me achieve more balance, while realizing the book will mean different things to different people.

And now I am grateful to you, for reading the published book, and I am eager to know what it means to you. Contact me awmpedalstory@gmail.com and let me know what you think!

AUTHOR PHOTO BY ERIC MUELLER.

ANNE WINKLER-MOREY has a Ph.D. in history and has been an activist scholar studying and participating in social movements since the 1980s. Her Minneapolis Interview Project is a collection of one hundred oral histories with a social justice lens. She is currently planning her next bicycle adventure. For more at the intersection of bicycling, oral and public history, sustainable economies, and social movements—or to book a presentation—visit annewinklermorey.com.